International African Library 36
General Editors: J. D. Y. Peel, Suzette Heald and Deborah James

MASQUERADES OF MODERNITY

The International African Library is a major monograph series from the International African Institute. Theoretically informed ethnographies, and studies of social relations 'on the ground' which are sensitive to local cultural forms, have long been central to the Institute's publications programme. The IAL maintains this strength and extends it into new areas of contemporary concern, both practical and intellectual. It includes works focused on the linkages between local, national and global levels of society; writings on political economy and power; studies at the interface of the socio-cultural and the environmental; analyses of the roles of religion, cosmology and ritual in social organisation; and historical studies, especially those of a social, cultural or interdisciplinary character.

MASQUERADES OF MODERNITY

POWER AND SECRECY IN CASAMANCE, SENEGAL

FERDINAND DE JONG

EDINBURGH UNIVERSITY PRESS
for the International African Institute, London

© Ferdinand de Jong, 2007

Edinburgh University Press Ltd
22 George Square, Edinburgh

Typeset in Plantin
by Koinonia, Bury, and
printed and bound in Great Britain
by Antony Rowe, Chippenham, Wilts

A CIP record for this book is available
from the British Library

ISBN 978 0 7486 3319 7 (hardback)

The right of Ferdinand de Jong to be identified
as author of this work has been asserted in
accordance with the Copyright, Designs and
Patents Act 1988.

For other publications of the International
African Institute, please visit their web site at
www.iaionthe.net

CONTENTS

LIST OF MAPS, FIGURES, PLATES AND TABLES

Plates

Plates are between pages 52 and 53.

Tables

ACKNOWLEDGEMENTS

How does society constitute itself in the current context of globalisation? This study demonstrates that secrecy is one of the means by which some societies in Senegal produce themselves as locality. Focusing on initiation rituals, masked performances and modern art, it shows that such secretive practices define identity and protect society against the homogenising forces of globalisation. The Jola and Mandinko peoples of the Casamance region in Senegal have always used their rituals and performances to incorporate the impact of Islam, colonialism, capitalism and, more recently, democracy. Their performances of secrecy have accommodated these modern powers and continue to do so today. The performers incorporate the modern and redefine modernity through secretive practices. This study attempts to show that performances of secrecy are historical practices that have enabled post-colonial subjects to come to terms with modernity.

This book has no linear trajectory. It is the result of the teachings of different teachers, intellectual exchanges in various intellectual environments, financial support from various institutions, and the unrelenting support of friends and family. It is based on several stints of fieldwork in Senegal, each of which provided new encounters and new interpretations. I spent five months in Casamance in 1990 and 1991. For my doctoral research I spent a full year (1994–95) in various villages and towns of Casamance. Since then I have regularly returned to Senegal for additional stints of fieldwork. Most recently, I was allowed to spend another year in this country, although that was for another project.

In Senegal, I have enjoyed the hospitality and friendship of many Casamançais, either in Casamance or in Dakar. I would like to thank my host and assistant Thioune Diatta and his family, who gave me a warm welcome during the celebration of the 1994 initiation ceremony and the various visits to Thionck and Dakar I have made since. I also thank Longe Diatta, with whom I spent quite a few afternoons talking politics in his well-visited sewing shop. I also spent many hours with Cheikh Abba Badji who explained to me his responsibilities as officiant of the sacred forest, and Sya Badji, his daughter, who was equally patient and willing to give me her – female – point of view. In Ziguinchor I spent a lot of time with Sidy Mohamed Mané, a devout and tolerant Muslim and the most gracious assistant who helped me navigate the rules of courtesy to be observed when visiting the town's dignitaries. I thank him and the Goudiaby family for their hospitality and friendship. In Ziguinchor I also lived with the late Salif Mandiang and his family, of which a few members have unfortunately died over the last few years. I remember the late Ibrahima Mandiang and the late Kinta Sonko. The artist Omar Camara has been a good friend and a chapter dedicated to him should return the gift of friendship and advice he offered me when I was in trouble. Of course, I should also mention Marie and Anne-Marie Cabo, their sisters, daughters and cousins, who have always given me the sense that I really was at home in Ziguinchor. There are many other people I need to thank here, including Yancouba Sagna from Diatock, Khady Diatta currently living in the Netherlands, Diarra Kébé in Italy, and several young men who found ways to escape Senegal's oppressive economic crisis.

The research for this study was made possible by the financial support of several institutions to which I am most grateful. First of all, I should like to thank the Netherlands Foundation for the Advancement of Tropical Research that has awarded me several travel grants. The fieldwork has been financed by the Amsterdam School for Social Science Research of the University of Amsterdam. I would like to acknowledge their unconditional support. In addition, the Amsterdam School has given me the most stimulating intellectual environment for writing a dissertation, for which I am most grateful. The various seminars at the Amsterdam School have enabled me to reflect on and develop my work. Beyond the Amsterdam School I participated in the research programme 'Globalization and the Construction of Communal Identities' of the Netherlands Foundation for the Advancement of Tropical Research. The numerous seminars and conferences in the context of this programme offered occasions for debate and inspired me in different ways. I also participated in several Satterthwaite colloquiums organised by Dick Werbner, where I presented some of material included here. Since 2000, I have enjoyed the company of the staff of the School of World Art Studies and Museology at the University of East Anglia. In this context I have been exposed to a series of new intellectual challenges which, I expect, will feed into my future work.

Beyond institutional support, I enjoyed the friendship and guidance of Jos van der Klei, who introduced me to the Casamance region. Since I started my research there, I have also benefited from the meticulous historical research by Peter Mark as well as his unfailing support. As supervisors of my dissertation, Wim van Binsbergen and Thoden van Velzen have played an important role in the making of this book, which is a substantially revised version of that dissertation. Their constructive criticisms and suggestions have helped me come to terms with my material. Many others have in one way or another contributed to the making of this book. Peter Geschiere has been a greatly appreciated mentor throughout the years. Drafts of various parts of this book have benefited from the constructive criticisms of Jan Abbink, Arjun Appadurai, Gerd Baumann, Marieke Bloembergen, Anton Blok, Mamadou Diouf, Remco Ensel, Abdoulaye Kane, Reinhilde König, Peter Pels, Marja Spierenburg, Maruška Svašek, Rijk van Dijk and Dick Werbner. Of course, none of them can be held responsible for the final result, which may not do justice to their incisive comments. I would also like to thank the two anonymous readers of the International African Institute for their helpful comments and contributions to this text, Mariane Ferme for her positive suggestions and the editor John Peel for his meticulous corrections. Nick Warr was an invaluable editor of the illustrations of this book. Finally, I would like to thank my friends and family for their patience and confidence. Never quite sure of what this was about, they nonetheless fully supported me, for which I owe them.

Versions of several chapters have appeared in edited volumes and journals. Chapter 3 appeared as 'The production of translocality: initiation in the sacred grove in southern Senegal' in *Modernity on a Shoestring: Dimensions of Globalization, Consumption and Development in Africa and Beyond*, eds Richard Fardon, Wim van Binsbergen and Rijk van Dijk (Leiden and London: EIDOS, 1999), pp. 315–40. Chapter 4 appeared as 'Politicians of the sacred grove: citizenship and ethnicity in Southern Senegal' in *Africa* (2002) 72 (2): 203–20. Parts of Chapter 6 were published as 'Secrecy and the state: the kankurang masquerade in Senegal' in *Mande Studies* (2000) 2: 153–73. Chapter 7 appeared as 'Trajectories of a mask performance: the case of the Senegalese kumpo' in *Cahiers d'Études Africaines* (1999) XXXIX (1) 153: 49–71. An earlier version of Chapter 9 appeared as 'The social life of secrets' in *Situating Globality: African Agency in the Appropriation of Global Culture*, eds Wim van Binsbergen and Rijk van Dijk (Leiden: Brill, 2004), pp. 257–76. Permission to reprint these texts is gratefully acknowledged.

ABOUT THE AUTHOR

Ferdinand de Jong received his doctorate from the University of Amsterdam and now teaches anthropology and art at the University of East Anglia. He has published on ritual and masquerade and has co-edited (with Geneviève Gasser) a special issue of the *Canadian Journal of African Studies* on the civil war in the Casamance region of Senegal, focusing on conflict resolution. Recently, he co-edited (with Mike Rowlands) a volume on heritage and memory in Africa, to be published by Left Coast Press. His current research focuses on the memory and heritage of the slave trade and colonialism in postcolonial Senegal.

PART I

INTRODUCTION

1

POWER OF SECRECY

Sacred forests constitute the traditional locus of political authority of the Jola population in the Casamance region of Senegal. The forests are strictly out of bounds to anyone who is not initiated into their secrets. In the 1980s separatists used the forests to organise their struggle for an independent Casamance. On 6 December 1983, policemen wanted to interfere with a secret meeting in the sacred forest of Diabir, close to the regional capital. The policemen suspected the members of the separatist movement of planning yet another subversive activity, and they thus entered the forest to arrest the suspects. This provoked an extremely violent reaction. Three policemen were killed on the spot with knives and machetes, four others were seriously wounded. The police reacted with a wave of arrests in town. Shortly afterwards, some deputies in the Senegalese parliament demanded that the Jola sacred forests be destroyed. The Senegalese government refrained from enacting this sacrilege but the demand for their destruction clearly demonstrates that the politicians viewed the sacred forests as loci of organisation, which they indeed were (Geschiere and Van der Klei 1988). The state recognised the sacred forests as sites of subversion.

In the Casamance region, secrecy is a widely shared cultural model of performance and certainly not restricted to the Jola. Mandinko perform secrecy too, in their masquerades and initiation ceremonies. Modernisation has not at all diminished their involvement in secrecy, as is witnessed by their reactions to violations of their secrets. Indeed, it is no exaggeration to state that politics in Casamance is shrouded in secrecy. In this respect I do not refer to the domain of politics as defined by the state, but to politics at large, *le politique*, as the French would have it (Bayart et al. 1992). For example, gender relations in Casamance are structured through secrecy. Practices of secrecy also provide the inhabitants of Casamance with a certain amount of leverage over the state. Moreover, secrecy enables its practitioners to come to terms with the market economy, that other inescapable reality of the global political economy. Secrecy can be a weapon of the weak (cf. Scott 1985). But there is a flip side to the power of secrecy: the state and market economy both penetrate the realm of secrecy, resulting in a continuous process of domains being interlocked. Practices of secrecy empower, and are subsequently disempowered. This book is about the dialectics of the expansion of secrecy into public spheres.

Such dialectics do not necessarily serve the reinforcement of boundaries of Casamance society and can in fact be compatible with the existence of the nation-state. In the process that led to the signing of a peace agreement between the separatist movement and the Senegalese government in 2004, the women of Ziguinchor played a remarkable role. Organising themselves in their sacred forests, these women made successful efforts to speak to their 'sons' in the guerrilla camps, convincing them to end their armed struggle. These women also made it possible for the oaths independence fighters had sworn in sacred forests to be undone. Most of these activities belonged to the realm of the sacred forests and were conducted in secret. In this case, secrecy ensured that the women could act independently. However, their operations have also been analysed as influenced by local politicians (Foucher 2003a). The women of the sacred forests have also received help from international non-governmental organisations. In various other ways too, the autonomy of the sacred forests is relative. For example, the women of the sacred forests have relied on anthropological texts to interpret their involvement in the separatist struggle in order to withdraw from that struggle. This suggests that the practices surrounding the sacred forests of today are actually constituted by anthropological knowledge and international donor money. Does that make these practices less authentic? No, on the contrary, I think that such entanglements demonstrate to what extent the sacred forests of the Casamance region are relevant to contemporary politics and the production of a postcolonial subjectivity (cf. Werbner 2002). The state and international non-governmental organisations instrumentalise all manner of 'traditions', such as joking relations, to reach the insurgents and tempt them to negotiate (de Jong 2005; Tomàs 2005). Likewise, the secrecy surrounding sacred forests is mobilised for intervention in the separatist struggle. In this particular place, practices of secrecy continue to shape the form of contemporary politics.

THE MODERNITY OF SECRECY

In Casamance secrecy is practised in everyday life and in a variety of ritual contexts: circumcision, initiation and masked performances. The study of rituals of this kind is not particularly fashionable in anthropology today. This lack of interest can be partly explained by the fact that in most societies the significance of these rites is on the wane. Many rituals of precolonial African societies have given way to other forms of public celebration. But there is another reason why less attention is now devoted to traditional life-cycle rituals. The study of traditional rites is increasingly unpopular because it allegedly portrays Africans as being stuck in tradition. Why, then, would anyone write a book on such an old-fashioned topic? I think there are several sound reasons. First of all, ritual and performance are still very much alive in contemporary Casamance. Rites of passage and masked performances are frequently staged in the villages and cities of this region. Secondly, it is not coincidental that these practices have survived. The people of Casamance do not perform traditional practices without reflecting upon them, simply because they were handed down from their ancestors. Casamançais use these practices critically and reflexively, giving them new meaning and pragmatic use. These practices represent their distinctive path through modernity (cf. Clifford 1988; Comaroff and Comaroff 1993). Old rituals persistently survive and receive renewed attention as identity markers in a rapidly modernising world. These observations not only pertain to the ritual practices of rural dwellers who, one might argue, live on the fringe of modernity (Piot 1999). Even in cities, these traditions are kept alive. In fact, it has been argued that traditions survive in cities more than anywhere else as valued forms of folklore (Bausinger 1990).

The sociological form of secrecy is certainly not unique to Casamance society. Georg Simmel argued that human life always requires a certain measure of secrecy (Simmel 1967: 335). Secrecy is indeed part of all contemporary societies. Espionage and trade secrets are vital to the sound operation of modern states and corporate enterprise. Secret societies abound in almost every modern society. The Ku Klux Klan, the Freemasons and the Mafia are some of the best known examples.[1] Secrecy can also be compatible with democracy. Habermas points out that the public sphere of the democratic state has gradually declined since the eighteenth century, and that secretive decision-making is vital to the modern welfare state (Habermas 1989). One could also argue that secrecy lies at the heart of democratic electoral competition: the voter casts the ballot in secret. Nothing suggests that secrecy is either a traditional affair or an African inclination.

Modernity is today's inescapable reality that remains hard to capture in a definition. Modernity is essentially plural and presents itself divergently in different places. I therefore refrain from defining modernity as a form of social life determined by a unitary Weberian rationality. I assume instead that modernity is a hegemonic discourse that labels some privileged societies as modern, while others are represented as fundamentally stuck in tradition. Modern societies are defined by history, which traditional societies are deprived of (Wolf 1982). As Dirks puts it: 'The modern not only invented tradition, it depends upon it. The modern has liberated us from tradition and constantly conceives itself in relation to it' (Dirks 1990: 27–8). Essentially, the modernist discourse posits that historical transformations are irreversibly heading towards the modern. The past was ruled by 'tradition', but the future is open to imaginations of all kinds. However, modernity distributes these imaginations unequally. While Western societies are commonly said to have invented modernity and to embody its vanguard, non-Western societies are perceived to be following in their wake. The only option left to the non-West is to copy the historical trajectory already accomplished by the West, merely performing a present that is always already the West's past. If anything, the discourse on modernity seems to define difference: between the West and the non-West, the vanguard and the rearguard (Mitchell 2000). We clearly need to think modernity differently. In this book I will use the term modernity as plural (Englund and Leach 2000).

In Casamance too, all structural transformations are seen as emanating from modernity. The state of turmoil many feel they are in is experienced as a consequence of *le modernisme*. The appropriation of the modernist discourse attests to its wide diffusion and the plurality of understandings of the modern that it has generated. However, most of its empirical referent *is* part of modernity by all understandings. Colonisation has profoundly affected the modes of livelihood in Casamance. The imposition of a central administration by the colonial state led to the transformation of historical structures of authority. State formation may therefore be considered one of the faces of modernity in Casamance, experienced as such by most Casamançais. Moreover, the encroachment of the capitalist mode of production – promoted by both the colonial and the postcolonial state – has led to increased labour migration and the production of cash crops. Although subsistence production still prevails in much of rural (and urban) Casamance, farmers have increasingly migrated towards urban centres, either temporarily or permanently, and have been subjected to capitalist relations of production. The market economy is one of those inescapable realities that one faces in contemporary Casamance. The increasing mobility also led to the disintegration of structural boundaries, which were increasingly replaced by symbolic boundaries (cf. Cohen 1989). More encompassing religious and ethnic categories, often invented and introduced by others, were appropriated by the local population. The state legitimises these new identities, while impressing its citizens with its own subjectivity through public education. Conversion to the world religions, the market economy and state formation should therefore be considered aspects of Casamance modernity. Indeed, these twentieth-century transformations are understood by the Casamançais themselves as constituting their modernity. Ethnicity, however, no matter to what extent it may have been 'invented', is never seen as 'modern'. Ethnicity constitutes for many Casamançais the domain of life in which traditions are maintained.

The idea that initiations and masquerades are part of the modern is not shared by the Casamançais. They objectify these performances as 'traditions'. In their theory of *le modernisme*, the Casamançais deny the modernity of their practices of secrecy. Paradoxically, this corroborates the modernity of these performances. After all, the conceptualisation of historical practices as 'traditions' is part of a modernist discourse, a discourse that emphasises a disjuncture between past and present, and a rupture between a world lost and an open future. The Casamançais certainly perceive their practices of secrecy as part of a vanishing world. But these traditions are not bound to vanish: they are historical practices with a future ahead of them. These practices are not modern inventions of tradition (Hobsbawm and Ranger 1983), but historical ways of dealing with modernity. All the practices discussed here incorporate the modern and constitute modernity at large (cf. Appadurai 1996). To be sure, the practices of secrecy may be considered modernity's malcontents (Comaroff and Comaroff 1993). Like so many other practices that seemed irreconcilable with modernity – witchcraft (Geschiere 1997), religion (Meyer 1999) or ethnicity (Cohen 1969) – practices of secrecy contradict common understandings of the modern as 'disenchanted'. It is this apparent paradox that I set out to fully explore. Practices of secrecy provide Casamançais with the means to produce an alternative modernity.

SECRETS AND THE SACRED

That practices of secrecy can be modern is an insight that is not shared by the performers of secrecy in Casamance. In their view Islam and Christianity are the modern religions, not the practices associated with a local cosmology. In the nineteenth and twentieth centuries, the large majority of the inhabitants of Casamance converted to one of these two world religions. Following Horton (1971), one could argue that they equipped themselves with a new system of explanation to cope with the novelties of modernity. Horton suggested that traditional cosmologies were well equipped for control over the microcosm, but not so much for agency within the macrocosm.[2] But in Casamance some of the practices central to the local cosmology are still performed today. We might make short shrift of the matter, arguing that these practices only serve concerns related to the microcosm. Yet I will suggest precisely the opposite. Following Baum (1999), I suggest that traditional practices of secrecy have retained their relevance because they offer their performers a means of coping with the radically transformed macrocosm. This, then, raises the question of how these practices relate to the other systems of macrocosmic explanation: Islam and Christianity. Early converts to Islam and Christianity were indeed inimical to traditional initiation ceremonies. The relationship between the monotheistic religions and the practices of secrecy underwent enormous change throughout the twentieth century. Today, they are thought to be compatible – although relations remain strained. In a number of cases, practices of secrecy have actually incorporated Islam. The universalist religion has been appropriated through particularist practices of secrecy. As I will demonstrate, secrecy has become a critical feature of Islam in Casamance.

Here, I would like to dwell a bit more on the relationship between the secret and the sacred. One of the reasons practices of secrecy are so persistent in Casamance society is that they are protected by prohibitions. Some ethnographic cues may give an impression of how I learnt about the sacred within the secret. We need to bear in mind that secrecy pertains in particular to sacred forests. Sacred forests are small tracts of dense forest on the fringes of Jola villages. Jola villages have sacred forests for each sex, strictly out of bounds to members of the opposite sex. The gendered nature of secrecy is most adequately demonstrated in the organisation of sacred forests. Before the Jola's conversion to Islam, the forests contained shrines. Sacred forests were places of worship, and they still are today. During my fieldwork, I discussed the meaning of sacred forests with some of my Jola interlocutors. The discussion focused on the contradictions between their Muslim faith and their practices in the sacred forests. The conversation was held in French. One speaker asserted that the forests were sacred (*sacré*) whereas other places of religious worship, such as mosques, were not sacred to him. I was puzzled. After all, these men were Muslims. But the conversation was going to lead me even further astray. I mentioned the existence of a mosque built at a location previously occupied by a sacred forest. This sacred forest had been cut down to build a mosque that was to serve the village-wide community of Muslims (see Chapter 2). To my interlocutors it was obvious that the mosque derived its sacredness from its location. They even argued that members of the Tijaniyya brotherhood, reputed for their fierce opposition to 'paganism', should refrain from praying at this mosque. The central argument – that the mosque was sacred since it was located at a spot formerly occupied by a sacred forest – turned up in other discussions as well. Some of my informants also suggested that the Kaaba at Mecca was in fact a transformed sacred forest and therefore sacred.

What was I to make of this conundrum? First of all, the arguments suggest that these Jola had a particular understanding of Islam. Having converted at the beginning of this century, the Jola appropriated this religion and gave it their idiosyncratic meanings. Yet what struck me most in these discussions was that mosques were not considered sacred in their own right. This is quite striking and certainly not in line with the piety of Jola Islamic practice. There must have been some confusion about the term 'sacred'. Indeed, my interlocutors had consistently confused sacred (*sacré*) and secret (*sécret*), two words with quite different meanings in French. They explained to me that they considered these terms synonyms. This suggests that for the Jola, the secret is certainly one quality of the sacred, and probably the most important one. The notions of the secret and the sacred are indeed inseparable in Jola society. What is secret must be sacred and vice versa, what is sacred must be secret. There is one Jola term that semantically denotes both: *nyau-nyau* ('forbidden'). This term can be translated as 'taboo' since it is always used to prevent pollution (cf. Douglas 1966).

The connection between the sacred and the secret is not restricted to Casamance society. The English term *secret* derives from the Latin *secretus*, the past participle of *secernere*, 'to set apart' or 'to discern' (Beidelman 1997: 257). The secret is something set apart. There is a striking analogy with the etymology of 'Holy'. Douglas observes that the Hebrew root of *k-d-sh*, usually translated as Holy, is based on the idea of separation (Douglas 1966: 8). Thus Holy can be translated as 'set apart'. The etymologies of sacred and secret reveal similar meanings. On the resemblances of the sacred and the secret Bok notes:

> The sacred and the secret have been linked from earliest times. Both elicit feelings of what Rudolph Otto called the 'numinous consciousness' that combines the daunting and the fascinating, dread and allure. Both are defined as being set apart and seen as needing protection. And the sense of violation that intrusion into certain secrets arouses is also evoked by intrusions into the sacred. (Bok 1982: 6)

It seems justified to consider the secret an aspect of the sacred. The secret is sacred to most Casamançais. And although the sacred cannot be reduced to the secret, the sacred always demands a measure of secrecy. Even today, Jola women are not admitted to mosques, which are defined as essentially secret to women. The Jola tend to consider places and practices related to Islam as secret. Another example pertains to the sphere of reproduction. Babies were formerly delivered in the female sacred forests. Today, men are not allowed to attend deliveries in hospitals, since they are defined as secret to men.

The secret is safeguarded by a series of taboos, thus contributing to the sacred nature of secretive practice. Participation in these practices therefore has sacrosanct consequences. The performance of secrecy sacralises the everyday life of Casamance and sanctifies the social structures that secrecy engenders (cf. Durkheim 1915). Having thus defined secrecy as a religious practice, we should also consider how secrecy relates to the social structure at large. I think that secrecy cannot be considered a theory that explains the world to the believers, as Horton's intellectualist theory suggests religion does. However, in keeping with Geertz's theory of religion, it can be assumed instead that secrecy does provide a model *of* the cosmic order – established in powerful moods and motivations – that spills over into ordinary life, thus providing a model *for* the same order (Geertz 1973). In this respect I recall Simmel's statement about the effect of secrecy: 'The secret offers, so to speak, the possibility of a second world alongside the manifest world; and the latter is decisively influenced by the former' (Simmel 1967: 330). The secret is present in the public sphere and can arouse strong moods and motivations, and thereby structures society. This is true even in societies that are generally thought of as secularised. In his most recent book Taussig (1999) conjures up a theory of secrecy that focuses on public secrets which consist of knowledge everyone knows but no one is allowed to speak about. His theory is based on the premise that the revelation of public secrets – their exposure – amounts to sacrilege, which he thinks is the closest secular society gets to the sacred. Even in secular society, the sacred seems preserved in the secret, or rather in its exposure.

THEORY OF SECRECY

Before going on to delineate the research problem, I shall clarify my own position by taking stock of the prevailing theories of secrecy. The first seminal contribution to the sociological study of secrecy was conducted by Simmel (1968 [1908]). He suggested that secrecy is in a particular way significant in the structuration of human interaction. By means of an extremely emphatic exclusion of all outsiders, the secret provides its owner with a strong feeling of possession. This possession thus creates a position of exception. Although this position is independent of the content of the secret, it has a profound effect on everyone who is excluded from the secret. From secrecy 'grows the typical error according to which everything mysterious is something important and essential' (Simmel 1967: 333).

The most widespread form of association based on secrecy is the secret society. When the secret becomes the principle of organisation of a collective, it has profound consequences for social relations. The secret structures relations internally among the members of the secret society, as well as externally towards non-members. Reciprocal confidence among the members is typical of the secret society (ibid.: 345). The trust that co-members are capable of keeping silent creates a strong bond, designated by Simmel as a 'moral solidarity' (ibid.: 348). This confidential nature of membership must also be ensured in the novices, and is usually achieved by means of an initiation consisting of an oath and systematic instruction in the art of silence (ibid.: 349). Externally, the secret surrounds the secret society like a boundary (ibid.: 362). This is perhaps best clarified in Simmel's comment on adornment. Adornment has a structure analogous to that of secrecy: 'It is the nature and function of adornment to lead the eyes of others upon the adorned' (ibid.: 338). The brilliance of jewels radiates towards others. Secrets, like jewellery, attract attention and demand recognition from the audience. The secret subordinates and, like elaborate jewellery, demands the recognition of the beholders.

In Africa, secrecy has been studied in everyday life as well as in ritual, notably in the context of initiation rituals and masquerades. According to Piot, there are four types of analysis of secrecy in African societies: structural-functionalist, Marxist, Freudian and semiotic (Piot 1993: 354). All these types of analysis – with the exception of the Freudian approach – are applied to the Poro secret society. The Poro secret society in Liberia, Sierra Leone, Guinea and the Ivory Coast is undoubtedly the most widespread secret society in West Africa. These Poro societies often cut across ethnic, linguistic and national boundaries. The structural-functionalist analysis of these secret societies consequently focuses on their role in the political organisation of segmentary societies (Little 1949, 1965, 1966; Fulton 1972). The Marxist analysis views Poro secrecy as a means of social control in a system of power relations: the elders maintain their privileged position by monopolising secret lore (Murphy 1980).[3] The semiotic approach analyses secrecy as a communicative system and focuses on how secrecy structures communication (Bellman 1984). All these studies analyse secrecy in ritual contexts, but Piot (1993) analyses secrecy in everyday life and suggests that secrecy is pivotal in the creation of ambiguity, a necessary feature of Kabre social relations. Likewise, Ferme (2001) has argued that the secret produces ambiguity among the Mende of Sierra Leone. In my own analyses, as pursued throughout this book, I adopt various theoretical stances. My approach is basically eclectic. However, instead of focusing on how secrecy shapes communication within Casamance society, I hope to highlight how certain practices of secrecy provide their performers with the means to engage with the wider world.

The most insightful work on secrecy as a system of communication is Bellman's monograph (1984), which incorporates Simmel's emphasis on form over content and recasts this observation in a linguistic analysis. Bellman studied secrecy among the Kpelle in Sierra Leone. He begins by noting that most definitions of secrecy are based on a differentiation of content. However, Bellman argues, any item of information can be the content of a secret. Secrecy should therefore not be viewed as a power struggle between those who know and those who want to know, but according to how concealed information is revealed (Bellman 1984: 5). Bellman then focuses on the Poro secret society among the Kpelle. He shows that secrecy not only applies to communication in everyday life, but also to participation in rituals (cf. Bellman 1979). He observes that 'everyone shares in the concealed knowledge'. His theory of secrecy could perhaps be summarised in one sentence: 'The *contents* of the secrets are not as significant as the *doing* of secrecy' (Bellman 1984: 17). Most authors on secrecy agree on the importance of form over content. In New Guinea, Barth notes that: 'The rite's aspect of "doing something" thus clearly predominates for the actors over its "saying something"' (Barth 1975: 221). This captures the essence of secrecy: it is a practice. In his study on Kaguru initiation, Beidelman notes that secrets must ultimately be disclosed to be considered secrets in the first place (Beidelman 1997: 14). The secret is created in the process of its transmission. Every theory of secrecy should take into account that revealing the secret is what secrecy is all about (Taussig 1999). Secrets need to be told if they are to be secrets at all. Secrecy is actually meant to create occasions of revelation.

Bellman argues that secrets are situationally defined. This has been confirmed elsewhere. Writing about secrecy among the Vagla of north-western Ghana, Poppi emphasises that secrecy enables initiates to see what they could formerly only look at. Whereas the information is available to everyone, its interpretation changes owing to initiation into its secret signifi-cance (Poppi 1993). I found that this observation is true in Casamance as well. Certain items of knowledge can be framed as secret, but become freely accessible in other situations. The first time I went to do fieldwork in Casamance in 1989, my intention was to study masquerading. To examine the history of the Kumpo masquerade, I was going to live in Diatock, a Jola village. My professor, Jos van der Klei, who had conducted fieldwork in this village, introduced me to a young man who was presumably involved in the masquerade and recommended me as a student of the performance. Van der Klei was cautious to point out that 'I had not come to discover secrets'. The man nodded: he had already understood. My professor had apparently found a way of speaking the language of secrecy. To me his words remained an enigma. Had I come to discover secrets?

As my fieldwork progressed, I gradually came to understand that the Kumpo masquerade was indeed shrouded in secrecy.[4] I consider this obvious today, since I now have a provisional command of the language of secrecy. However, at the time I was still unaware of how secrecy struc-tures communication with regard to masked performances. Witness, for instance, my naiveté in confronting my research assistant Jimmy Carter with a question that had long since been on my mind. Suspecting the secret but tempted by my good relations with my assistant, I asked him who was actually dressed in the Kumpo costume when the mask performed at the village square. Feigning surprise, he replied: 'What makes you think that a man stages Kumpo?' Although his smile revealed that my question was well taken, Jimmy Carter clearly did not want to divulge secrets and suggested that the mask was actually not a human being. I was left with a mystery. But I noticed that other men, notably elders, were not so reticent and freely discussed the intricacies of the masquerade. I learnt that the young men had a vested interest in the masquerade and were not willing to share their knowledge of it, whereas the elders whose interests were not promoted by the masquerade freely talked about backstage matters. To what extent knowledge is secret, I learnt, depends on the context.

My experience thus far corroborates Bellman's theory but also indicates that secrecy cannot be understood without considering power relations. Some of my experiences clearly contradicted his assertion that secrecy is a form of communication. Bellman was initiated into Kpelle secret societies and thus acquired proficiency in talking secrets *and* the right to do so. This might explain why he focuses on concealment and revelation as the essential elements in the language of secrecy. In Casamance, I found that secrecy not only pertains to knowledge. Places are also shrouded in secrecy, especially the sacred forests in Jola villages. What happens in these small tracts of dense forest remains concealed to non-initiates. Since I was not initiated, the sacred forests were out of bounds to me. When attending initiation ceremonies, time and again I was sent away when the others headed for the sacred forest. My otherwise extremely hospitable Jola hosts would not let me into their sacred forest. I was and remained an outsider. I encountered the same boundaries around Mandinko initiation camps, even when these were established in rooms 'set apart' in compounds in the city of Ziguinchor. I did manage to enter some of these camps but I was eventually sent away, seriously reprimanded and fined for having violated a forbidden boundary. I thus concluded that the secret is used to reinforce boundaries.[5] When secrets are transmitted to some people but concealed from others, strong bonds and boundaries develop. These bonds and boundaries emerging in the practice of secrecy have pragmatic value to the holders of the secret.

I became sensitive to the extent to which the secret constitutes a virtually impenetrable boundary, at least for the outsider. The anthropologist Fabian had a similar experience in his fieldwork on the Jamaa religious movement in Zaire. Jamaa leaders sometimes refused to engage in conversations about the movement, leaving his questions unanswered. They would turn the tables on him and tell him to listen and answer their questions. In their performance of secrecy, the issue at stake was the power of self-assertion. Thus, while secrecy is a form of communication, an emphasis on communication does not eliminate the problem of power relations (Fabian 1998: 55–6). In this study I depart from Bellman's emphasis on secrecy as a form of communication, and stress how practices of secrecy establish relations of power. I examine how historical practices of secrecy retain their relevance in contemporary circumstances and serve as powerful techniques for self-assertion. I am particularly interested in instances where secrecy provides the organisational principle for political action (Bayart 1983a, 1983b, 1986; Bayart et al. 1992).[6] Practices of secrecy may be historical, but some of them evolved into contemporary modes for the expression of discontent with postcolonial governments. I hope to demonstrate that these practices have a long history of providing organisational principles for contestation. Indeed, this study seeks to demonstrate the historicity of resistance through secrecy (cf. Bayart 1993).[7] But it should be noted that the very same practices that resist incursions by the colonial and postcolonial state also incorporate the market economy and the state, and accommodate these encompassing structures. The fact that agency in performances of secrecy is often concealed makes these practices very productive. The very unpredictability of performances of secrecy empowers its performers. In this respect I recall Ferme's emphasis on ambiguity in political struggles in Sierra Leone: 'The effective use of ambiguity has been – and continues to be – more productive than the pursuit of social ideals of transparency' (2001: 2). In this book I attempt to show how secrecy empowers its performers in Senegal's public sphere.

LOCALISING THE SUBJECT

While situating practices of secrecy in the post-colony, this study should also take into account the argument that postcolonial nation-states in Africa have become increasingly unstable. In addition to the privatisation of the state, the impact of which is much stronger in some other African states, the process of globalisation is thought to subvert nation-states everywhere. The theory of globalisation has drawn attention to the growing flows of people, commodities and images all across the globe. The various 'scapes' in which people's lives are situated (finanscapes, mediascapes, ethnoscapes, etc.) have lost their former isomorphism and display disjuncture (Appadurai 1996). Unpredictable connections between the various flows have unforeseen consequences for identity politics. Equipped by modern means of transport and communication, transnational diasporas sustain long-distance nationalisms (Anderson 1992; Appadurai 1996: 195–6). Whether they consist of war refugees or labour migrants, diasporas establish various connections to their homelands and produce divergent imaginations of community (Malkki 1995). Globalisation has indeed led to the 'deterritori-alisation' of identity (Gupta and Ferguson 1992). People increasingly work and live in places far removed from their kin, friends and community. Yet in the face of these accelerating flows of people and commodities, there is an intense awareness of identity and a forceful, increasingly violent assertion of boundaries (Meyer and Geschiere 1999). We therefore need to think of the production of cultural difference while abandoning received ideas of localised culture (Clifford 1997). Gupta and Ferguson suggest that 'instead of assuming the autonomy of the primeval community, we need to examine how it was formed *as a community* out of the interconnected space that always already existed' (1992: 8). I will try to do so by employing Appadurai's notion of locality (1996), which I will discuss at length since it is a pivotal notion in this study.

Studies on globalisation reflect a common interest in localisation (Hannerz 1987, 1990; Friedman 1990, 1994). Globalisation and locali-sation are considered a Janus face, leading some scholars to remark that the global is in the local and, vice versa, that the local is the global. Of course, what is global must – if we have social formations in mind – also be local (Fabian 1998: 83). This study therefore seeks to account for the process of globalisation in a local context *without* assuming a juxtaposition of the local with the global. We need to think the local as an instance of the global, or, in other words, how the local is produced within the global. In a fascinating essay, Appadurai has examined what *locality* might mean in a situation of transnational destabilisation (Appadurai 1996: 178). The author examines the various modalities of the production of locality in the contemporary context of globalisation. Locality is used by Appadurai to refer to a quality of social life consisting of a sense of social immediacy brought about by certain forms of sociality, thus generating itself as context.[8] Locality, Appadurai states, is a social achievement. To view locality as a social construct implies that all social and symbolic behaviour previously understood as activities in the production and reproduction of society should also be seen as actions by which subjects deliberately define themselves and their society.[9]

Locality produces a context for local subjects within which meaningful social action can be generated and interpreted (Appadurai 1996: 184). Yet as local subjects engage in the activities of production, representation and reproduction, they contribute to the creation of contexts that might exceed the existing boundaries of the community and thus provide context to others: communities as context produce the context of communities. Social activities are therefore both context-driven (signified within the community) and context-generative (signifying to others). The problem addressed in Appadurai's essay is that in the face of larger-scale social formations, small-scale societies lose their capacity to generate context. The capability of communities to produce local subjects is profoundly affected by the locality-producing capabilities of larger-scale social formations (e.g. nation-states). In the contemporary process of globalisation the production of locality increasingly becomes a struggle.

Appadurai argues that rites of passage have traditionally been appropriate techniques for the production of locality by inscribing particular subjectivities onto the bodies of the members of specific communities (ibid.: 179). But he is rather pessimistic about the prospects for small communities to maintain their ability to produce local subjects. It is indeed obvious that the techniques used by the nation-state to discipline its citizens – education, registration, mass media, to name but a few – are overwhelming to the local community. Nonetheless, in this study I will argue that rites of passage are still excellent techniques for the production of a sense of social immediacy. My problem with Appadurai's theory is that he does not sufficiently examine the dialectical relationship of locality and contexts (cf. ibid.: 187–8). If rites of passage produce locality, they do so under ever-changing conditions. It has been amply demonstrated that ritual is historically contingent. Minor transformations in ritual structure can generate immense changes in meaning, if only because the context changes (Bloch 1986). Rituals may even be completely modelled on symbolic material derived from beyond the confines of local communities, but once they are appropriated, they empower *against* the context the material was originally taken from (Comaroff 1985; Werbner 2002). What we need to account for, when studying the techniques for the production of locality, is the local appropriation of context. Only if we acknowledge that the techniques for the production of locality are flexible and subject to change will we be able to grasp how locality is produced and reproduced.

To complement Appadurai's theory of locality, I use an idea derived from French political theory (Bayart 1993). In Bayart's view, African societies are conceived of as traditional, but have in fact always been open to external determination. In fact, the leading actors of sub-Saharan societies have tended to strengthen their positions by means of strategies of *extraversion*, mobilising resources derived from the external environment.[10] The internal structure of African societies thus stems from its relationship with the global political economy (ibid.: 27). Bayart goes on to demonstrate how this principle can be traced in the organisation of African states. This theory may seem radical in its refutation of any African authenticity, but the principle of extraversion can also be traced in other spheres than political structures: in dance (Ranger 1975), dress (Gandoulou 1989), music (Hannerz 1987), masquerading (Argenti 1998; Nunley 1987) and religion (Van Dijk 1997; Meyer 1999; Pels 1999). As Bayart argues, the adoption of foreign cultural elements was never an expression of the hegemonic power of colonialism, but of the extraordinary flexibility of the people in its grasp (Bayart 1993: 28). Shouldn't we apply the same principle to African ritual? Performances of secrecy, I argue, are increasingly extraverted towards the wider world and incorporate context to produce locality. While secrecy is commonly associated with closure and concealment, it may come as a surprise that practices of secrecy are in fact opening up societies to the world at large and incorporating the global into the local in order to produce locality.

THE PROBLEM OF 'TRADITION'

This study examines the role of practices of secrecy in the construction of locality in Casamance. My approach departs from Bellman's analysis of secrets as texts and examines practices of secrecy as signifying practices (cf. Comaroff 1985). In practices of secrecy local subjectivities are constructed that structure their performers' implicit habitus and sometimes direct them towards explicit self-assertion. The practices of secrecy provide locality and empower their performers in and sometimes against the encompassing contexts engendered by the contemporary global political economy. Secrecy sets the subjects of a particular community apart.

The locality of small-scale communities is often threatened by the process of state formation. In producing a subjectivity that undermines the subjectivity required and produced by the nation-state, practices of secrecy may counter the quest for state hegemony. The practices of secrecy are studied here in so far as they resist or accommodate state incursions. In

Senegal's post-colony, one discourse is particularly relevant to the study of the secret's capacity to produce locality. I am referring here to the culturalist discourse that is largely inherited from Senegal's first president, Léopold Sédar Senghor. His philosophy of *Négritude* and African socialism provided the basis for a cultural discourse on *enracinement et ouverture*. This ideology embraced the assimilation of Western values into African civilisation, which should essentially be rooted in local culture (Snipe 1998). While inimical to ethnicity, the policy founded on this ideology embraced expressions of local culture as 'traditions'. Traditions have therefore been incorporated in state policies and have been made part and parcel of the state's nationalist ideology (de Jong 2005). Consequently, a popular discourse on *retour aux sources* legitimises the performance of traditions within a national context. Nowadays many inhabitants of Casamance perceive their practices of secrecy as 'traditions'. The 'nationalisation' of tradition is therefore part of all performances in Senegal. Moreover, part of the cultural heritage of the Jola and Mandinko in Casamance is the product of anthropological canonisation. This anthropological canon has subsequently served the Catholic Church in its attempt to vernacularise Christianity (Foucher 2003b, 2005). This suggests that the practices of secrecy performed in Senegal, are to some extent the product of anthropological imagination, the Catholic Church's authorisation and subsequent reappropriation. This raises the question to what extent these traditions can still be ways to counter the nation-state's project. If 'traditions' have been inscribed into national and international discourses on culture, to what extent can they still be performed to assert difference?

Whereas the culturalist discourse in contemporary Senegal may have a particular trajectory, the reification of cultural practices is obviously part of a global modernity (Appadurai 1996). The selection of cultural practices and their reification into 'cultural heritage' is today part and parcel of the nationalist projects of states and separatist movements (Handler 1988). 'Culture' has become a tool in the political battle for access to resources (Baumann 1996). In this process an obvious irony is implied: while anthropologists either discard the notion of culture or attempt to redefine it, state bureaucracies and their subordinates increasingly use the notion in its old-fashioned essentialist mould. Cultural practices are increasingly objectified and commodified in this process, not only in the West but all across the globe (e.g. Errington and Gewertz 1996; Van Binsbergen 1994). Every single cultural practice can now be objectified and brought into circulation. The practices of secrecy in Casamance are facing this predicament. One of the issues to be explored in this study is how the state-sponsored discourse on 'culturalism' impacts on the objectification of sacred performances. To what extent are performances of secrecy subordinated to this culturalist discourse? Can such performances escape Senegal's cultural policy? Do these performances continue to provide moments of freedom (Fabian 1998)? I will demonstrate that performances of secrecy – initiations, masquerades – cannot escape their canonisation as 'traditions'. Yet, secrecy as a cultural model of performance remains elusive to other projects and continues to infuse reified traditions with a potential for counter-hegemonic subversion. The question to be addressed in this study can therefore be formulated as follows: how do practices of secrecy contribute to the production of locality in the face of overwhelming contexts produced by the nation-state and the global market economy? The multitude of possible answers makes any detailed elaboration of this question unfeasible. Moreover, totalising interpretations do not help us situate the locus of struggle. The answers are sought in historically contingent moments of conflict, creolisation and contestation.

FIELDWORK AND SECRECY

As rituals, performances of secrecy are framed events set apart in time and space (Turner 1987). Rituals direct our attention to the aspects of social life that are of paramount importance to the people we are studying since they themselves take the effort to perform them. While acknowledging the importance of ritual, I do not hold that rituals reflect social structure, as Durkheimians claim. In fact, a one-to-one correspondence between religious practices and the social structure – characteristic of a Durkheimian approach – should never be assumed (Van Binsbergen 1981; Thoden van Velzen and van Wetering 1988; Baumann 1996). Of course, the rituals and performances described and analysed below are not mere representations. They are events in the ongoing process of context production. These performances not only indicate what the Casamançais think and feel is important, they structure and signify their social life (Geertz 1973). This assertion should then also be understood to account for historical change. As I will try to demonstrate, performances of secrecy shape how the Casamançais come to terms with their changing reality.

If this study is an ethnography of performance, I should hasten to add that it is not a performative ethnography (Fabian 1990, 1996). However intriguing and challenging an epistemological approach to ethnography *as* performance can be, this study does not represent dialogues from the field. There is no doubt that conversation was a prerequisite for the making of this study. While I acknowledge the dialogical nature of ethnography, I do not employ the tropes proposed by some of its advocates. At various moments my project nonetheless came close to the projects of the people I was studying. My research on local traditions was sometimes seen as supporting the local politics of creating 'heritage'. Various men expressed a need for written records of the contemporary rituals. In their opinion, these records needed to be produced right now, before the rituals would vanish for good. They thought future generations would need documents on their cultural past (cf. Van Binsbergen 1985, 1992). Ethnography was solicited to save practices expected to vanish in the onslaught of modernisation. On various occasions my interlocutors wanted to help me represent *their* traditions, and some even claimed a right to edit the present text. One man in particular expressed an urgent need for records of the history of his village. He felt the community needed a *carte d'identité*. This clearly demonstrates to what extent 'traditions' serve to legitimise one's place in the nation-state, and the precariousness of that place. Others, perhaps more confident about the survival prospects of their traditions, were not prepared to talk with me. Fieldwork is not always a matter of dialogue. In the field I frequently found myself confronted with secrecy. Men and women denied me access to certain places and performances. The present text is consequently the result of dialogue *and* its negation, silence.

In this respect it is interesting that Appadurai reinterprets the ethnographic project as basically isomorphic with the social projects it seeks to describe: 'The ethnographic project is in a peculiar way isomorphic with the very knowledge it seeks to discover and document, as both the ethnographic project and the social projects it seeks to describe have the production of locality as their governing telos' (Appadurai 1996: 182). The history of anthropology may indeed be considered an accumulated effort to 'write locality'. In the context of this project, these isomorphic goals inevitably led to confrontations between the observer and the observed, me and them. When subjects sought to exclude me from secret places and performances, it might be argued that my exclusion was part of their performance of secrecy. The process of excluding me, or anyone else, constituted their secret. What follows therefore presents my own exclusions as moments of the performance of secrecy. Obviously, my exclusion implied that I was not always capable of generating the cultural knowledge that ethnography requires. Nowhere was this more apparent than the impossibility of researching female performances of secrecy. Although my participation in male initiation was seriously restricted by secrecy I was nonetheless allowed to talk secrets, as long as none of this was framed as an intrusion (which it was, at other times). Female performances of secrecy were, however, strictly out of bounds to me, and this book therefore only cursorily addresses such performances.

This ethnography examines secrecy in so far as it confronts overwhelming contexts through negation or appropriation. This approach does not privilege the representation of local society as a time-honoured formation as in more conventional ethnographies; instead it invents a society in the making (cf. Clifford 1986: 19). By examining how secret boundaries are produced, one observes how society invents itself under the condition of modernity. A focus on extraversion implies recognition of the transformative potential of performance, which is indicative of the flexibility of a society that remains 'local' owing to its continuing capacity to produce locality. This book does not portray local society as basically embedded in its own 'pure' logic. Instead I try to capture moments of extraversion that are indicative of creolisation. Purity is to be found in authentic modes of creolisation. As an ethnography that recognises the performative mediation in distinct and dispersed practices of secrecy, this study makes an effort to capture the moment of extraversion.

OUTLINE

A brief outline of the study may help direct the reader. This book can be read as a series of essays, each of which deals with yet another aspect of practices of secrecy. The practices of secrecy discussed here essentially comprise Jola and Mandinko initiations as performed in Thionck Essyl and Ziguinchor, and the Kumpo and Kankurang masked performances as performed in Diatock, Ziguinchor and some other localities in Casamance. The research for this book was conducted in a number of towns and cities and this monograph may therefore be considered multi-sited. However, the Jola and Mandinko initiations and the Kumpo and Kankurang masquerades are not performed in isolation and their performers reflect upon their differences. The various practices of secrecy constitute each other through inclusion or exclusion of the ethnic other. These performances define and defy ethnic boundaries and are understood by the Casamançais themselves as constituting their ethnic 'heritage'. The various initiations and masquerades discussed in this book should therefore be seen as interrelated practices that sustain rural–urban migrations, contest the production of national subjectivity, and produce transnational localities. Although each of the chapters can be read independently, they are presented in an order that makes an accumulative argument. The chapters are presented in three parts: Transitions, Trajectories and Traces.

The first part consists of three chapters that deal with one aspect or another of the transitions brought about by the Jola male initiation ritual. Chapter 2 describes the male and female initiation ceremonies as performed in Thionck Essyl, a Jola town in the Boulouf region. These two performances are contrasted to reveal that they accomplish different transitions in the participants. Remarkably, the Jola male and female initiations do not produce complementary, gendered subjectivities, but in fact engender antagonistic subjectivities. This first chapter on Jola initiation may serve as background for the next two chapters. Chapter 3 analyses the participation of urban and international migrants in the male initiation ceremony. Although such participants may never have lived in the village, they are eager participants in the initiation ceremony. I demonstrate that their participation is a precondition if they are to define themselves as Jola. To that

end, the ritual script has been fully accommodated to ensure their participation in the performance. This goes to demonstrate that migrants return
to take part in a ritual that produces a translocal subjectivity, performed in
a village that is transformed into a site for the enactment of the initiation
of city-dwellers: a virtual village. Chapter 4 also examines the Jola initiation, in particular the participation of politicians in that ritual. Whereas
Chapter 3 demonstrates that the ritual is accommodated to reinforce the
relations between villagers and migrants in order to produce translocality,
this chapter demonstrates that participation in the ritual is important for
politicians to create a relationship with their electorate. The electorate, in
its turn, relies for its access to the state on the participation of politicians.
This goes to show that initiation and political representation have become
increasingly intertwined. The Jola initiation ceremony, then, appears to be
a means for the incorporation, in a literal and figural sense, of the world
beyond the sacred forest.

In the second part of this book, Trajectories, we turn towards rituals
enacted in Ziguinchor, the largest city of the Casamance region. In both
chapters, I describe historical performances and suggest how these sequences
of performances suggest particular, urban trajectories. Chapter 5 describes
the trajectory of the urban rite of passage for boys, usually referred to as
the 'Mandinko circumcision'. I analyse its introduction in Ziguinchor and
the various historical transformations it has been been subject to in order
to demonstrate how the performance, at different moments in the twentieth century, produced different senses of locality. In Chapter 6 I analyse
the historical trajectory of the Kankurang, a masquerade that is held to
protect the initiates of the 'Mandinko circumcision' against witchcraft. The
masquerade is usually performed in the context of initiation, but may also
be staged at other occasions. Importantly, those who the bring the mask
out enjoy immunity and therefore act with licence. I examine historical and
contemporary cases of how the mask has been used to oppose the king and,
today, the state. The debate focuses on the interpenetration of the masked
performance and politics, and the subversive nature of the secret in political
society. However, as we will see, the secret is increasingly domesticated by
the state.

The third part, Traces, deals with transformations of secretive practices
that turn the secret into a sign. These practices are strictly speaking not,
or no longer, practices of secrecy because the secret is recontextualised in
practices of representation. The secrets are no longer a presence, but in fact
representations of local society. Chapter 7 provides an analysis of the Kumpo
masquerade and its trajectories in the market economy. Here we have a
masquerade that at various moments in its history empowered young men
in their attempt to deal with the impact of the market economy. The performance of the masquerade was used to renegotiate relations between gender

and age categories. Nowadays, however, the masquerade is also increasingly staged in order to express local identity within the context of the Senegalese state, or to perform locality for an audience of tourists. The second chapter of Part III examines the trajectory of the secret into modern art. Inspired by the initiation ceremonies and masked performances discussed so far, artists in Casamance depict these rituals in their art. I analyse how these works of art are given various, contradictory meanings depending on the context in which they are shown. The chapter shows how the depiction of secret rituals is part of the widely shared sense that such rituals will eventually vanish in the process of 'modernisation'. It is feared that such 'traditions' come to signify 'locality', even if they are not capable of producing it. However, this book demonstrates that, in spite of the modernist expectation that rituals will disappear in the onslaught of 'modernisation', they do in fact have a future as 'traditions' and continue to escape their contextualisation.

Finally, the last chapter deals with the representation of secrets in writing and reflects on the moral ambiguities involved in writing secrecy. While many anthropologists claim that they have been initiated in the secrets and are therefore not allowed to reveal them, I suggest that such rhetoric of secrecy in fact serves to enhance their authority versus the reader, turned into a non-initiate. While I recognise that the representation of secrets is a morally ambiguous area, I suggest that the performance of secrecy is in reality intersubjective. Writing secrets participates in the performance of secrecy.

PART II

TRANSITIONS

JOLA INITIATIONS, GENDERED LOCALITIES

There are various ways to travel from the national capital Dakar to the remote region of Casamance. Many tourists go on daily flights operated by Air Sénégal. However, most Senegalese cannot afford this luxury and travel by road. The journey takes one through a dry and dusty savannah dotted with occasional baobab trees, to a lush landscape of forests and valleys of rice paddies along tidal creeks and rivers. However, before arriving at one's destination in Casamance one needs to traverse The Gambia, the state that separates the southern region from the rest of Senegal (see Map 1). This idiosyncratic legacy of colonialism continues to haunt the postcolonial present. The journey through the Gambia is a time-consuming affair as the ferry that takes you across the Gambia River often causes considerable delay. The ferry is a nuisance to Casamançais, as they are looking forward to their arrival. Going south is going home, and arrival is anticipated with impatience. But the state of the road and the ferry thwarts their expectations of modern transport and infrastructure. A ferry connecting Dakar and Ziguinchor used to provide a welcome alternative to travel by road. Unfortunately, in September 2002 *Le Joola* capsized on its way to Dakar, resulting in an official death toll of 1,863 passengers. Apart from killing an entire generation of students – on their way to the capital to pursue their academic studies – this immense tragedy also aggravated the isolation of the Casamance region.

Undoubtedly, the geographic separation of the Casamance region has generated sentiments that contributed to the making of the separatist movement. Originating and operating in the Casamance region of Senegal, the Mouvement des forces démocratiques de Casamance (MFDC) has called for the political independence of the region, claiming that Casamance was never part of Senegal. The MFDC puts forward a number of grievances, including the accusation that the Senegalese regime has consistently failed to invest in the economic development of the Casamance region. The first public protests took place in Casamance in 1982, to which the Senegalese regime reacted with political oppression and military interventions. In 1990, the MFDC officially declared that armed struggle would be the only way to achieve independence. Since then, Casamançais have been living in a climate of insecurity, fear of armed robbery by rebels or bandits, and

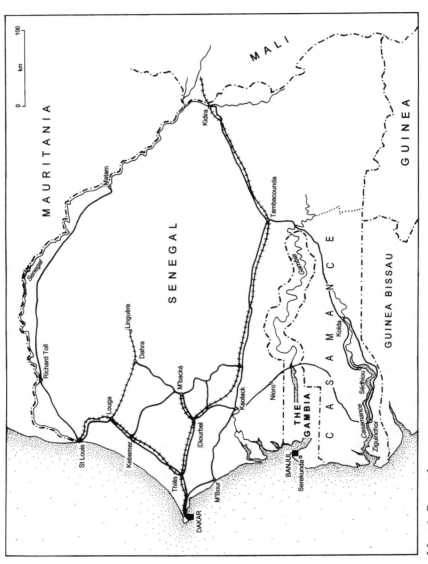

Map 1 Senegal

human rights violations by government forces. Normal economic activities have been very difficult to maintain. The local infrastructure is in decay and the growth of a promising tourist industry has been interrupted. Over the years, the parties have committed themselves to numerous ceasefires, which many times failed and led to renewed fighting. But the latest developments in Casamance suggest that peace has finally been established (De Jong and Gasser 2005: 214). The causes of the Casamance conflict have been well researched. While all researchers agree that the failing integration of the Jola in Senegalese society is the reason for the insurgency, they disagree about the root causes for this lack of integration.[1] But it seems that the geographic isolation of Casamance, although not the most important factor, has played a significant role in the instigation of the insurgency.

In spite of the hardship of the journey, most Senegalese of Casamance origin living in Dakar will continue to travel south, as kinship ties them to their place of birth. Many Casamançais make the journey home to attend religious holidays such as Korité, the festive ending of the Muslim Ramadan, or Noël, Christmas. Another ritual that all Jola migrants attend is the male initiation ceremony in their village of origin. Every Jola village celebrates its male initiation approximately once every twenty-five years. Jola male initiation is a baffling ritual that involves virtually everyone born in the village. The entire initiation cycle requires vast human efforts over a long stretch of time and the preparations start years in advance. In contrast to the frugal life villagers live throughout the years, life during the initiation ceremony is characterised by excess. Families destroy much of the wealth they have accumulated. The villagers and their guests feast on enormous quantities of meat and rice. The male initiation ceremony has its female equivalent. However, Jola female initiation is less of a potlatch and involves fewer people. Yet in many respects it is the complement to male initiation. Many men and women make the journey across Senegal and the Gambia to attend the male and female initiation ceremonies in their village of birth in Casamance.

Rites of passage are particularly suited to the production of local subjects (Appadurai 1995: 205). This chapter examines how the male and female initiation rituals produce distinct gendered subjectivities. The argument will be that the performances of secrecy bring about ritual separation between men and women. Everything that happens at the male sacred forest is kept secret from the women and vice versa, everything related to female initiation is kept secret from the men. Yet, while secrecy may be a shared discourse for the production of gender, its practices are not uncontested. Although Jola have practised ritual secrecy since times immemorial, Jola men contest female initiation for its alleged 'foreign' origin. In this chapter I will unravel why.[2] In my analysis I rely on the male and female initiation rituals I witnessed in the village of Thionck Essyl, located in the Boulouf area of

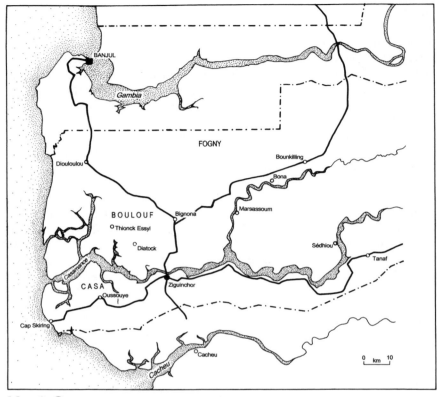

Map 2 Casamance

the administrative region of Ziguinchor (see Map 2). In July 1994, Thionck Essyl celebrated its male initiation ritual, or *garur*.[3] Three years later, in July 1997, the women of Thionck Essyl celebrated *gassus*, their counterpart to male initiation. The ceremonies staged in Thionck Essyl were unique performances and my description of the rituals differs from the descriptions of initiations in other villages provided by other anthropologists. This chapter starts with a brief introduction to Thionck Essyl's economic, political and religious life, before proceeding to describe the male and female initiations as I witnessed them. Finally, the two performances will be contrasted as rituals for the production of competing subjectivities.

THIONCK ESSYL, A JOLA TOWN

Thionck Essyl is situated in the western part of the densely populated Boulouf plateau, north of the Casamance River. It is very different from most Jola villages. In contrast to the picturesque Jola villages that attract tourists, Thionck Essyl has a distinctly modern outlook. In most Jola

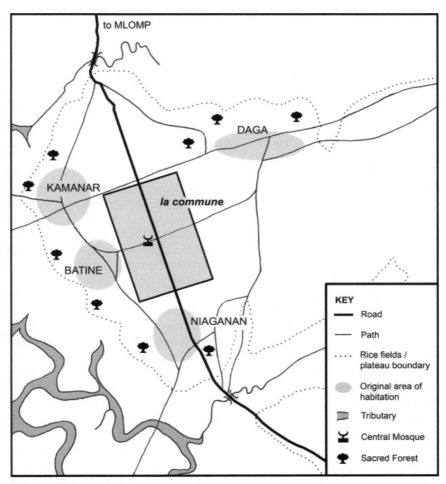

Map 3 Thionck Essyl

villages the anthropologist is easily lured into believing that village life is perpetually repeating itself, but Thionck Essyl does not encourage one to make that mistake. The village layout consists of a rectangular network of streets that give access to square lots of equal size. The main street that leads through the village is straight, from the southern tip to the northern end of the village (see Map 3). The road connects Thionck to the nearby villages of Mlomp and Tendouck, and beyond them to Bignona, the capital of the *département*. This road was constructed under colonial rule as one of the *pistes de production* to facilitate the transportation of market produce to the regional market town of Ziguinchor. The rectangular grid of Thionck, however, is a product of postcolonial policy. In the 1970s, this grid was made conditional for the construction of electricity and water networks. After a protracted debate between the various wards of the village, three out of four wards accepted this condition and relocated themselves in the area they now inhabit. The majority of the houses of the remaining ward, Batine, are currently still situated in their original location, without access to either running water or electricity.

The relocation involved the redistribution of land and the attribution of lots to the various households. The villagers thus moved away from their original wards situated near the rice fields towards the new residential area (referred to as *la commune*) built around the central mosque. Today the mosque is still the village centre, and around it are situated a Koranic school, a library and a few other facilities including a bus station. It should be said, however, that few cars pass through Thionck Essyl and passengers waiting for an opportunity to travel just wait at the roadside. Another symbol of Thionck's attempted modernisation is the large construction that was meant to house a market. However, economic production and consumption in the village were never commercialised to the extent as to require a marketplace. In spite of its ambitious modernisation projects Thionck essentially remains a large village. At the time of the 1988 census Thionck Essyl had 6,467 inhabitants (République du Sénégal 1988b: 15) and it allegedly was Senegal's largest village. However, as many members of the population engage in temporary labour migration or have permanently settled elsewhere, this figure only gives a rough indication of the number of people who consider themselves members of the community. Many of these community members live in Dakar, but remain committed to the economic development (*le développement*) of the village. The relocation, for instance, largely sprang from the imagination of Thionck's city-based migrants and reflected their interest in the modernisation of their village of birth.

Thionck Essyl has recently been assigned the administrative status of *commune*, which allows its citizens to elect their own mayor. Thionck's inhabitants are proud of this administrative status, even though all it led to was a splendid city hall that was blown up by the MFDC in 1997. The attack was a warning to Thionck's citizens who, after years of refusal, had once again started paying their taxes. This demonstrates that postcolonial forms of authority are contested, if not by the villagers, then by the separatist movement that can exert considerable pressure on the inhabitants of Thionck. However, even if the authority of the postcolonial state is not fully acknowledged, precolonial forms of authority have lost much of their legitimacy. In precolonial times, the village (*esuk*) of Thionck Essyl was composed of four wards (*galol*, plural *ulolau*) that are still political units today: Niaganan, Batine, Kamanar and Daga. The wards used to be highly autonomous political units but some political power was vested in a village-wide council of male elders (Mark 1992: 22). Matters pertaining to the

Figure 2.1 Central mosque of Thionck Essyl, next to the overgrown sacred tree (Photo: Ferdinand de Jong)

village as a whole, such as initiation and warfare, were decided upon by this council, which held its meetings in the central sacred forest. As a social unit the village also shared the office of a rain priest (*oeyi*) (Mark 1985: 8), but this institution is now defunct. Indeed, most of the precolonial and colonial political and religious institutions have been replaced with bureaucratic structures. While the colonial regime installed a *chef de village* as mediator between the village and the colonial administration, Senegal's independent government imposed various other administrative structures (Darbon 1988; Gellar 1995). Hence the central sacred forest lost its role as the focus of the political process. As a result of conversion to Islam, the central sacred forest was destroyed and replaced with a mosque. One sacred tree remains untouched, however, and still stands upright next to the mosque, in the centre of the village. As its destruction would entail mystical consequences, no one dares to cut it down (see Figure 2.1).

The village of Thionck Essyl, then, comprises four wards, each of which is divided into several sub-wards composed of several residential descent groups. Among the Jola descent is reckoned in the male line, but all anthropologists writing on the Jola make the point that the Jola do not memorise their ascendants' names. Thus Linares notes that 'beyond three generations of ascendants, everything fades into vague notions of brotherhood' (Linares 1992: 105). How, then, is social life in Thionck organised if agnatic descent

Figure 2.2 Bridge towards the rice fields of Thionck Essyl (Photo: Ferdinand de Jong)

is not the dominant structuring principle? In contrast to earlier authors who consider Jola kinship a classic patrilineal segmentary system (Thomas 1959, I: 236–57), later authors emphasise that the Jola place much more importance on residential patterns than on descent: the pivotal social unit has always been the residential unit.[4] In Thionck Essyl this residential unit is termed *fukelum*. A residential unit consists of a male elder, his wife, their married sons and in-married wives, and all their unmarried children. The *fukelum* comprises various households, each with its own premises located around a central courtyard, which is why Schloss refers to this residential unit as a House, a corporate group (Schloss 1988). Ideally, the male members of the *fukelum* share the same patronym and belong to the same lineage, but the largest of these residential groups may include unrelated men and their dependants. These unrelated members nevertheless express their affiliation in an idiom of kinship and practise exogamy. The idiom of kinship is always used in such a way as to turn the residential group into a patrifilial group. However, due to the relocation of Thionck's wards to the new residential area, the specific residential pattern typical of the House no longer exists. In everyday social life the critical social unit is the household. However, the organisation of rituals such as male initiation revolves around the patrifilial group (*fukelum*) and to some extent reveals the continuing existence of this unit.

With the exception of a few Fulani shopkeepers, all permanent inhabitants of Thionck Essyl are farmers. Their wet-rice agriculture is based on the laborious construction of dikes to reclaim rice fields from tidal waterways. The paddies are located on islands across the tidal waterways that criss-cross the lower Casamance region and expand inland towards Thionck Essyl. Long wooden bridges are in place to access these islands and their paddies (see Figure 2.2). Upon his marriage a son sets up his own household and receives rice paddies from his father so that he can assume responsibility for his own subsistence production.[5] His spouse moves in to live and work with him – all the Jola are virilocal – but she retains her father's patronym and remains a member of her patrilineage. The wife brings in her own rice paddies.[6] The household functions as a self-subsistent unit of production and consumption. Sometimes households do not have sufficient paddies to cultivate but through borrowing, all the households can have as much land as they need for subsistence production. The critical aspect in the number of plots cultivated by the household is therefore not the number of plots it has, but the availability of labour (Loquay 1979; Van der Klei 1989).

Jola wet-rice cultivation is characterised by sharp sexual division of labour. Men build the dikes and plough the fields whereas women plant seedlings and harvest the rice. Male labour is organised at the household level. Women generally form labour associations based on age sets at the sub-ward level. These associations work collectively on the parcels of their respective members. Men and women share the responsibility for sustaining the household. The man provides his household with rice during the rains, but his wife cooks her own rice to feed the household members in the dry season (Loquay 1979: 272). However, ever since the droughts of the 1970s, many households have not been able to cultivate enough to sustain themselves, and most of the inhabitants of Thionck are periodically forced to buy imported rice. As the cultivation of rice is the ultimate signifier of independent adulthood, the purchase of rice is considered shameful and even today people are very discreet about it. But there is no denying that the cultivation of rice has gradually declined over the last few decades. While most men and women born in Thionck spend part of their life cycle in the city, labour has become increasingly scarce in the village and few villagers actually manage to produce enough rice for subsistence. This has also led the villagers to diversify their household economies. In addition to rice, several other crops are cultivated in Thionck Essyl. Since the 1920s, the farmers have grown groundnuts as a cash crop, but groundnut production has declined over the past thirty years due to the falling price on the world market. For cash, the men increasingly rely on orchards of oranges, lemons and mangoes. The women collectively engage in horticulture and produce tomatoes and lettuces for the urban market. Men or women are occasionally lucky and make a lot of money through such cash crops, but most farmers have great difficulties ensuring their subsistence. In fact many households depend for their livelihood on remittances they receive from urban kin (Lambert 2002).

The surpluses of rice harvested throughout the years used to be stocked in rice granaries that were only accessible to their owners, who would never make the contents of their granaries public knowledge. Today it is increasingly difficult to create a rice surplus, as labour is in short supply. For men, cattle are now the primary means of accumulation (women do not inherit cattle). The Jola of Thionck Essyl do not use their cattle for animal traction in agricultural production and they are solely kept as accumulated wealth. The owners cautiously hide their property from the jealous eyes of their peers and guard their herds in neighbouring villages, or even in the Gambia (Van der Klei 1989: 195). Of course, other prestige goods have been introduced into the village such as corrugated iron roofs and electronic equipment (transistor radios, televisions and telephones). But in the egalitarian Jola society, accumulation of wealth is generally looked upon with suspicion. The demonstration of one's wealth is only possible through its redistribution at community-wide celebrations. Before Thionck's inhabitants converted to Islam, the funerals of elders (*nyunkul*) used to be the ultimate occasions for the ostentatious redistribution of wealth. Today, only the male initiation ritual has retained this potlatch nature.

SACRED FORESTS

The spatial focus of the initiation is the sacred forest (*gureng*). As irrefutable markers of the landscape, sacred forests are ecological signs of major importance in the production of locality (Appadurai 1995: 208). The sacred forests of Thionck Essyl consist of huge trees overgrown with ivy and they are virtually impenetrable due to the thick undergrowth. The forests are up to two hundred metres in length and have a diameter of at least one hundred metres. The centre of the forest usually consists of a huge silk cotton tree planted many generations ago. Before Thionck's relocation, the dwellings of each ward used to be situated right next to its sacred forest (see Map 3). Historically, a settlement's political independence was established by the erection of an initiation shrine in a male sacred forest (Baum 1999: 150). The sacred forest as the central sanctity of a ward symbolically refers to the act of the ward's foundation because in the forest the ward's relationship to protective spirits is acknowledged.

Before the introduction of the world religions, Jola communities probably regulated their entire social, economic and political life by means of shrines (Linares 1992; Baum 1999). Thionck Essyl's social life was historically organised around spirit shrines (*buneti*, plural *sineti*), located in houses or courtyards, or at the base of large silk-cotton trees.[7] However, the entire population of Thionck now professes either Islam or Christianity and shrines are no longer openly venerated. Whether they still venerate the shrines in the sacred forests has remained a mystery to me. Thionck's Muslims state that all the shrines have been destroyed but the public denunciation of pre-Islamic practices does not preclude the shrines continuing to have a secret life. To make the veneration of spirits compatible with the new religious convictions, palm wine libations have been replaced by sacrifices of kola nuts and prayers to Allah. Thionck's Muslims and their imams generally feel that the initiation ritual at the sacred forest is compatible with their Muslim conviction, but there are certainly contradictions. That conversion to Islam was to have profound consequences for the meaning and practice of initiation is obvious and these will be discussed in Chapter 3.

Interestingly, while some spirit shrines are accessible to mixed congregations, the ones at the sacred forests are only for the members of one sex and are strictly out of bounds to members of the other. The sacred forests demarcate separate ritual domains for men and women. Formerly, female sacred forests were the appropriate place for women to deliver, and male sacred forests were and still are the sites for the enactment of the male initiation ritual. One begins to see that the sacred forests are important places for the separation of the sexes, as symbolised through their roles in reproduction. Later we will see that beliefs relating to the sacred forests indeed separate the reproductive capacities of men and women.

The sacred forest used for the male initiation ritual is always taken care of by a male elder who is referred to as *afan gureng*: 'grandfather of the forest'. In Thionck, it is usually the oldest member of one particular lineage in a sub-ward who is responsible for its sacred forest. The office is inherited along the male line of descent. Upon the death of the officiant the office is inherited by his brother, and successively by his eldest son, etc. If the lineage responsible for the forest of a sub-ward dies out, the responsibility can be given to the officiant's sister's son (*assebul*) and thereby become hereditary in another lineage.[8] This particular lineage is said to be the 'owner' of the forest and also 'owns' the drums to be used during the initiation ritual. Every sub-ward has a pair of drums (*emumbi*, a wooden slit drum, and *fujundum*, a huge wooden cylindrical drum with a leather drumhead). Both of the drums are considered sacred (*nyau-nyau*).[9] They are carefully hidden from women and other non-initiates in the interval between initiations.

Some sub-wards do not have their own proper forest and share a forest with other sub-wards, but sub-wards belonging to different wards do not have forests in common. For example, in the Niaganan ward three sub-wards (Boutem, Djiwat and Dialil) share one sacred forest that the officiants (*ufan gureng*) of the respective sub-wards take care of. The fourth sub-ward (Kafanta) has its own forest. In Batine ward, the sub-ward Ba has its own forest, and the two other sub-wards (Balinkine and Elogogne) share a forest. Thus some sub-wards share a sacred forest and others have their own. The reason for this lack of equality lies in the segmentary nature of village politics. Conflicts within a ward easily lead to fissure and the departing section may establish its own sacred forest. The pattern of relationships between sub-wards and forests exhibits a strong tendency towards fission and the process of fusion is never strong enough to result in a communal forest for all sub-wards in a ward.

A sacred forest can be abandoned if it does not adequately meet the needs of the inhabitants of a sub-ward. For example, three Niaganan sub-wards with a communal sacred forest were confronted with numerous afflictions and a high mortality rate, and decided to relocate their sacred forest. Since sacred forests can be shared with other sub-wards, established and abandoned, the relation between a sub-ward and a sacred forest is unstable. Moreover, as a result of conversion to the world religions and the integration of the Jola into the state, the sacred forests lost their pivotal role in the political process. The village of Thionck used to have one central sacred forest (Badiangusor) where the council of elders decided village matters, but the villagers destroyed the forest in 1952 and replaced it by a central mosque. Clearly, the site of the mosque is still the most important sacred site of the village but it is no longer a site where all village matters are discussed and decided with the authority formerly associated with the central sacred forest. Today, the remaining sacred forests of the sub-wards do not stand in a hierarchical relation to each other. They are no longer used for political meetings. The initiation ritual is the only occasion when the entire community of Thionck Essyl focuses on its sacred forests. The sub-wards that share a sacred forest then unite in a single congregation.

Lush vegetation is an important feature of the sacred forest in preserving its secretive quality. If a sacred forest has recently been established and dense vegetation is still lacking, artificial devices are used to ward off the inquisitive glances of non-initiates. When the three sub-wards of Niaganan ward decided to relocate their sacred forest, they chose a large silk-cotton tree as focal point. However, the site's vegetation was not dense enough and fences were used to keep non-initiates from getting a glimpse of the secret activities in the forest. The officiants also planted trees to make it grow impenetrable. Everything that happens inside the forests is shrouded by strict secrecy. Women and non-initiates are not supposed to know or are expected to feign ignorance about what is going on in the men's forests. Women's sacred forests are equally mysterious to men. The ritual separation of men and women is reinforced by beliefs and practices that make people even more afraid to approach the sacred forest of the opposite sex. The secrecy of everything related to the forest is denoted by the term *nyau-nyau*. While the forest's sacredness may theoretically derive from the presence of a shrine at its inner core, its sacredness is naturalised through the performance of secrecy outside the forest. The secrecy pertaining to the sacred forest is primarily observed during the ritual seclusion of novices. At other times, during the interval between initiations, the sacred forest is not cared for and is left to run wild. But everyone can tell a sacred forest apart, and no one will venture into it.

MALE INITIATION

Today's forests are still sacred for Muslims and Catholics and initiation rituals are still performed in them. The moment of their performance depends on the sequence of a regional cycle. This sequence is prescriptive but the exact year of initiation in a particular village depends on the decision by the sacred forest officiants (*ufan gureng*). In July 1994, Thionck Essyl celebrated its male initiation ritual or *garur* for the first time since 1962. However, as a result of dissension three sub-wards of Niaganan (Boutem, Djiwat and Dialil) had held their initiation in 1990. The fourth Niaganan sub-ward (Kafanta), together with the other wards of Thionck (Batine, Kamanar and Daga), performed the initiation in 1994. Jola villages are always divided into two factions and the decision regarding the year of initiation is always contested among the factions. It thus happens that the factions organise their initiation at different moments, as was the case in Thionck Essyl. The reasons for this conflict will be examined in Chapter 4. Here, I provide a description of the 1994 performance. As the performance of the ritual depends on the improvisation skills of its organisers, there is considerable variation in the ritual practices between villages and, due to the autonomy of the wards, even within villages. In this respect it is important to note that I lived in Kafanta, and my account may reveal this. I should also note that due to my research schedule, I arrived on the eve of the initiates' entry to the sacred forest. Although most visitors arrived on that day, it should nonetheless be noted that I had missed out on many of the preliminary rituals. Based on what the participants told me about them, I can only briefly relay them. What should also be mentioned is that I did attend the ritual retreat for its full duration. Even though I was befriended by some of the villagers, however, I was not allowed to enter the sacred forest. The following impression is therefore written from the edge of the sacred forest.

Preparations

After the rainy season of 1993, with what promised to be an abundant harvest, the initiation ritual was publicly announced. One morning, the men assembled at ward level and each of the wards took off to a place called Fundim, located outside the village. While walking, the wards made sure not to encounter each other and followed a prescribed order (Niaganan, Batine, Kamanar and Daga). This avoidance by the wards expressed their independence in the upcoming collective ritual action. Only the novices and initiated men took part in the procession as Fundim was taboo (*nyau-nyau*) for women and guests. After their visit to Fundim, where all were blessed by an officiant, the congregations returned to their respective wards. There, the officiants of the sacred forests publicly announced the upcoming initiation to the audiences gathered at the public spaces of the respective wards. The announcers spoke in metaphors, saying: 'This year our children have grown up, we are going to bathe them.' Any explicit references to the initiation ceremony were considered mystically dangerous for women. Moreover, the use of metaphors was designed to conceal the exact nature of the upcoming event from women and other non-initiates.

The public announcement was a great event to which numerous high-ranking officials were invited, and was publicised on the local radio station. The event also marked a change in the status of the novices, who were now considered taboo (*nyau-nyau*), indicative of their liminal state. However, the ritual did not really affect the behaviour of novices and they barely adhered to the rules imposed on them. After the announcement, most of the migrant novices left the village and returned to their homes in their cities of residence.

While the officiants of the sacred forests held their secret meetings in the forests, public preparations consisted of dancing exercises (see Plates 1 and 2). Preparatory dances were not only held in Thionck Essyl but in all the cities with substantial numbers of migrants from Thionck Essyl. Thus novices regularly danced in various towns across Senegal and the Gambia (Bignona, Ziguinchor, Dakar and Gunjur). During these exercises 'guardians' taught the novices the initiation dance and ostentatiously rebuked and humbled them. The novices were made to respect their guardians, who had themselves been initiated in 1962. The guardians thus exercised their authority over the novices, though they themselves were subservient to the male elders who had been initiated in 1940. The preparations for *garur* clearly reinforced the classification of men into various male age grades. The age set of men initiated in 1940 secretly directed the ritual preparations while the age set of men initiated in 1962 were concerned with the daily supervision of the novices. While the preparations reinforced the hierarchy between males, the guardians themselves often dressed up as women or had their faces painted to contribute to a carnivalesque atmosphere of role-inversion (see Plates 3, 4 and 5).

By July 1994 the migrant novices started coming back to Thionck and the village was getting increasingly crowded. In the last couple of days before the entry into the sacred forest, a final preparatory ritual was performed. In *buyeet*, the novices were accompanied by their agnatic kin and visited their matrilateral relatives. The ritual lasted for several days, with visits to villages throughout the entire region. The novices were brought to the compounds of the lineages that had once upon a time given a wife to the novice's lineage.

This was to remind the novices of the ties that linked them to these lineages of wife-givers. Every time the assembled men of a particular lineage arrived at the compound of the wife-givers, they formed a phalanx and threatened to invade the compound by force. After some make-believe fights the novices and their kin were welcomed by a senior woman in the compound, carrying white cotton clothes. The novice's maternal uncle then shaved the eldest novice's head and tied a cloth around the young man's waist, admonishing him to remember his roots in this compound (see Plates 6 and 7). The novice then performed a vigorous dance in the middle of the compound (Mark et al. 1998: 39–40). This ritual emphasised the relation between the maternal uncle (*mamai*) and his sister's son (*assebul*), which is an important one in Jola society. The *assebul* has numerous obligations to his maternal uncle (e.g. to assist him in cultivation and other work), while the uncle in turn has to lend his nephew rice fields and give him his daughter as wife if the *assebul* wants him to (Van der Klei 1989: 93–4). In the *buyeet* ritual the maternal uncle and the sister's son are reminded of these mutual obligations, and the two lineages commemorate how they have become affines (Van der Klei 1989: 162–4).

The last day before the entry into the sacred forest – Friday, 15 July – was dedicated to an assembly of thousands of people in front of the village's central mosque, the former site of Thionck's central sacred forest. Thionck's imam, several marabouts and a male elder from each ward made speeches and blessed the novices. But the guardians, who continuously fired their shotguns, made most of the speeches inaudible to the audience. The atmosphere was one of general excitement.[10] By noon, everyone returned to their compounds, which were bursting with visitors, and the women had a hard time feeding them. The cooking was done in the kitchens set up in the compounds that had been selected by the lineages as their places of assembly. At night, the novices were secluded in this compound, in eager anticipation of their entry into the sacred forest.

Entering the Forest

The day of entry (*bunokhen*) started with the killing of bulls. Every lineage killed as many bulls as it needed to feed the members of the family and their guests (*ajangarur*, plural *ujangarur*). The more bulls killed, the wealthier the lineage, whose members kept track of the number killed. In the afternoon, everybody gathered at the ward common. By now, everybody had become very excited and especially the guardians seemed elated, irregularly firing their – often self-made – guns, causing confusion among the audience. Some of these gunmen gave the impression of being intoxicated. A special kind of fermented millet beverage (*bunkaye*) was served, which was believed to strengthen the men. Some men carried bottles of water and roots. I am not sure that the bottles said to contain water did not in fact contain *cana*, a spirit made from sugar cane. Others chewed roots that were said to eliminate fear and promote a state of excitement (*neeneeken*). All ran around nervously, carrying numerous weapons including shotguns, knives, swords and spears. To demonstrate their invulnerability, some men pretended to saw at their limbs with knives. Although amulets allegedly made the men invulnerable, some men inevitably wounded themselves but this was blamed on the occult treachery of enemies. The guardians demonstrated the courage and virility required of warriors, adorned with amulets that were made to render them invulnerable (see Plate 8). In contrast, the supple and muscular bodies of the novices represented the ward's future force, still to be forged into men. The novices were very nervous. They were about to enter the sacred forest, a domain of unknown powers and secrets. Their dancing became ever wilder up to the point when some of them panicked (see Plate 9). The elders then decided to take them away. The drums were silenced and some of the elder men threw their spears in the direction of the sacred forest. A procession left for the sacred forest, headed by the elders, the novices surrounded and protected by their guardians (Plate 10). Women and other non-initiates, including myself, followed. When the procession approached the sacred forest, the guardians turned to the women and sang: 'From now on the novices are ours.' Women were not allowed to proceed beyond that point. (I had been stopped long before then.) They witnessed their sons and brothers being taken into the sacred forest and remained uncertain about what was to become of them. For weeks on end, nothing was heard about the novices in the village.

Seclusion

The next day, most visitors went home. But novices under the age of eight were taken to the forest, accompanied by novices from other villages, who for one reason or another preferred to be initiated in Thionck Essyl. In the following weeks, novices delayed by exams or work in the formal economy kept arriving in the village and were quickly taken to the forest. This clearly illustrates the extent to which the ritual has been adapted to suit the demands of the market (see Chapter 3). Yet the majority of the young men spent a full three weeks at the forest. In the village, the women spent some of their time in the kitchen of the lineage compound where the food for the novices was prepared. Since all contact between the women and the novices was to be avoided, guardians took the meals to the forest. Water was transported to the forest's edge by pre-pubescent girls. While male elders spent most of their time in the forest, instructing the novices, the guardians were in charge of the daily logistics, performing the tasks assigned to them by their elders. Life in the village revolved around the ritual, but the proceedings at the forest were not discussed in the village. However, at night the beating of drums in the forest could be heard.

As noted above, I never entered the sacred forest. What happens at the sacred forest is defined as secret, although some men occasionally discussed the proceedings in the forest with me. I have very little to say about what went on in the sacred forest. As established in the anthropological literature, initiation usually imbues esoteric lore (La Fontaine 1985). In Thionck, the elders probably instructed the novices. What this instruction entailed, how elaborate it was and whether the knowledge was shared by all the novices are questions I cannot answer. Presumably, the transmitted lore pertains to procreation as this activity is made formally accessible to the novices through initiation (even though quite a few novices had already gained some informal experience). If the contents of such lore remain uncertain, we can be sure that its transmission is part of drilling exercises. The drilling has the express purpose of creating an *esprit de corps*. The young men of the ward are forged into an age set, the members of which will always remember that they were together subjected to the terror of their elders.

Assaye

Jola male initiation creates a ritual separation between the sexes through secrecy (Schloss 1988). Let me invoke yet another performance of secrecy to illustrate how this works in Thionck's initiation. On the second night of the novices' seclusion, everybody in my compound was attentively watching the World Cup soccer final on television. Needless to say, men paid more attention than women. But a strange thing happened during the match. An unfamiliar noise was heard outside the compound. Suddenly the women were very excited. They claimed Assaye had passed by. Windows and doors were immediately closed, lights and television switched off, and everybody went to bed. It was a rather unexpected end to a World Cup final. The next day and for weeks to come, people continuously talked about this thing called Assaye. The men enjoyed impressing me with lengthy descriptions of Assaye's supernatural qualities. As a mystery associated with the sacred forest, talking about it extended their authority vis-à-vis a non-initiate like me. But I quickly understood that Assaye was a bull-roarer. Bull-roarers, I knew, are widely used in West African initiations to scare women and novices.

Assaye was also named *afan gureng*, 'master of the forest'.[11] His appearance was much feared by the women. Whenever people whispered that the 'master' was approaching, they fled and hid in a house. One night a fight broke out between a woman and her niece, and all of a sudden everyone heard the 'master' make his way to the compound. Everybody went inside and locked the doors: the fight was immediately over. Sometimes, the mystery intervened among the villagers to punish wrongdoings. For instance, if a meal for the novices was poorly prepared or late, the 'master' punished the responsible woman by imposing a fine on her entire age set. The fine could amount to as much as a bull. Such fines were also imposed if the women quarrelled. Since women should never see the 'master', the 'master' communicated with the women through a male mediator. Assaye did not only inculcate a general compliance with ritual activities among the women, he presumably also did so among the novices. The novices were told that the 'master' protects them against evil forces.[12] Although the novices received protection from the 'master', they were nevertheless scared to death by the unfamiliar sounds produced by Assaye. Hence the secret of the 'master' was used to inspire fear among the women and the novices alike. However, while the women were permanently deceived by the secret, it was revealed to the novices. By the end of their seclusion, some of the eldest novices were taught the working of the mechanism.

Women consider the 'master' a threat to their reproductive capacity. Exposure to Assaye and everything else related to the male forest is thought to turn women barren. The 'master' reinforces the female fear of the male sacred forest. The danger of pollution is mediated through very basic emotions. But not only women fear contamination of their capacity for reproduction. Indeed, the men believe that the women want to discover the secrets of male initiation and transform themselves into animals to enter the sacred forest at night. Formerly, when circumcision was still practised during the initiation retreat, the novices would be recovering and were considered especially vulnerable to the attacks of witches. Assaye was there to curb female transgressions into the space where boys were made into males capable of reproduction. The bull-roarer is therefore performed to counter the alleged mystical and potentially nefarious powers of the women. Secret domains are protected by means of secrets (the 'master'), but the performance of such secrets is intrinsically related to a belief in the uncontrolled mystical powers associated with the opposite sex. The performance of secrecy in the context of Jola initiation reinforces the ritual separation between the sexes and naturalises gender categories.

Coming Out

After two weeks of seclusion, all novices were taken out of the forest and allowed to wash in a creek. This ritual washing of the novices (*gatas umanja*) marked the first step towards their coming out of the forest. The next morning, they had their first public appearance in a celebration at the edge of the sacred forest. All the women and girls went to the sacred forest and lined up in front of a 'gate'. Inside the forest the novices were waiting in line, dressed in lianas (*gatombol*, plural *utombol*) that covered their heads and bodies. Some of the initiates carried *ejumbi* masks (see cover of this book). One by one, the novices were led out of the sacred forest where their guardians took off the upper part of their costume, revealing the novices' faces. After their momentary revelation, their faces were immediately covered and they were taken back into the forest.[13] In the past, the initiation lasted for several months, during which time women were not informed about the health of their sons. This ritual – *ganghalen*, the demonstration – was the first opportunity for the mothers to find out how their sons were doing. The period of seclusion has, however, been drastically reduced and modern medicine is now available at the forest, so the chance of a novice dying during the ritual seclusion is now very small. But the ritual separation of more than two weeks still arouses fear among the novices and their mothers, which explains their joy at recognising each other. In 1994 the *ganghalen* ritual in Kafanta took a long time, since more than four hundred novices were to be shown. It should be noted that this is the number of initiates in the sub-ward Kafanta alone. The number for Thionck as a whole may have exceeded 3,000 initiates.

Towards the end of the initiation retreat, kin and guests who had attended the entry into the forest returned to the village again to attend the coming out ceremony. The number of languages spoken in the village increased significantly and hip female urbanites, fashionably dressed for the occasion, transformed the village into a cosmopolitan catwalk. The four-wheel drive vehicles that arrived attested to the interest of high-ranking civil servants in the ritual. After a three-week retreat, the novices were expected back in the village. The youngest boys and 'strangers' came out two days before the general coming out ceremony (*gapurem*). Their coming out was not as spec- tacular as that of the elder novices on 6 August, a day of great excitement. In the afternoon of that day, all the villagers and guests walked up to the gate of the sacred forest. The women formed two lines, creating a closed space in front of the gate. They clapped a rhythm and sang the songs composed during the 1922 and 1940 initiations, to commemorate the grandfathers of today's initiates. The guardians danced vigorously. Again they chewed roots and carried guns which were fired at irregular intervals. Some of them were dressed as transvestites, prolonging the liminality of the ritual process. *Kanyalen* women also entertained the crowd and continuously surprised the audience with self-humiliating horseplay. Many of the villagers and guests carried video recorders and cameras. The male elders who had been responsible for the novices' training came out of the forest first, with an air of proud directors. The novices followed them and silently lined up before the gate just outside the forest. They were dressed in black cloths with a red fez, and held decorated sticks in their right hands while their left hands and their faces remained hidden under their cloths (see Plate 11). The women were not yet allowed to recognise them. Then the guards started a dance, creeping on their knees in front of the forest, singing, 'Kafanta, put your sons on the ground!' The tension gradually rose. Then all of a sudden, all the guardians discharged their guns, producing an overwhelming noise and clouds of smoke. The coming out was a fact and the initiation was completed. Everybody danced. There was laughter and joy, and constant gunfire. Whoever had a camera took pictures.

After a while, the novices formed a long single file and were taken back to the village (see Plate 12). The novices walked two by two, in a quiet and disciplined fashion, and put down their staffs in unison, marking their progression by the rhythm. The women and girls followed the procession headed for the sub-ward's central square, where the novices' journey had started three weeks earlier. Upon arrival at the square, the novices were welcomed by their mothers and sisters (see Plate 13). This was also a photo opportunity to celebrate the transformation of boys into men, brought about by the elders (see Plate 14). Finally, the novices were divided into groups of agnates and taken to their respective lineage compounds. In the compounds, the novices were allowed to show their faces to their mothers and sisters, though they were not yet to be greeted (see Plate 15). For the guardians and elders as well, the ritual was now completed and they put on new caftans. The men were proud of the successful completion of the initiation and the hospitality they had offered to so many guests. The fathers of the initiates had lived up to their most important responsibility towards their sons.

The next day, the mothers and sisters were allowed to greet the initiates and present them with gifts. The initiates' newly acquired status was a clear source of pride for their mothers and sisters. The initiates were given scarves that they attached to their staffs. They then walked through the ward and visited the various compounds, receiving gifts and greeting everybody in their new capacity as adults (*furemben*, plural *guremben*) (see Plate 16). The next day, they took off their black cloths and put on a new caftan, which marked their final integration into adult society. Their successful journey into adulthood was then continued with a variety of festivities: soccer matches were held between the various wards of the village and at some of the youth centres in Thionck, the young initiates danced with their girl-friends all night long. However, these pleasures did not last long, as most of the visitors, including the girls, went back home to their cities of residence shortly after the coming out ceremony. In fact, most of the initiates themselves returned to the cities they had come from. A few days later, all the compounds looked eerily deserted.

MALE LOCALITY

The initiation ritual is a performance of the ideal structure of Jola society. All the important categories of Jola society are made manifest in the performance of initiation (cf. Durkheim 1915). The Jola male initiation reproduces these categories and inculcates in the initiates a sense of belonging to particular corporate groups. Here, I would like to examine which categories of Jola society are reproduced in male initiation and how these categories are natu-ralised in the experience of its participants.

In the initiation ceremony, people were constantly moving through the village in an orchestrated fashion. Processions were a recurrent phenomenon in the *garur*. The core of the procession always consisted of the novices, who were uniformly dressed and had similar haircuts. The core of novices was surrounded by men who had gone through the previous initiation (Fas-Fas in 1962). These guardians were there to protect the novices, in a physical and mystical sense. To enhance their frightening performance, they carried home-made cannons and shotguns that were fired at irregular intervals, contributing to the carnavalesque atmosphere. In contrast, the elders generally had a solemn look and headed the processions, giving directions and leading the entire ritual. The elder men belonged to the age set initiated in 1940 (Bagonbane). Finally, at the rear of the procession, the women did most of the singing and dancing, while tapping old shovels for rhythmical accompaniment. The rigorous spatial organisation of the processions categorised the participants according to the principle of initiation itself. The men were differentiated into age grades according to their moment of initiation and the women constituted the category of non-initiates. Most of the guests easily found a place among their peers in the same category. However, I was myself neither a novice nor an initiated adult. While I was allowed to attend the processions, I found myself negotiating a place between the non-initiates (the women) and the initiated men of my age. Clearly, I did not fit in.

The goal of male initiation is to forge all the young men into one age set and to elevate the age set to adulthood. The ritual emphasises the young men's equality and obligation to help each other, imbuing them with age-set solidarity. In Thionck, the 1994 initiation was given a name that will forever remain with the newly forged generation (Matkane: 'That will never happen' – see Chapter 4). The young men are now entitled to marry and set up their own households. The elders will now recede from public life and probably pass away before the next initiation. The formerly intermediate generation of Fas-Fas will now assume its social and moral responsibilities. The entire age grade system thus reproduces itself and the cycle of life is continued (Van der Klei 1989: 179–80).[14]

In addition to the age-grade system, the lineage is another category reproduced in *garur*. The organisation of the *garur* largely results from the cooperation between members of the lineage, tapping their individual and collective resources. The collaboration of members of the House (*fukelum*) is also expressed in the construction of a central kitchen (*ewayn*) in one of the lineage compounds. Rice and ingredients are stocked in the kitchen where the women cook the meals to be transported to the sacred forest. In this central compound, agnatic novices are secluded before their departure to the sacred forest. Here too, they spend the nights after coming out from the forest. This central compound thus serves as the focus of the ritual activities of the House. As noted before, initiation is also an opportunity for the ostentatious display of the House's wealth. The number of bulls killed by each lineage, the number of guests received and the quantity of food offered are tokens of the lineage's prestige. This rivalry reveals that *garur* is not only an initiation, but a potlatch where the honour of the House is at stake (cf. Mauss 1954: 4–5).[15]

We noticed that the processions in the initiation ceremony categorise the participants into gender and age groups. But the processions do not only reinforce these structuring principles of Jola society, they also make visible the segmentary structure of Jola society. Throughout the initiation ceremony, processions assemble initiates in corporate groups at different levels of aggregation. Processions always depart from the central compound of the House and take the initiates to the ward's central square, and vice versa. At one particular ceremony – the meeting at the central mosque – the initiates were first taken to the ward's central square and from there onwards to the village square in front of the mosque. This goes to show that the initiates always need to assemble at the aggregate level of the ward before they can join the congregation of the village. The initiates are made to embody the political structure of the village by processing between the places associated with the different levels of aggregation.

While the processions formally recognise the segmentary structure of Thionck, the ritual procedures also evoke a potential hierarchy among the wards, either in attributing wards specific ritual responsibilities or in giving a ward the right of first enactment. For instance, Niaganane claims to organise *fundim* and Batine claims to lead *etep emano*. The entry into the sacred forest (*bunokhen*) also occurred in a set order, with Niaganan entering its sacred forest first. Individuals sometimes question the privileges of other wards by downplaying the importance of rituals led by others while emphasising the importance of the rituals led by themselves. There is a strong spirit of competition among the wards. However, all wards do meet for the village-wide celebrations and the communal prayers at the central square of the village. In spite of inter-ward competition, initiation involves the entire village and through its enactment reproduces the village as a social unit.

Finally, the initiation ritual also reproduces the region as a social unit. The villages of the Boulouf region belong to a regional ritual cycle in which each village has an assigned position, determining when it has to celebrate its initiation. The untimely organisation of an initiation is generally felt to call down misfortune on the village. Thionck Essyl violated the order by celebrating its initiation in 1994 while Diégoune and Djimandé which were scheduled to perform *before* Thionck were still at the preparation stage. The awareness of a ritual cycle nonetheless inculcates a sense of regional identity. The initiation thus produces in the initiates a sense of belonging to House, ward, village and region. While male initiation enables the transition from boys into adults, it simultaneously incorporates them into the structure of Jola society and makes them embody that very structure.

FEMALE INITIATION

Three years after the celebration of male initiation, the female initiation (*gassus*) was held in Thionck Essyl. According to my female interlocutors, female initiation is a relatively recent innovation and was performed for the first time in the 1940s. Since its introduction the performance follows the cycle of male initiation, with *gassus* happening two or three years after the male ritual. Despite its recent introduction, the women consider *gassus* a full-fledged initiation. One woman asserted, '*gassus* is our tradition that we respect and will never give up!' I attended the female initiation performed in 1997, three years after the male initiation. Although I attended the entire ritual, the following description is very brief in comparison to my description of male initiation. This is partly because my enquiry into female initiation was restricted by the secrecy women observed vis-à-vis all males, myself included. I was not even informed about its date of performance. One woman nevertheless alerted me to the upcoming event, which I would otherwise have missed. Because of the secrecy I faced when talking about the ritual, my description is mostly based on observations made in the public domain. However, I should emphasise that *gassus* is not comparable to the male initiation in terms of ritual elaboration, investment of time and money, and interest on the part of the community (cf. Linares 1992: 110). Male migrants do not bother to return to the village to attend *gassus* and even women are more apt to attend male initiation than *gassus*.

   On the eve of 13 July 1997, all the participating girls, all between ten and twenty-five years old, were assembled in their respective paternal compounds. Adult women danced all night at the ward's square where a hut (*diudiu*) was constructed for the seclusion of the girls. At midnight the women started a procession through the ward accompanied by three drummers playing the *kutiring* (Mandinko drums). Young men initiated in 1994 fired guns, as this was now their prerogative. The procession was halted at all the compounds where the girls of a lineage were assembled. The girls were then incorporated into the procession, which went on until late at night, after which the girls were secluded in the initiation hut. The next morning all the girls were led into the female sacred forest (*kuyangba*). The drummers played a variety of rhythms, some of which were typical of Thionck's fertility dances (*enyalenay*), others of Jola dances (*bugarabu*), others again of Mandinko initiation rites (*diambadong*): the selection of rhythms was rather eclectic. The women and novices spent the entire day at the forest and returned to the village towards sunset, a pattern to be repeated throughout the entire week. The women spent the day at their sacred forest and the night in their hut at the ward's central square. At some distance from this hut, a provisional kitchen had been constructed where young men prepared the meals for the girls in the hut of seclusion. At night, the beating of drums in the hut could be heard throughout the ward.

The female initiation was performed by the women of the ward who organised the ritual on behalf of their daughters who, unlike themselves, are female agnates of the ward (cf. Linares 1992: 110). During the ritual process contact between the girls and ordinary men was taboo but the female initiation in Kafanta was led by a male 'stranger' from Fogny. The women claimed he had a mystical capacity, a 'wide head' (*kunfanunte*) that enabled him to protect the novices from evil forces. The man was in charge of the entire ritual and was paid for his work. The mystical protection of the novices was not limited to the presence of this man. In some wards an anvil was placed on the ground near the novices' hut, which was regularly beaten by the leading novice (*kuya mansa*, 'the queen of initiation'). The mystical power associated with the anvil (and the forge) and the 'wide head' of the stranger were supposed to drive away sorcerers. However, the association of the forge with initiation and the concept of the 'wide head' are more current among the Mandinko than among the Jola of Boulouf.

After a week of seclusion, the novices left the sacred forest. Like the male initiates, the girls wore black cloths that covered their faces. They walked into the village in two files. Young men initiated in 1994 shot their cannons to celebrate the coming out while the mothers expressed their joy by dancing. *Kanyalen* women did their utmost to give the event a carnivalesque atmosphere by forms of compulsory buffoonery. After they arrived at the central square of the ward, the novices took the black cloth off their faces and photographers were allowed to take pictures of the initiates. Led by the 'queen of initiation' (*kuya mansa*), the initiates then danced the *eking* (from Mandinko, *kin*), the appropriate dance for the closing of Mandinko initiations. Only some of the elder men of the ward attended the ritual and none of the men of the Fas-Fas generation showed up, but a considerable number of local politicians from the ruling Socialist Party made sure they were seen celebrating the coming out of the girls. The day after their coming out, the initiates were dressed in new clothes. They wore elegant *grands boubous*, colourful umbrellas, new artificial wigs, make-up and jewellery, high-heeled shoes and fashionable handbags.[16]

The female initiation is a puzzling phenomenon. For a number of reasons, it is unclear why it is performed and what it is meant to achieve. First, although the initiation ritual might be assumed to provide the ritual context for women to excise their daughters, excision is practised on girls independently of and prior to their initiation. In Thionck Essyl, girls are normally excised at about the age of six. Excision (*sunno*) is done at home or in the female sacred forest, either individually or collectively.[17] The event is not elaborately ritualised. Only excised unmarried girls are allowed to participate in female initiation (cf. Linares 1992: 176). So excision is a condition for participation in initiation, but not part of it. Second, while a young man acquires adult status through initiation, a girl has to give birth to qualify as an adult woman and obtain the right to attend the secret rituals at the female sacred forests. *Gassus* does not mark the girls' transition to adulthood. Third, attendance at the female initiation is not compulsory and some uninitiated women do not bother to return to their village to be initiated. Although I did not observe any feelings of doubt or ambiguity surrounding the rite, as Linares found among the women of Jipalom (Linares 1992: 111), it is obviously not unequivocally considered an indispensable transition to adulthood. This leaves one to wonder to what extent female initiation should be considered the equivalent of male initiation. In their account of circumcision among the Mandinko of Pakao, Schaffer and Cooper argue that 'the girls' circumcision parallels that of boys and evokes similar images of maturation' (Schaffer and Cooper 1980: 99). Yet they recognise that, despite structural similarities between the male and female rituals, there are important differences. To give just one example: female initiation does not inscribe identities associated with the structure of Jola society. In patrilineal, virilocal Jola society, the inscription of a sense of belonging to the lineage and other residential corporate groups is primarily of interest to men. It is telling, in that respect, that the female initiates uncover their faces when arriving at the ward common, at which point their new identities are photographed. Male initiates, in contrast, are only allowed to uncover their faces once they have arrived in the lineage compound. After their seclusion in the forest, their reincorporation into society necessarily happens in the space associated with the patriline. In contrast, a woman is incorporated into a lineage at marriage, when she moves to her husband's compound. Virilocal marriage, not initiation, affiliates women with their husband's residential descent groups. This explains Linares' remarks on the meaning of female initiation. According to her, the girls' initiation does not turn the novices into independent adults, but makes the girls available to become dependent wives (Linares 1992: 110).

Female initiation affects the status of the individual girl, but the meaning of the ritual is not fully understood if we do not examine it in terms of collective gender relations. Why do women practise excision and initiation? Women argue that excision (*sunno*) and initiation (*gassus*) are Islamic obligations. Non-excised girls are considered impure (*seenya*) and referred to as *solema* (uncircumcised). Excision and initiation purify the girls. This ritual purification is the most important reason for women to practise excision and initiation. However, this religious meaning is profoundly embedded in contingent and contested gender relations. Conversion to Islam has meant that the most authoritative ritual responsibilities have been monopolised by men. With the incorporation of Jola society into the state, men have also monopolised the formal political process. While men transferred the political and ritual process from the sacred forests to the institutions of the state and Islam, the parallel political structure of the female sacred forests was marginalised. Subjection to the state and conversion to Islam have been detrimental to the position of women. However, by adopting new rituals such as circumcision and initiation, new forms of authority have been created. I therefore hold that women have adopted these rituals so as to recast their ritual, religious and political independence. Accepting these new ritual obligations, women redefine gender separation on their own terms. It is no coincidence that many of the elements of *gassus* resemble parts of the men's *garur*: women aspire to create a ritual of equal grandiosity. Indeed, one of my female informants considered female initiation a sign of female 'emancipation', borrowing from an idiom not usually associated with support for female excision. Linares emphasises that the women's initiation stresses compliance and submission rather than maturity and independence (1992: 176). This may indeed be what female initiation means in terms of the socialisation of girls (just as male initiation teaches submission to male elders). For the women involved, however, the ritual is a counterpart to male initiation, meant to recapture women's independence. This is well understood by the men, who absent themselves from its performance.

GENDER, ISLAM AND ETHNICITY

From the many Mandinko terms used in female initiation it may be surmised that female initiation is in fact borrowed from the Mandinko. Jola initiations indeed situate the participants in an ethnic field and engender ethnic subjectivities. It may therefore be hypothesised that male initiation is an occasion for the exclusion of ethnic others. When I started my fieldwork, I expected participation in the initiation to be restricted to Jola men. To my surprise, this was not the case. Ethnic identity was not a criterion for exclusion. Thionck's male initiation ritual was open to guests – men who could not trace their descent to one of Thionck's lineages through their father. These guest novices, who were referred to as *uteyemo* (singular *ateyemo*), could legitimise their participation in Thionck's initiation in a variety of ways and their participation as 'strangers' fully qualified them as men. Although the Jola male initiation is open to any man irrespective of his ethnic extraction, initiation *is* an important marker of Jola identity. Here I would like therefore to pursue the relationship between initiation and ethnicity a little further, especially because gender and ethnicity have been demonstrated to be intricately related (Hodgson 1999).

Guests of various ethnic extractions were initiated in Thionck's male forests. In fact, so many strangers were initiated that it might justifiably be argued that anyone could enter the sacred forest and become initiated.

This is indeed what the officiants of sacred forests told me. Although we may conclude that ethnic identity as such was not an important criterion for exclusion, this does not imply that ethnicity was irrelevant. I encountered one young man who was explicitly denied access to the forest. Originating in Bona, a village on the Soungrougrou River in Fogny, he had come to Thionck Essyl to accompany a friend who was to be initiated. It was not entirely clear to him why he was denied access to the forest, especially since he was a Jola man initiated in the sacred forest of his home village. However, Bona is located in an area considered profoundly 'mandinkised'. It was therefore argued that he should not learn the secrets of Thionck's initiation. Paradoxically, the only man to be denied access to the sacred forest considered himself a Jola. But in fact the boundary established by his exclusion was an ethnic boundary vis-à-vis the Mandinko. Jola initiation does symbolically define the boundary of the Jola ethnic group.

For centuries, relations between the Jola and the Mandinko have been antagonistic, especially in Fogny. Towards the end of the nineteenth century, Mandinko marabouts started a jihad. Mounted on horses, these holy warriors propagated the Holy Book, while raiding Jola villages and enslaving captives. The Jola resisted conversion by the sword and the jihads remained ineffective.[18] However, the colonial pacification resulted in more exchange of all kinds, even between the Jola and Mandinko. Soon after the pacification, the Jola started migrating towards the Gambia to work on the Mandinko groundnut estates. At the start of each rainy season, young Jola men from villages on the north bank of the Casamance River travelled to the Gambia and offered their labour to the Mandinko groundnut producers. Many of these young men converted to Islam during their stay among the Mandinko and returned as Muslims. In the 1930s, older men and women swiftly followed suit and Islamisation gained a momentum of its own (Mark 1978: 11; Pélissier 1966: 808). Most of the Jola joined the brotherhood of their Mandinko instructors, the Qadiriyya *tariqa* (Linares 1992: 98).[19]

The intimate relations with the Mandinko led to a profound transformation of the Jola way of life. Land tenure patterns and the organisation of labour associations changed dramatically and the relation between the genders – notably the sexual division of labour – altered as well (Linares 1992). In mandinkised Jola villages, the men gradually abandoned the cultivation of rice and specialised in the cultivation of millet and groundnuts. Mandinkisation thus led to an increased burden of labour for women and faltering subsistence production (Pélissier 1966: 804–806). Many other transformations in Jola society have been attributed to the contact with the Mandinko (Mark 1985: 100). It is possible that the Jola deliberately adopted Mandinko customs because of their sense of inferiority vis-à-vis a civilisation they deemed superior, as Pélissier suggests (1966: 798). Yet in a situation where 'Mandinko' had become synonymous with 'Muslim', it probably was hard to draw a distinction between Mandinko practice and Muslim presciption. To convert to Islam was 'to become Mandinko'.

Mandinkisation was a process intimately related to the integration of the Jola into the global political economy (cf. Linares 1992: 101; cf. Pélissier 1966: 808). But the mandinkisation of the Jola was an uneven process that implied a certain extent of regional differentiation.[20] The most profound consequences of mandinkisation were geographically restricted to the zones of intense inter-ethnic contact north of the Casamance River (Kombo, Fogny and Kalounayes). South of the Casamance River, the Jola remained hostile to mandinkisation. Even today groundnut cultivation in this area is limited, nor is Islam a widespread religion. In this scheme of differentiation, the Boulouf region in which Thionck Essyl is located presents an interesting case. The inhabitants of Boulouf believe that Fogny was 'colonised' by the Mandinko and that its population was converted by force. The same inhabitants of Boulouf pride themselves on having resisted invasions by the Mandinko. They believe that their grandfathers and fathers voluntarily converted to Islam. Within the Jola ethnic group, remembering the mode of conversion to Islam articulates an internal boundary. Remembering conversion to Islam is problematic as it reminds the Jola of Mandinko domination and, in spite of recent expressions of dissatisfaction with 'Wolofisation', the Mandinko have remained the Jola's most significant other. Below, I suggest that the relationship with the Mandinko is reflected in the subjectivities produced by Jola initiations.

GENDERED SUBJECTIVITIES

While male initiation requires the full cooperation of women in their capacity as mothers and affines (Mark et al., 1998), most men do not participate in the female initiation. Moreover, many men raised objections to female initiation and deliberately failed to attend the public celebrations. Men argued that female initiation is a mere copy of male initiation and they considered the ritual a waste of time and money. Most importantly, they perceived the female initiation as contrary to Jola traditions. It is indeed true that the female initiation has been introduced in Thionck Essyl fairly recently as part of conversion to Islam. Excision and initiation are considered Islamic precepts, part of a Muslim faith that was propagated by the Mandinko. This is corroborated by the diffusion pattern of excision and female initiation. Today the excision of girls is practised in many Jola communities, yet restricted to the ones where the population was converted to Islam through contact with the Mandinko. Female excision is not practised in villages south of the Casamance River where conversion to Islam is limited (Baum 1999: 205, n. 147; Mottin Sylla 1990). Excision and female initiation may therefore rightfully be considered Mandinko traditions adopted by Muslim Jola women (cf. Linares 1992: 110, 176). Indeed, the form of and most of

Plate 1 Dancing exercises for the initiates, Tendouck (Photo: Ferdinand de Jong)

Plate 2 Initiates with *usikoi* caps, Tendouck (Photo: Ferdinand de Jong)

Plate 3 Guardians applying face-paint, Tendouck (Photo: Ferdinand de Jong)

Plate 4 Guardian ready for celebration, chewing a fortifying root in Tendouck (Photo: Ferdinand de Jong)

Plate 5 Guardian dressed up as palm wine tapper wearing a football as hat, Tendouck (Photo: Ferdinand de Jong)

Plate 6 Initiate being shaven prior to entry into sacred forest, Thionck Essyl (Photo: Ferdinand de Jong)

Plate 7 Initiates posing for photograph, Thionck Essyl (Photo: local photographer)

Plate 8 Guardian on the day of entry, wrapped in protective amulets, Thionck Essyl (Photo: local photographer)

Plate 9 The initiates dancing prior to the entry into the sacred forest, Kafanta, Thionck Essyl (Photo: Ferdinand de Jong)

Plate 10 Procession of initiates to the sacred forest of Kafanta, Thionck Essyl (Photo: Ferdinand de Jong)

Plate 11 The initiates coming out of the sacred forest, Kafanta, Thionck Essyl (Photo: Ferdinand de Jong)

Plate 12 Procession of initiates back to Kafanta (Photo: Ferdinand de Jong)

Plate 13 Women celebrate the coming out of their sons with clapping and dancing (Photo: Ferdinand de Jong)

Plate 14 Photo session at the central square of Kafanta, Thionck Essyl (Photo: Ferdinand de Jong)

Plate 15 The initiates arrive at their family compound, tired and dazed
(Photo: Ferdinand de Jong)

Plate 16 The initiates celebrate with decorated initiation sticks (Photo:
Ferdinand de Jong)

the terms associated with female initiation are of Mandinko origin.[21] Men are opposed to female excision and initiation precisely *because* these practices are part of a Mandinko tradition. To them, female initiation represents a pollution of Jola identity.

Men consider *gassus* a Mandinko tradition and perceive the practice as a result of the cultural domination by this significant other. The women in turn consider the ethnic origin of this practice completely irrelevant. To them *gassus* is primarily an Islamic obligation. Although the men identify this practice in ethnic terms, women identify the same ritual in religious terms. The women design their own Muslim identity, asserting their own ritual competence, cast in a performance of secrecy. Interestingly, the practice of ethnic boundary maintenance is at the heart of both male and female initiations. As we saw above, a Jola man originating from Fogny was excluded from the sacred forest in which his best friend was initiated, while a 'stranger' from Fogny was given the responsibility of protecting the female initiates against the nefarious attacks of witches. The female initiation seems to amount to an inversion of male initiation. Male and female initiation should therefore not be interpreted as complementary forms of ritual separation. Men perceive female initiation as a Mandinko practice, while their own male initiation inscribes a Jola identity. Male initiation demarcates an ethnic boundary, while female initiation negates this boundary. Female initiation produces an alternative subjectivity that subverts male subjectivity.

3

OUT OF DIASPORA INTO THE FOREST

Jola rites of passage produce local subjects. However, many members of the Thionck Essyl community no longer live in the village and are dispersed across all Senegal and beyond. We therefore also need an assessment of how a diasporic community reproduces itself in the face of the long-distance migration of its members. Chapter 2 demonstrates how male initiation reproduces local society. Contrary to Appadurai's rather gloomy view of the decreased capability of local communities to produce locality (Appadurai 1996: 178–99), this chapter takes the point further and attests to the continued capacity of a *translocal* community to reproduce itself within overwhelming global contexts. I show that in the contemporary context of globalisation, male initiation can still be a social technique for the production of subjectivity. The initiation ritual transforms young men into adults who properly belong to a diasporic community. This is why the ritual has retained its relevance for young men born in the diaspora. My approach is to focus on the historical transformations of local society brought about by the incorporation of local society into the global. The chapter goes on to analyse the translation of these transformations into the ritual process. Like *ngoma* in colonial Tanganyika, the rite of passage discussed here has mediated the historical transformations of society by including these changes in the ritual (Pels 1996). The ritual practice has been transformed to produce a translocal subjectivity.

CONCEPTUALISING JOLA INITIATION

Jola male initiation has attracted the attention of numerous scholars.[1] This scholarship has resulted in a debate on the plausibility of a particular historical transformation in Jola initiation. Some authors have suggested that the Jola traditionally practised an 'open' sort of initiation (*kahat*) which was subsequently replaced by a 'closed', secretive initiation (*bukut*).[2] The *kahat* consists of circumcision, followed by a short ritual seclusion and a longer period of initiation in which novices are allowed to wander through the village. *Kahat* is still practised today in several towns to the south of the Casamance River (Baum 1999: 218). Why *kahat* gave way to *bukut* remains an enigma as far as Thomas is concerned (Thomas 1965, II: 706). Girard suggests that the introduction of *bukut* was a reaction to colonisation. Under colonial rule, women benefited from opportunities provided by the emergent labour market in the port of Ziguinchor. Girard explains the introduction of *bukut* as a device for the restoration of a strong bond among disempowered men (Girard 1969: 89). Whereas Girard dates the introduction of *bukut* to the early twentieth century, Baum suggests that it had already been adopted by the close of the eighteenth century (Baum 1999: 101–2). Yet Girard and Baum agree that the lengthier seclusion of novices in *bukut* was primarily designed to create a stronger cohesion among them. The need for a bond among men arose from the changing relationship between the sexes in a period of social instability (Baum 1999: 102–3). Yet, however relevant these observations may be with regard to the Jola who practised *kahat*, scholars working among the Jola north of the Casamance River have found no evidence whatsoever that *kahat* was ever practised by them (Mark 1976: 35; Van der Klei 1989: 152). Sapir (1970) and Linares (1992) do not even mention the word. In Thionck Essyl, no one was familiar with the term *kahat*. We can conclude that *kahat* initiation was never practised north of the Casamance River.

Among the Jola of Boulouf the male initiation ritual has been practised for several centuries at least (Mark 1985: 21–2). Notwithstanding this continuity, several transformations can be observed in the Jola male initiation. Scholars have consistently conceptualised these transformations in terms of an opposition between tradition and modernity. Modernisation was thought to have a detrimental effect on traditions, leading to their disappearance. Indeed, that is what Thomas – observing a *bukut* in 1965 – expected to happen. He predicted that this tradition would not survive (Thomas 1965). Others have perceived the initiation as a tradition that would survive in spite of modernisation. Mark, for instance, interprets the male initiation as a means for preserving tradition (1985: 122). In keeping with a widely shared view that initiation rituals manifest traditional authority and preserve tradition (Turner 1967; La Fontaine 1985), Van der Klei (1989) analyses the male initiation as a ritual in which male elders reinforce their authority. Most authors nevertheless recognise that the Jola male initiation is not a static but indeed a dynamic ritual. Indeed, the Jola male initiation is a ritual practice that is subject to change. While the ritual manifestly celebrates the structure of traditional Jola society as a gerontocracy – as demonstrated in the previous chapter – it also incorporates historical change. To analyse the male initiation as a modern ritual is precisely what I set out to do. Jola male initiation is a ritual that is designed not so much to preserve tradition as to incorporate modernity. Therefore I argue that the secrecy surrounding male initiation is not a consequence of modernisation. In contrast, secrecy enables the Jola to appropriate the modern on their own terms.

A TRANSLOCAL COMMUNITY

Ever since the start of the colonial period, the Jola have increasingly participated in production for the market economy. From the beginning of the
twentieth century, seasonal migration to the areas of groundnut cultivation
in the Gambia provided an opportunity to earn a monetary income (Mark
1976, 1977, 1985). From the 1950s onwards, the migration that had formerly
revolved around the rural production of groundnuts shifted towards the
urban economy. Most of the migrants were employed by the Senegalese
state. The educational policy of the independent Senegalese state created
many jobs in primary and secondary education. In addition, posts in the
Senegalese administration that had been formerly held by Frenchmen were
now occupied by Senegalese (Van der Klei 1989: 227-30). The national
army and police also employed a considerable number of educated young
men. This situation meant the men had to leave their villages and settle in
the towns, but they retained close ties with their kin in their home village.

Despite Senegal's economic stagnation since the 1980s (Gellar 1995:
55 ff.), the urban economy still attracts young villagers. The constraints
and hardship of a farmer's life are well-known to the villagers, and a future
in the urban economy evokes dreams of possible wealth and status. Young
men's migration, however, is proving progressively less rewarding, and leads
some of those who have spent several years in town to return to the village
and settle as farmers. Young female migrants are less concerned with their
professional prospects than with finding a husband. They settle in town
with the intention of earning an income that will allow them to buy clothes
and cosmetics and attract a wealthy husband. The girls envisage a marriage
to a civil servant and certainly not to a farmer (Van de Laar 1995; Lambert
2002).

Since the economic prospects in Senegal are anything but encouraging, more and more young people now want to leave for Europe or
North America. By the 1970s, labour migration to France was already
taking place. Using Dakar as an intermediate place of residence, men from
Thionck Essyl made their way to the French *Métropole* and were soon
joined there by their wives. The first international migrants benefited from
the growing European economy and the demand for unskilled industrial
labour. However, migration prospects have since worsened. Using established intercontinental kin ties, some young men still manage to make their
way to Europe. In addition, students travel abroad on grants and some
individuals contract marriages with Europeans and subsequently move to
their partner's home country. Thus, while at least half of the members of
the Thionck Essyl community now live in Senegalese cities (Ziguinchor and
Dakar), a growing number of them are moving abroad. The first generation
of migrants often married in their urban place of residence, and the second
and third generations are now growing up in many Senegalese cities. Their

cousins are growing up in the Ivory Coast, Gabon, Morocco, Algeria, Libya, Saudi Arabia, Russia, France, Italy, Canada and the Netherlands. Some of them are unemployed, but most earn incomes far higher than the farmers back home. Part of the salaries earned abroad is used, either in currency or kind, to support family members in the village.

With so many members of the Thionck community living in diaspora, the community has become deterritorialised. How do the members relate to each other nowadays? How is the social reproduction of their community organised? Social and economic relations are strong among all the people born in the same village, even if they move to urban areas. Though young men and women born in town do not want to live in the village and become farmers, their lives are still very much embedded in networks focused on the village. The networks not only comprise those born in Thionck Essyl, but also include their children born in town. Members of this network are referred to as *ressortissants* (community members) of Thionck Essyl. In addition to the informal networks in the towns of residence, the Association pour le Développement de Thionck-Essyl is a more formal network. Membership in this association is mandatory for all the *ressortissants* and entails annual membership fees. The association contributes to the village's economic development. Every village in Lower Casamance has this kind of community-wide association comprising villagers and migrants (cf. Reboussin 1995; Lambert 2002). The associations have sections in all the cities where a substantial number of migrants from a particular village reside. The association of Thionck Essyl has sections in Bignona, Ziguinchor, Dakar, Gunjur, Serekunda (the Gambia) and France. The sections exert social control on the migrants and their children born in town. Migrants in the diaspora are thus grouped in communities of people from the same village.

In addition to the association, there are other ways of reinforcing relations between villagers and migrants. For instance, people frequently travel from the village to the city and vice versa. Visits can last up to several months, and with regard to some people it is hard to tell where their home is (cf. Ferguson 1999). These visits to kin and friends enhance the community's overall cohesion, since visitors often take letters with them and convey messages. Moreover, all the community members are suitable subjects for gossip. Now that several families in Thionck have telephones, migrants are also beginning to use them for conveying the most urgent messages. However, since the cost is often prohibitive, handwritten letters carried by friends are still the normal way for migrants to communicate with their kin back home. Visits are most frequent during the rainy season, when some of the young urban dwellers return to the village to help out with the rice cultivation. The school holiday period coincides with the rainy season, and is the most suitable time for visits to kin and friends and the social events where relations can be reinforced. For instance, the village association usually convenes its annual meeting in August. The meeting takes place in the village and draws many people who have moved to towns.

The most important occasions when people gather and a sense of belonging is reproduced are religious holidays and rites of passage. For instance, an elderly person who has passed away in the diaspora may be buried in the ancestral soil of the village, provided the kin can afford the cost of transport to the village. Such a funeral procession usually includes many city dwellers. Marriage is another ritual event that many people participate in. As mentioned before, Muslim holidays such as Korité (the end of Ramadan) and Tabaski (the commemoration of Abraham's near-sacrifice of his son) also motivate people to travel and celebrate with close kin in the village. Although regular communication of this kind enables villagers and migrants to keep in touch, participation in the communication network is limited to direct kin and friends. Moreover, neither workers with regular jobs nor migrants abroad can ordinarily visit their village of origin for extended periods. The long-distance migrants therefore only participate in the networks in a very limited sense. They may not even attend the rites of passage of their direct kin. There are no occasions when all the *ressortissants* participate, save one: the male initiation ritual. Thus the social reproduction of the community has come to predominantly rely on the male initiation ritual that all the *ressortissants* participate in, men and women alike. The initiation ritual has evolved to reflect the changing economic activities and residence patterns of Thionck's community members.

INITIATION AND THE MARKET ECONOMY

Male migrants who have left Thionck Essyl and settled elsewhere still have to go through initiation to acquire adult status. Thus far, no man has ever been exempted from the initiation ritual, no matter how much of his life he has spent abroad. The ritual's organisation has undergone several changes to accommodate the restrictions the capitalist economy entails on participation in it. First, the timing and duration of the sojourn at the sacred forest have been modified. Formerly, initiation took place during the dry season just after the rice harvest. The period of seclusion lasted for at least two months. With the introduction of state schools, pupils could no longer spend two months at the sacred forest and the ritual is nowadays scheduled in July and August to coincide with the school holidays. This rescheduling also enables civil servants and workers with limited holiday periods to participate in the ritual. Since this moment coincides with the start of the rainy season and the ploughing of the rice fields, the duration of the seclusion has been shortened to two or three weeks. In the 1992 initiation of Tendimane, the period of seclusion was even reduced to one week.[3]

Another modification pertains to the admission standards. Formerly, the initiation was organised once every twenty years. No man could get married before his initiation, and fathers could not initiate their sons in the *garur* after their own. Their sons had to wait until the following initiation (Mark 1985: 122). The interval between a man's initiation and his son's could be up to forty years. If an uninitiated man wanted to get married and the village initiation was not scheduled for any time in the near future, he could have himself initiated in another village. Back in his home village, the initiate was supposed to sacrifice a bull as compensation, and would then be considered a full-fledged member of the male age set previously initiated. In this way, young men of comparable biological age were included in the same classificatory age grade. Apparently, initiation in other villages was widely practised after 1940. A considerable number of young men had been conscripted into the French army and were abroad when the 1940 initiation was celebrated. Upon their return home, they had themselves initiated in other villages. Since they could not be held responsible for their absence, they were exempted from the compulsory sacrifice of a bull in their native village.

In the 1962 initiation, the rule that prohibited a young man's initiation in the initiation following his father's was abandoned. So all the young men were initiated regardless of when their fathers had undergone the initiation. This change might be an indication of the shifting balance of power between the male age sets (Van der Klei 1989: 156). Participation in the market economy and increased wealth had made the young men eager to have their new status reflected in the traditional promotion to adult status. Their independently acquired wealth and decreased dependence on rice land increased their influence in the negotiations with the male elders. Migration and participation in the market economy were reflected in earlier access to social adulthood for young men. One consequence of the modification was that the number of young men initiated in neighbouring villages dropped dramatically. Nowadays all the young men can be initiated at their village of birth (or at their father's village of birth) before they reach marriageable age.

In the 1962 *garur*, there were modifications in some of the other regulations as well. Individual migrant novices were allowed to enter the sacred forest at a moment of their choice, and to exit when their leave or furlough was over. The name given to the age set forged in this initiation reflects the fact that many migrants were returning to their urban occupations before the ritual was over: Elando (*elaan* = to return). In short, in various ways the ritual process was made compatible with migration and participation in the market economy. We now need to examine other transformations in ritual practice that attest to its accommodation to the requirements of adherence to a world religion.

ISLAM AND INITIATION

Most Jola on the northern shore of the Casamance River are Muslims today. Aside from the inhabitants of a couple of small Catholic sub-wards, the same holds true in Thionck Essyl. The population of Thionck converted to Islam in the first decades of the twentieth century (Mark 1985: 110–12). Initially, Islam mostly attracted uninitiated young men engaged in labour migration. Conversion meant an alternative means of access to adult status. The male elders, whose authority was vested in the care of shrines, reluctantly accepted Islam. Likewise, women stood to lose much of their authority by converting to a religion that denied them ritual responsibilities. Thus Islam provided alternative sources of authority that changed age-grade and gender relations. According to Mark, conversion also led some of the first Muslims to reject the initiation ritual (Mark 1985: 112–15).[4] They considered the ancestral tradition incompatible with Islam. Although rejection of the initiation ritual may have characterised the attitude of the first Muslims, some elements of the pre-Islamic ritual were quickly adapted to the demands of the new religion. For example, Jola Muslims do not drink alcohol. Palm wine libations have therefore been suspended during the retreat at the sacred forest.[5] Mark holds that sacrifices are still made, but suggests that palm wine has been replaced by water or kola nuts (1992: 57–8). In their prayers at the forest, Muslims probably address Allah, although they generally do not deny the existence of the spirits (*ajino*, plural *sijino*) that are still believed to live in the forest. In other respects, pre-Islamic traditions have been continued. Masking is an important feature of the initiation cycle, notably at one particular ceremony (*ganghalen*) that marks the beginning of the novices' reintegration into society when the novices wear masks. Since iconic imagery is formally forbidden in Islam, the preservation of masquerading at the Jola initiation is surprising but it has been established that the participants in the initiation consider masquerading entirely compatible with Islam (Mark et al. 1998).[6]

Although the initiation ritual is potentially at odds with adherence to the world religions, Muslims and Catholics do participate in initiation. Nowadays only members of the Tijaniyya brotherhood object to initiation. They do so at the risk of being rejected by other members of society. No Jola father would consider allowing his daughter to marry an uninitiated Jola man. Consequently, Tijanis who have not been through the initiation can only marry daughters of other Tijanis. Nor are uninitiated men allowed to attend the secret meetings that only the initiates have access to. Apart from some Tijaniyya opponents, all the Jola men have their sons initiated. Older men still consider the initiation and the Muslim faith as contradictory, yet they frequently recite Muslim prayers for the novices. The guardian of one sacred forest even invited a number of marabouts (Islamic learned men) to bless the novices. Many younger men, however, do not see any contradiction between initiation and Islam. They think of initiation as a tradition, the purpose of which is to educate and socialise novices to be responsible members of society. To them, initiation represents tradition (*ado*), and tradition belongs to a different realm than religion without being contradictory to it. Initiation marks the transition to adulthood through the acquisition of secret knowledge. Enacted vis-à-vis women and the uninitiated, secrecy is not incompatible with the Muslim faith. Thus, more than fifty years after the population of Thionck Essyl converted to Islam, *garur* is maintained as a 'tradition'. The justifications for the preservation of this ritual vary and contradict each other and may even be perceived by some as invalid. The legitimation is clearly problematic. However, by adapting some parts of the ritual practice, the initiation has effectively been accommodated to suit Muslim precepts.

The relationship between initiation and Islam is not exhaustively examined without mentioning one radical modification related to Islamic precepts. The novices were formerly circumcised on the first day of their retreat at the sacred forest.[7] Since circumcision is considered an Islamic obligation and a condition for the proper conduct of prayers, boys are now circumcised between the ages of five and ten. In addition, circumcision is no longer carried out at the community level but at the household level instead (see Chapter 5). In Thionck Essyl, the 1940 *garur* was probably the last initiation in which circumcision was practised. Nowadays, circumcision is no longer performed during the initiation retreat and some of the younger novices may therefore go through the initiation uncircumcised. Circumcision is no longer the essential bodily marker of initiation. This said, it is surprising that the act of circumcision should still be so much shrouded in secrecy, even today. Even now that circumcision is considered a Muslim obligation and is no longer done in the sacred forest the men still refuse to talk about it. Since circumcision is regarded as secret, I suggest that this practice amounts to a Jola initiation. To which status, then, is circumcision the necessary rite of passage? The answer must be that circumcision initiates boys into Islam. The Muslim faith of the Jola should thus be conceptualised as a new trajectory of their traditional practices of secrecy. Without a secretive initiation, a Jola cannot be a proper Muslim. Secrecy has provided the Jola with a model for appropriating Islam. The culturally embedded practice of secrecy has incorporated the Muslim faith as yet another form of initiation (cf. Pels 1999). This corresponds to my suggestion that, for the Jola, the sacred must necessarily be shrouded in secrecy.

To summarise, the physical removal of the foreskin is now perceived as an Islamic obligation. The secrecy that surrounds circumcision also defines Islam as a Jola religion, into which secretive initiation is required. Circumcision (*sunno*) and the initiation at the sacred forest (*garur*) should be considered commensurate initiations. Apparently, the ritual practices at the sacred forest may change to the point of omitting what was previously the most important marker of initiation (circumcision). The physical endurance required for circumcision is no longer tested in initiation. Today's production of masculinity through initiation is in fact based on an illusion of male endurance. Secrecy is enacted to conceal the fact that circumcision is no longer practised in the sacred forest.

PURITY AND POLLUTION

For at least three centuries, Jola initiation has marked accession to adulthood (Mark 1985: 20). In the past thirty years, however, the male initiation has become more important as a marker of identity. In the context of increased Jola self-assertion, initiation has recently emerged as the cornerstone of Jola identity (Mark 1992: 55; and Chapter 2 of this book). Thus, not only has the form of the ritual undergone substantial changes in the face of conversion to Islam and migration, the meaning too has shifted. Part of this shift is related to how the Jola experience and interpret modernity. Today, many Jola feel they have become uprooted. Urban dwellers feel they no longer live up to the obligations of the old customs and consider the countryside the repository of traditional culture. This is why my interlocutors consistently advised me to do my research on 'tradition' in the countryside. Their discourse situates ethnic purity in the countryside and ethnic impurity in the city (cf. Van Binsbergen 1999). But the countryside is not conceptualised as uniformly authentic. Authenticity is attributed to particular places and mapped on the land.

Conversion to Islam implied multifarious transformations of the Jola life style. Today, the inhabitants of Thionck recall that converts started wearing Muslim dress. Although suited for activities like prayer and religious discussion, the same dress was an impediment for agricultural labour – especially for ploughing paddies. Thus Muslims remember how their fathers and grandfathers, once they had converted to Islam, stopped doing any of the heavy work in the rice paddies. Indeed, the Jola consider their conversion to Islam – their 'civilisation' – one of the reasons why they are no longer self-subsistent today. The Jola were dedicated, self-sufficient rice farmers and have become 'civilised' but 'decadent' Muslims. The introduction of Muslim dress, some would argue, led to the Jola dependence on store-bought rice. In this understanding Islamic purity has led to the 'pollution' of Jola identity. As conversion to Islam resulted from contact with the Mandinko, the purity of Jola identity is defined as the inverse of mandinkisation. Mandinkisation, Jola think, is reflected in the variety of practices associated with the male initiation ritual. Jola locate the 'purest' form of initiation in Casa south of the Casamance River, where few Jola have converted to Islam. The initiations of the northern Jola are considered 'polluted' by mandinkisation.

Although Jola, even Muslim Jola, feel that the initiation ritual has been contaminated by Islam, the ritual has nonetheless come to be seen as the authentic expression of Jola-ness. The sense that initiation is the only remaining relic of Jola tradition is shared by migrants who adhere to very few cultural practices that can be considered specifically Jola. They perceive their urban way of life as 'modern' and consider the initiation as their 'tradition'. For instance, a Jola migrant from Paris told me he would certainly bring his sons back home to be initiated and thus familiarise them with 'their culture'. When asked why initiation would be the appropriate way to do this, he answered: 'Initiation is all that is left of our culture.' It is true that the initiation ritual is one of the few remaining pre-Islamic forms of performance. But this alone does not explain why initiation has become such a pivotal symbol of Jola identity. One of the reasons is that the making of Jola nationalism has greatly contributed to an interest in Jola tradition (Foucher 2003b). This is true even for Muslim Jola. Among many of my interlocutors I witnessed a reorientation towards 'tradition' and a reconsideration of their 'pagan' past. Shrines associated with the vener-ation of local spirits were demolished in the past, but are now considered typical of the ancestral religion. The number of Jola who turn away from Islam is increasing (but still limited) and many Jola do recognise shrines as important relics of what is now referred to by some as 'the Jola religion'. Even the Muslim Jola consider the continued reverence of spirit shrines as evidence that the original Jola religion still exists. Thus some Jola have started to view their conversion to Islam as basically at odds with their 'true' and hidden identity and re-evaluate traditions as expressions of Jola authen-ticity. In this process, the initiation ritual has come to define the boundary of the group (cf. Barth 1969; Cohen 1989). A Jola man must be initiated and cannot avoid this obligation. The ritual represents a recently acquired pride in the Jola cultural heritage and is undergone as a confident assertion of Jola identity in Senegalese society. Today, undergoing initiation not only leads to adulthood, but specifically to Jola manhood.

MIGRANTS IN THE 1994 *GARUR*

Some of the young urbanites might have been reluctant to undergo initiation, but only one young man told me so. Most of the novices considered their initiation a moral obligation and looked forward to their social promotion. I was quite surprised that even young men who had only occasionally visited the village considered their initiation a matter of course. Virtually all the 'sons of the village' came to be initiated. Even boys born in Paris were there. Only a few *ressortissants* were not. For some the travel expenses were prohibitive. Others were unable to attend because as illegal aliens in their country of residence, a journey to Senegal would preclude their return to their host country.

Most of the migrants only stayed in the village for three weeks. Some of the novices even arrived too late to take part in the *buyeet* ritual, which is so important for the affirmation of ties with their maternal uncles. Others did not even make it on time to participate in the formal entry of the sacred forest. Upon reaching the village, they were quickly taken to the forest. By then soldiers whose furlough was over were already leaving the forest to return to their posting. Men constantly entered and left the forest throughout the three weeks of seclusion. In the ritual's aftermath, no one bothered to stay in the village any longer than strictly required. Within a week after the exit from the sacred forest, Thionck Essyl was almost deserted. The farmers remained in the village, as did the elders and the youngest children. They had to work the rice fields and the rainy season was already well underway. The farmers expected their rice harvest to be very poor. Fortunately, the rains were late and the farmers nevertheless had a very good harvest. In general, however, in a year of initiation agricultural production suffers from the celebration (Van der Klei 1989: 186).

In the organisation of the initiation ritual, migrant participation is obviously a top priority. The incorporation of migrants in the urban market economy is fully acknowledged. What is sacrificed is the rice cultivation of the villagers. This does not mean that only the migrants benefit from their participation in the market economy. In fact, they do contribute substantially to the initiation costs. Men who work in the formal economy are expected to contribute extra bulls to be slaughtered during the rite. Some of the migrants buy enormous quantities of rice. The overseas migrants are especially afraid of appearing poor and do their utmost, working extra hours and night shifts, to outdo their relatives in their contributions. One migrant who lives in the Netherlands, for instance, added four bulls to the number of animals for sacrifice in his House. My host's fifth wife, who lives in Paris and has a thriving business as a practitioner of traditional medicine, had two sons initiated in the 1994 initiation. She alone contributed one ton of rice and a barrel (200 litres) of cooking oil. The value of these gifts amounted to 250,000 West African francs (approx. US$450). Indeed, the potlatch nature of the initiation ritual is demonstrated by the slaughter of hundreds of heads of cattle and the consumption of tons of rice that would be impossible without the revenues from the market economy.

Though some of the successful migrants may contribute substantially to the initiation costs, many are unable to make more than the compulsory contribution. The novices themselves do not make any material contribution, since most of them are students or unemployed. This is surprising if we bear in mind that the elders used to allocate the labour force of their unmarried sons in the cultivation of rice paddies. The elders thus accumulated a surplus which they converted into prestige goods (Van der Klei 1989). Their sons' migration to urban areas put a radical stop to this mode of production. Migrants still return to the village to assist their fathers in ploughing the rice fields but the young men increasingly spend their holidays in the city. In 1994, most of the initiates immediately returned to their urban homes after leaving the sacred forest. The elders who had destroyed their livestock capital at their sons' and grandsons' initiations, silently hoping the young men would subsequently settle in the village and provide labour for rice cultivation, certainly did not envisage this hasty departure. One of the elders grudgingly told me: 'We wasted everything!' The elders provided the ritual knowledge for the performance of the initiation without being compensated with labour in return.

The initiation ritual used to reproduce a system of authority, and even today principles of gerontocratic authority are still expressed in the ritual performance. But the city-based novices no longer contribute to the costs of their own initiation. The ways in which urbanites participate in the initiation ceremony has significant implications for our conceptualisation of the traditional system of authority. Marxist-inspired studies on the Jola and their neighbours suggest that male elders continue to extract a surplus from young men's labour (Van Binsbergen 1984; Van der Klei 1989; Van der Drift 1992). To my surprise, I saw nothing in the 1994 *garur* to corroborate their common hypothesis of a viable gerontocracy that exploits the labour of non-initiates.[8] Thus young male city-dwellers no longer remunerate the elders for their ritual expertise. The larger share of the initiation expenses is borne by the successful migrants who work in the formal economy. These middle-aged men thus pay for the initiation of their sons.

For the migrants, the initiation is the occasion par excellence to visit their native village. Indeed, among the men previously initiated, the opportunity to meet relatives was the most frequently mentioned reason for attending the ritual. The reaffirmation of kin ties has a very practical relevance to villagers and migrants alike, as it enhances the opportunities for mutual support. Yet we should clearly distinguish the various interests at stake. The initiation enables migrants to reaffirm their membership in the Thionck Essyl community. In particular the well-educated men who work in the public sector and sometimes hold high offices in the government manifest themselves during the initiation and assert their identity as 'sons of the village' (Van der Klei 1989; Mark 1985). Through their participation in the *garur* the migrants, who face many insecurities in the urban lives they live, acquire a sense of rootedness. In fact, 'se resourcer' is the Senegalese expression for participation in traditional performances of this kind. The villagers, however, regard the migrants as alienated from village life and question their status as 'sons of the village'. Instead they refer to them as 'strangers' (*anaya*). The villagers state that the migrants do not master the ritual knowledge to perform initiation and depend on the villagers' know-how. In addition, I overheard villagers complain about the rather modest financial contributions made by some of the wealthy migrants. Their complaints about the migrant participation clearly reflect an attempt on their part to emphasise the migrants' dependence on the villagers. While an ideology of ostentatious loyalty to the rural home community has been forged, the interests of villagers and migrants may clearly be antithetical.[9] The ritual provides the migrants with an occasion to stake their claims to 'roots' and this is something they are made to pay for. In all this, the generation of elders is now marginalised. The ritual performance still affirms the principles of gerontocratic authority, although the system itself has become obsolete. The structure of the ritual is nonetheless maintained as a necessary requirement for the celebration of an idealised village, however virtual that village has actually turned out to be (cf. Van Binsbergen 1999).

The contradictions in the relations between villagers and migrants should not cloud our view of the ritual's major significance in a context of migration. The initiation enables villagers and migrants to reaffirm their relations with each other, even when the participation of migrants is rather restricted. The participation of migrants is in fact entirely centred on the seclusion at the sacred forest, at the expense of the numerous rituals that reproduce the relations with other wards and other villages. The meaning of the ritual has thus substantially changed for the migrants. *Garur* used to be a ceremony where relations with other wards and villages were reproduced. For the migrants, however, the ritual has become a ceremony reinforcing the relations between kin. Today, the initiation has become a reunion for the members of a translocal community, performed in the village that has been turned into a ritual site for the migrants (cf. Piot 1999).

TRANSNATIONAL SECRECY

Having established the initiation's role in the production of translocality, the question still remains as to why secrecy is so important in creating translocality. The retreat to the sacred forest used to last over two months and was long enough for secret knowledge to be imparted. Today, the age of the novices (some are toddlers) and the duration of the retreat (sometimes just one night) makes this transmission unfeasible. The transmission of secrets cannot be the crux of the matter. However, as I noted above, it is not the content of the secret that is important. The men act together to preserve an illusion of dangerous secret lore and through the production of this illusion they create complicity and mutual dependence. An initiated man is expected to remain silent about the activities at the sacred forest and, as long as he obeys this rule, he will be respected as a man capable of keeping a secret. Trust in their co-initiates travels with the initiated men wherever they go.

Secrecy creates boundaries between the people who know that nothing special is concealed and the people who don't. Obviously, to keep the non-initiates ignorant, they have to be excluded from the sacred forest. Non-initiates are therefore never allowed to enter the forest. I myself became particularly sensitive to secrecy as a critical aspect of initiation. Every time the novices were led into the sacred forest I was denied access to this mysterious place. A young man would walk up to me and say: 'Whites are not allowed to go any further!' Sometimes women would tease me, asking me why I was denied access. They suggested that a man my age should have been initiated by now, although they would never expect a white European to be initiated. In an ironic way, the women identified with a ritual that was designed to exclude them. Others did not really appreciate the irony of their exclusion. A Frenchman married to a woman born in Thionck was not at all amused at his exclusion. He had once spent a year in Thionck and had now come to visit his affines for the initiation celebration. The poor man was outraged about being denied access to the sacred forest and was determined to seek revenge. His excitement need not surprise us. Although he was obviously not familiar with the rules of access to the sacred forest (previous initiation), he considered himself a member of the local community so felt he was unjustly excluded. His case demonstrates how much the denial of access contributes to the idea that the most important of all activities take place at the sacred forest. Secrecy is indeed important for the establishment of boundaries, especially vis-à-vis the descendants of the former colonisers.

Yet, even if this explains why secrecy is necessary for the creation of solidarity among Thionck's men, it does not explain why male secrecy also creates translocality for women. Women are de facto excluded from the secret. However, by expressing their allegiance to the rules of male secrecy, the women are included in the ritual congregation. The next case illustrates the secret's capacity to include women in the congregation and demonstrates how much such inclusion depends on a particular sense of propriety in performance. A Jola woman in Amsterdam has a copy of an anthropological study on the Jola's male initiation (Van der Klei, 1989). Although she perfectly understands the language the study is written in, she refrains from reading it. She is afraid of learning secrets that are the prerogative of initiated men. This shows the power of secrecy to include a migrant in the diaspora – in this case a female *ressortissant* – in a translocal community. Interestingly, she also confided to me that she does not want the secret to be exposed out of fear that it will then lose its mystery. While it might be argued that secrecy has cast a spell on her, her respect for the secrecy of initiation demonstrates that she is in fact complicit in its performance. She is held in suspense, but deliberately does not want the mysteries to be revealed to her. Women are members of the community through a commitment to men's secrets.

Secrecy includes the male and female members of a community, and extends to places far removed from the sacred forest. The next case demonstrates the secret's capacity to reach out to Europeans. A young man born in Thionck Essyl is married to a Dutch woman and has settled in the Netherlands with her. At the time of Thionck Essyl's *garur*, the couple had two children, one of them a two-year-old boy. The father was determined to initiate his son at the sacred forest. His wife, holding an MA in anthropology, feared that her son would be circumcised at the sacred forest (apparently misled by the French term *circoncision* used for the initiation ritual). She was concerned about her child and did not want him exposed to unsanitary conditions that might endanger his health. Her husband flatly refused to inform her about the proceedings at the sacred forest and said it was men's affairs. His wife unwillingly accepted the situation. When I met her in Thionck Essyl a few days before her son was to be taken into the sacred forest, she was quite worried about the ritual's consequences for her son. I tried to reassure her and gave her a copy of the ethnography written by the Dutch anthropologist to read. Soon afterwards, she had to leave Thionck Essyl and took the book with her to the Netherlands. Later on, after I returned to the Netherlands, I called her and asked for the book. A few days later her husband showed up and handed over a parcel carefully wrapped in tape. After his visit, I opened the tightly wrapped parcel that contained the secret knowledge: the ethnography on Jola initiation. The woman had carefully wrapped the book so as not to reveal to her husband that she had learned the knowledge forbidden to her. I, for sure, had betrayed the men's secret. By transmitting esoteric lore to a woman (secrets which I myself was not entitled to know), I had violated the rules of secrecy, even though the book was already in the public sphere. However, I also felt I had acquired a certain competence in the performance of secrecy. Our violation reinforced our sense of exclusion from the community of Thionck Essyl (though only secretly), but we had become competent practitioners of secrecy ourselves. Our practical competence in the performance of secrecy helped conceal our knowledge of secrets. This shows that the performance of secrecy includes those who are nominally excluded. So, initiation includes all male initiates, no matter where they are born or currently live, and excludes all others as non-initiates. But non-initiates are included in the community as long as they conform to the rules of secrecy.

MODERN SUBJECTIVITY

For centuries, initiation has been the central rite of passage in Jola villages. In the past, many young men got married soon after the initiation, received rice fields from their fathers and founded their own households. Nowadays, the lives of most of the young men do not change in any practical sense. These men live in town and attend school, they may have a job or be unemployed. Initiation will not change their formal economic position, nor will it affect their marital status. Today, many uninitiated young men have children before they get married. Their marriage depends less on their initiation (though this remains a *conditio sine qua non*) than on their financial position. In terms of impact on the economic and social status of the young men, initiation is largely symbolic. Yet, exactly how initiation transforms the novices is a question that still remains to be answered. How are initiates transformed into male adults? How is their initiation made effective (cf. Kratz 1994)? And how is participation in the ritual made meaningful to the initiates?

It is quite understandable that young men born and raised in the village should wish to participate in this one-time ritual to acquire adult status. But what about the young men born elsewhere, in Ziguinchor, Dakar or Paris? The cultural fabric of these cities does not in any way reflect the beliefs and practices of Jola village life. However, villagers do travel back and forth between the village and the city and the distinctions between Jola village life and Senegalese city life are diminishing. For instance, many young Jola men and women prefer to speak Wolof instead of Jola. Wolof has become the lingua franca of Senegal, notably of the large urban centres. The Wolof language is identified with modernity and urbanity, and attracts speakers of other languages (Fall 1989; McLaughlin 1995; Cruise O'Brien 1998). Some young Jola born in Dakar do not even speak their parents' language and only speak Wolof. Wolof has also become the lingua franca among Ziguinchor's youth, and even in small Jola towns Wolof is widely spoken (Juillard 1991, 1994; Moreau 1994). Labour migration has resulted in the rather puzzling phenomenon of young Jola speaking Wolof in their villages of origin. This 'wolofisation' of Jola youth can be observed in various other cultural practices too (food, dress, music), and is in fact a sign of their integration in Senegalese society. Youth generally consider it more important to be proficient in Wolof than to be knowledgeable about 'traditional' cultural practices. What then makes them interested in participating in the initiation? Some of the young men born in urban areas have not visited the village for years. The cultural, social and economic orientations of these urban youth reflect an interest in a distinctly urban life style with parameters of social status that are quite different from the ones prevalent in the village. Yet most of these young men remain eager to experience initiation. What does this traditional ritual offer them? By examining the young men's discourse about initiation and how their bodies are ritually transformed in a sequence of changing styles of dress, I would like to suggest that the initiation produces a kind of subjectivity that fits the urbanites' experience.

When asked about the ritual, many young men stressed its aspect of tradition. To most of them, the ritual performance signified following the path set out by the ancestors. Some young men, however, viewed the initiation as an educational exercise and therefore considered it the equivalent of the state school system. Others emphasised the discipline imposed on the novices and compared the initiation with military service. Still others offered an even more refined analysis by likening the initiation's hierarchical organisation to the state government. They thus legitimised this 'traditional' custom by comparing it to institutions widely associated with *civilisation* and *le modernisme*. Of course, socialisation and intricate social organisation are indeed important features of the ritual. Comparisons like these demonstrate that the participants believe initiation is an expression of Jola society that is as legitimate as institutions associated with modernity. In addition to this secular interpretation of initiation, parts of the ritual are believed to bear a striking resemblance to aspects of Islam. For instance, before entering the sacred forest the novices dance three circles around a sacred site. Men compare this dance to the circles Muslim pilgrims make around the Kaaba in Mecca.[10] They believe initiation is the authentic Jola counterpart of Islamic practices. Some young men place Jola practices on an equal footing with Islam and Christianity.[11] The comparisons serve to reaffirm the contemporary relevance of the initiation which, as a result of its constant incorporation of historical transformations, the ritual had never lost anyway. Paradoxically, while the ritual incorporates modernity, the participants perceive it as the authentic Jola counterpart to modern secular and religious institutions. The ritual assumes a new meaning in idioms derived from modernity.

This conception of initiation must also affect what the initiation does. I therefore suggest that the initiation transforms the novices into men who embody modernity. In other words, the initiation enables the novices to appropriate modernity on their own terms. The bodies of the novices are transformed through metonymic references to the history of Jola society. Initiation provides the novices with a formalised entry into the modern world through a metonymic re-enactment of the various stages of Jola history. This is apparent from the bodily transformations the novices go through during the ritual process (Van Gennep 1960). As soon as the initiation is formally announced, the initiates are regarded as taboo (*nyau-nyau*) and interaction with them is subject to various rules. They are set apart from society. On the day they enter the sacred forest the novices are barechested and wear only raffia skirts. Thus in the rite of separation the status of the novice is expressed by dress that refers to his 'uncultured' nature. They re-present the stage in Jola history when the ancestors had not yet become cultivated men. The transformation from 'uncultured' to 'cultured' is symbolically brought about through the initiation ceremony and related to permanent settlement. The entry into the sacred forest can be understood as a re-enactment of the initial act of 'colonisation' of the land. I recall that the elders throw their spears in the direction of the sacred forest, which clearly signals the force that was required to conquer the land. While they sojourn in the forest, the initiates are familiarised with the spirits of the land with whom their ancestors struck an alliance. What is also conveyed is the secret history of settlement and the resultant relationships between 'land-lords' and 'strangers'. This historical knowledge is imparted to the initiates for them to transmit when they themselves become instructors. When the novices leave the forest, their impending status is expressed by a new style of dress and accessories to go with it. Standing at the gate of the sacred forest, they each carry a white, decorated stick, reminiscent of the circumcision formerly practised at the sacred forest (Van der Klei 1989: 165–6). Their heads and bodies are covered with black cloths (*jebil ganyuget*), above which they wear a red fez.[12] These black cloths are generally viewed as 'traditional' Jola dress. Metonymically, the cloths and fez express that the novices have been 'cultured' during their seclusion at the sacred forest. As 'cultured' men, they walk back to the ward in a solemn procession. Their new status is reflected in the cloths they wear, but they are not yet allowed to speak. Only after a night spent at their patrilineal compound is this right conferred on them, which suggests that the men should assume moral responsibility as members of their House. The novices only wear the black cloths for one day and then change into a new caftan. In Casamance this dress is asso-ciated with Islam, so the caftan metonymically refers to the Jola conversion to the Muslim faith. The custom of wearing a new caftan to celebrate one's initiation began at the 1940 initiation, when most of Thionck's inhabitants had converted to Islam. At the time, Thionck also had a large minority of Catholics. Not surprisingly, they wore European dress to celebrate their newly acquired adult status. The sequence of stages as expressed by dress conveys that adulthood can only be obtained by miming the various stages of Jola history. Thus the novices have to be cultured at the sacred forest where they are symbolically circumcised before they are allowed to enter the ward in 'traditional' dress. Then they have to be reintegrated into their House before they are to be allowed to dress in a caftan. Their kinship is affirmed before their religious affiliation. In the very last stages of the rite of passage are included the most recent gadgets that can be obtained at the cosmopolitan markets of Dakar.

In the days after their exit from the sacred forest, many initiates carry colourful umbrellas like the ones adult men carry to the Friday service at the mosque. Some initiates have received sunglasses as a present, others wear glasses without corrective lenses. Some of the initiates wear new *babouches* (slippers of North African origin), others sport trendy Nike sneakers. In the choice of clothing and other accoutrements at the final stage of incor-poration the initiates not only express their Muslim identity but also their allegiance to the capitalist world represented by consumer goods. The rite of incorporation is marked by hybrid dress of diverse origins. The initi-ation thus transforms a young man from an uncultured person into a Jola

Muslim and an acknowledged participant in the global capitalist economy. This status is conveyed metonymically by dress and other symbols of capitalist consumption and registered by modern means: many initiates are photographed when fully dressed and decorated at their rite of incorporation. This is quite surprising, if we bear in mind that photographs are only taken at the most important Christian and Muslim holidays and during *soirées dansantes* in clubs. Photographing the initiation ritual communicates that the Jola initiation is as important as the celebrations associated with the world religions. For the individual initiates, however, the photographs provide tangible proof of their becoming modern Jola men. Initiation has incorporated the signs of modernity that are subsequently conferred on the initiates at the moment of their incorporation into society. The male initiation remembers the Jola past (cf. Connerton 1989), but it does so as a series of events metonymically remembered through dress and demeanour. Through the embodiment of the subsequent stages of Jola history, initiation produces a historical subjectivity. In that respect, male and female initiations are comparable and accomplish similar goals.

CONCLUSION

In the course of this century, Jola society and the initiation have both undergone profound transformations. The community of Thionck Essyl now not only encompasses the villagers but also its *ressortissants*: the members of the community who live in urban areas in Senegal, Europe and beyond. Within the global contexts that encompass the community of Thionck Essyl, the production of a sense of social immediacy is organised in a ritual focused on the sacred forest. The initiation does so, we might argue, by representing community life as stable and unchanging (Hobsbawm and Ranger 1983). The model of the social structure that is affirmed by the initiation is indeed derived from the past and symbolically refers to an outdated and virtual model of society (cf. Van Binsbergen 1999). However, the ritual has also been transformed so as to accommodate modernity and to incorporate historical change in its ritual script. Most of the participants are aware of these modifications. To them, initiation does not represent an unchallenged tradition. Nor would they believe that community life continued unchallenged throughout the twentieth century. The initiation is not a remnant of the past. A balance between continuity and change has been found so that the ritual suggests continuity with the past and includes societal transformations. The subjectivity produced by the initiation ritual is indeed historical.

Inevitably, the capacity of the community to produce local subjects is profoundly affected by large-scale social formations and its capacity to produce locality seems critically diminished. The conversion to Islam, the subjection to the postcolonial state, migration and the dominance of the market economy attest to the globalisation of Thionck Essyl. Today, the members of this community are cosmopolitan Muslims, Senegalese citizens and Parisian *africains*. However, the community's central ritual has been adapted to include the global. The initiation ritual of Thionck Essyl has retained the capacity to produce subjects that embody translocality. Even so, it should be recognised that such translocality is focused on a virtual village, the existence of which can only be ensured through the assistance of migrants living in cities.

4

POLITICS OF THE SACRED FOREST

Being a good politician requires multifarious personal qualities, some of which depend on the cultural context of the political contest. One specific requirement for politicians operating in Casamance is that they have to be initiated. This chapter deals with the participation of a Senegalese politician in the Jola initiation, and the consequences for a local political contest. The politician is Robert Sagna, the former Senegalese Minister of Agriculture and the present mayor of Ziguinchor. He is a long-time member of the Socialist Party, the party that dominated Senegalese politics until early 2000. Robert Sagna has had a successful career, in the party and the state apparatus, resulting in several highly prestigious positions in the Senegalese government. At the age of fifty-five, he had himself initiated in the traditional Jola male initiation, and in September 1994 he was led into one of the sacred forests of Thionck Essyl. We might wonder why a Minister of Agriculture felt a need to be initiated. With his high status, income and privilege, he could well have considered initiation a relic of the past, part of a tradition modern statesmen do not have to conform to. The clue lies in the realm of ethnicity that has been an increasingly important feature of social life in Casamance since the rebellion against the Senegalese state in 1982. I suggest it was necessary for Robert Sagna to enter the sacred forest to assure his political position. We might also wonder why the people of Thionck Essyl were so eager to initiate this Minister of Agriculture. Obviously, the villagers considered good relations with the Minister important and this is why they welcomed him. Moreover, Sagna's initiation was so important to the villagers that the event became a major issue in a local election campaign. Surprisingly, the people who had initiated Robert Sagna supported his opponents within the Socialist Party. Why did they suddenly shift their allegiance? The electorate of Thionck Essyl led Sagna into the sacred forest, but they also used other strategies to accommodate national politics. In this chapter, Sagna's initiation and its consequences for the local political contest are evoked to demonstrate that a local electorate uses a combination of strategies to come to grips with elusive politicians.

The case might be dismissed as idiosyncratic. However, Sagna's initiation illustrates a more general interest on the part of Jola politicians in male initiation. Senegalese politicians are keenly aware of the need to play a role in events of this kind. They have to be accountable, even in 'traditional' matters. So they have to comply with the standards set by their ethnic compatriots. This has partly been a result of the pressure by the international donor community on the Senegalese government. So, one of the paradoxes of globalisation is that the International Monetary Fund and the World Bank make Senegalese politicians accountable to their voters, and that the voters express their political preferences in unexpected local idioms. Robert Sagna's initiation can be explained as resulting from the combination of global pressure for political transparency and the increased ethnicisation of local politics.

ETHNICITY AND CITIZENSHIP

This chapter analyses an encounter between politicians and members of the Jola ethnic group in terms of state–society relations. The issue at stake is the extent to which ethnicity can be a discourse enabling subjects to exert pressure on the state. In other words, can subjects make their specific subjectivity instrumental in their performance of citizenship (cf. Mamdani 1996)? I am not referring to the formal recognition of ethnicity as a political principle in the organisation of the state, as it is pursued in Ethiopia (Abbink 1997). I rather examine how ethnicity provides the idiom of the interaction between citizens and politicians.

Ethnicity has often been conceived by scholars and politicians alike as a threat to the state's integrity. Fear of the powerful force of ethnicity was especially strong when African colonies were achieving independence. At the time, scholars considered tribalism a primordial attachment and felt that tribal ties were incompatible with national citizenship. But tribalism was soon revealed to be an ideology (Mafeje 1971; Godelier 1973), a social construct rather than a primordial given. In the 1980s, many authors demonstrated that tribes had in fact been created by the colonial administration, showing tribalism to be an entirely modern phenomenon (Amselle and M'Bokolo 1985; Vail 1989). As far back as 1963, Geertz had already recognised that ethnic identification was stimulated by the process of state formation, 'because it introduces into society a valuable new prize over which to fight and a frightening new force with which to contend' (Geertz 1973: 270).

Since ethnicity and state formation are so intricately intertwined, Bayart correctly argues that ethnicity cannot be studied as a self-contained social field (Bayart 1993: 49). Ethnicity cannot provide a basic reference point for our comprehension of African politics, but it is a social process within the state to be reckoned with. Of course, we should be careful not to reify ethnicity and to fully acknowledge its historicity (Burnham 1996: 161–2). Ethnicity may then be shown to be a variable in people's perception of the state and their strategies to confront or appropriate the state. Indeed, we need to analyse ethnicity as one of the keys, but not the only one, to political behaviour. Ethnic affiliation may only be situationally activated (Werbner 1996: 1). In this respect, Mbembe convincingly argues that 'the postcolonial subject mobilises not just a single identity, but several fluid identities which, by their very nature, must be constantly revised in order to achieve maximum instrumentality and efficacy as and when required' (Mbembe 1992: 5). Subjects can situationally shift their attitude vis-à-vis the state. They can be ethnic subjects as well as citizens and, as I will demonstrate, alternate between these positions (cf. Mamdani 1996).[1] Jola ethnicity may thus be analysed as an interface that functions in sometimes diametrically opposed ways. In many ways Jola ethnicity has shaped the political struggle for secession, as is witnessed by the separatist struggle led by the MFDC (Marut 2002; Foucher 2002a; Gasser 2002). However, in this chapter I examine Jola ethnicity as an interface that contributes to incorporation into the Senegalese state.

ROBERT'S INITIATION

Three wards of Thionck Essyl had initiated their novices in 1994. The novices of these wards who, for one reason or another, had not been initiated in July could still enter the sacred forest in the following months because the sacred forests were not immediately 'closed'. Robert Sagna used this possibility and was initiated two months after the big event in July, and one year before the Socialist Party elections. I could not attend his initiation and only afterwards was I told that I had missed an important occasion. Several men who had attended the event themselves provided me with information afterwards. A photographer who had been there to take pictures of the Minister's initiation gave me some twenty photographs of the celebration. As a matter of course, Sagna's initiation can only be critically analysed if we relate it to the usual way young men are initiated. Since I had attended the public part of the July initiation I pretty well knew what was supposed to go on and what actually did. So it was not hard for me to figure out what made Sagna's initiation so peculiar.

Robert Sagna was initiated at the sacred forest of Kafanta sub-ward (Niaganan ward). Sagna arrived in Thionck Essyl on 30 September. He was courteously received by the officiant of the Kafanta sacred forest. The next afternoon, three young novices (*kambaj*) were led into the sacred forest in a festive procession from Kafanta's common. Robert Sagna, however, was taken to the sacred forest by car, accompanied by the forest's officiant, a few respectable village elders and several of his political allies. He spent the night in the forest, and left it the next day with the three other initiates. Villagers who were incredulous when they first heard about Sagna's initiation now appeared in large numbers at the forest's edge. Proud of the initiation of the most prominent Jola, they led Sagna back into the village. Photographers took numerous pictures. After some courtesies, Sagna left the village and returned to his usual business in the capital. Shortly afterwards, Robert Sagna was on television addressing the Senegalese Parliament, his head shaved as evidence of his initiation.

When I talked to the inhabitants of Kafanta about this rather unusual event, they showed great pride in Sagna's initiation. People who were not born in Thionck Essyl were far more sceptical and suspected that the Minister's initiation was a purely political act. Before interpreting his initiation in this sense, I would like to examine how it diverged from the usual practice. First of all, it should be noted that Sagna's sacred forest retreat lasted only one night, whereas other novices were obliged to stay three weeks in the forest. Second, novices are usually led into the sacred forest in a festive procession starting at the ward's central square. Initiated men surround them to 'protect' them, and by instructing them, demonstrate the initiates' inferior status. The status of the novices is also accentuated by their physical appearance: they are bare-chested and wear raffia skirts. Since Robert Sagna was taken to the forest by car, it was impossible for bystanders to witness his status of novice. Yet while his status of novice was carefully hidden from the public eye, a whole show was made of Robert Sagna's new status of initiate. When novices exit from the sacred forest, they usually wear black cloths that cover their faces. Robert Sagna, however, wore the black cloths in such a way that everyone recognised him as soon as he exited the sacred forest. Was this a carefully orchestrated way of publicising his initiation?

Robert Sagna was initiated at the age of fifty-five. In the past, men could indeed be initiated at a rather advanced age. However, due to modifications in the standards of admission, nowadays most men are initiated before their thirties. Why was Sagna initiated at such an advanced age? Sagna was born in Brin, a village on the southern shore of the Casamance River, the Catholic son of Catholic parents. Catholic missionaries used to condemn pagan practices such as initiation, which is why Sagna's father forbade his son's initiation. When Brin held its initiation in 1976, Sagna did not enter the sacred forest. So when he decided to be initiated, he had to look for an opportunity elsewhere. Why did he want to be initiated in Thionck Essyl? Sagna himself suggested that he preferred to be initiated there because of the special relationship between the villages of Brin and Thionck Essyl. Historical relations do exist between Thionck Essyl and villages on the southern shore, but Brin is definitely not one of them.[2]

Finally, Sagna was married and the father of four children. However, in Thionck Essyl, men are not allowed to get married before their initiation. Although many young men now do have sexual intercourse and father children before their initiation, no man gets married before entering the sacred forest. The standards of admission to initiation do, however, exhibit considerable variations and I was told that this rule is not observed in Brin.

The officiant of the Kafanta sacred forest argued that if married men were allowed to enter the sacred forest in Brin, Robert Sagna should also be accorded this liberty when he came to Thionck. I found people considerably less lenient with regard to the rules of the sacred forest when it came to strangers of lower status.

THE APPROPRIATION OF A POLITICIAN

Sagna's career testifies to his intelligence and competence. He was raised in a Catholic family and went to Catholic primary and secondary schools, which are better than public schools. He subsequently studied in Belgium and France and was awarded a PhD in economics in Paris. Upon his return to Senegal, he was a civil servant in the Senegalese bureaucracy and soon he became Secretary of State. Since 1978 he has been Minister of Transport and Equipment (three times), Minister of Fisheries, Minister of Tourism, Minister of the Senegambian Confederation (twice), Minister of Communication and Minister of Agriculture (twice). In addition, he has held several positions in national commissions and has been mayor of Ziguinchor since 1984. Of course, he is a member of the Socialist Party *bureau politique*. Why did this Minister of Agriculture feel a need to be initiated? Presuming political motives, I was eager to interview Sagna, and he kindly consented. Yet he felt uneasy with the questions I posed. When I suggested that he had been politically motivated, Sagna said that anything about his initiation was a secret, thus shifting identity from a politician to an initiated man (vis-à-vis a non-initiate like myself). Sagna denied that political opportunism had motivated him to be initiated.

The most important reason for Sagna's entry into the sacred forest must be that initiation has recently become an important symbol of Jola identity (see Chapter 3). For a man like Robert Sagna, raised in a Catholic home, it may have been appropriate not to undergo initiation, but he may have felt increasingly uneasy with his status of non-initiate. This might have been why Sagna was initiated at his rather advanced age. However, his position as mayor of Ziguinchor and high official in the Socialist Party may also have played a part. Robert Sagna was already facing practical problems as a non-initiate. Today it is increasingly common for politicians to attend initiation rituals, and give handouts and congratulate the initiates on their new status. Sagna did this too, but could never enter the sacred forest himself and had to send representatives. There were rumours about his status as non-initiate. Other politicians had begun to refer to Sagna's status as non-initiate, suggesting that he could not properly represent the people. Landing Sane, another prominent Jola politician at the SP who headed another faction, openly ridiculed Sagna for his status of *ambaj*. For Sagna remaining non-initiated entailed a risk of being ostracised.

Sagna's initiation became all the more urgent in view of the increasing pressure from Western donors and Senegalese citizens on the Senegalese government to enhance its democratic procedures, especially to make the electoral process more transparent. The Socialist Party was taking the argument seriously and trying to democratise the procedures for its internal elections. This meant politicians needed to have a personal appeal to the electorate. Moreover, changes in the national political system created a new local arena for political rivalry. There was about to be an administrative reorganisation in Senegal: *Régionalisation*.[3] The regional administrations were to be governed by newly established regional councils. Sagna would certainly be an excellent candidate for the council of the *région* of Ziguinchor, which was to be established in 1995. He was close to President Diouf and had strong popular support in the region. In addition he was leading the negotiations with the MFDC and had turned out to be an acceptable negotiator. Undoubtedly, Robert Sagna was the most eminent Jola politician on the national political landscape and the most popular SP candidate in the Ziguinchor region.

Initiation was a crucial prerequisite for Sagna's future political career. Most of his electorate in the Ziguinchor region are of Jola extraction. His initiation at a Jola sacred forest made him more trustworthy to the local electorate.[4] Moreover, his initiation reinforced his position in the Socialist Party, because he would continue to draw considerable electoral support in Ziguinchor. His initiation qualified him even better as an interlocutor for the MFDC, the leader of which had already suggested that any politician who had not been initiated at the sacred forest should be considered untrustworthy (Lambert 1998: 592).[5] Although it seems that Sagna's initiation only contributed to maximising his credibility, I should acknowledge that the political competition within the Socialist Party was severe and no one's position was ever stable. Sagna's position within the SP may have been reinforced within one faction, but not necessarily within the entire SP. Indeed, after his initiation several accusations were voiced against him. Some newspapers accused him of being a prominent rebel. Thus his entry into the sacred forest meant an increasingly narrow identification of Robert Sagna with the Jola ethnic group (and of his possible sympathy towards the rebels) (Marut 1995: 167). The Minister walked a thin line, carefully maintaining his trustworthiness with the Senegalese government, the MFDC and the Jola electorate. On the whole, however, his initiation reinforced his political position with his political base.

THE PRESENCE OF POLITICIANS

Robert Sagna's case may be idiosyncratic, but the participation of state officials in the 1994 *garur* was not restricted to his initiation. Many politicians had been to Thionck Essyl to show their commitment to the village's most important celebration. The public announcement of the initiation (*fundim*), a year before the actual retreat, was an occasion for many dignitaries to come there. That day, Thionck Essyl welcomed two Ministers (Robert Sagna and Landing Sane), several Members of Parliament, local administrators such as the prefect, and the governors of the administrative regions of Ziguinchor and Fatick (Saliou Sambou, who was born in Thionck Essyl himself).[6] The officials carefully selected the individuals they associated with. They visited their political allies in the village and showed respect for the sacred forest officiants and the former *chef de canton* by visiting them. In addition, gifts were given in kind and currency. The former *chef de canton* received fifteen tons of rice for distribution among the village wards: a gift made by the Socialist Party. Another five tons were given by Landing Sane. The gifts may have been funded by the government or the Socialist Party (the two are often confused by villagers and politicians alike). What matters to the villagers is which individual donated the money or goods.

Officiants with responsibilities for the ritual's successful performance knew exactly why particular politicians were invited. Their support was needed for several reasons, the most important of which was the free import of rice and cattle from the Gambia. At the beginning of the twentieth century, young men temporarily migrated to the British colony to earn a monetary income by cultivating peanuts for the Gambian hosts. Some of the cash they earned was invested in cattle that were left in the care of the Gambian hosts. Even now Thionck's villagers still have cattle in the Gambia. Some of the cattle had to be led to the village for slaughter during the initiation. Moreover, many community members now live in the Gambia. They too wished to import cattle and rice, which were cheaper there, into Senegal. High-ranking politicians and civil servants were therefore invited to attend rituals to make sure they 'arranged' for the community members living in the Gambia to freely cross the border and import rice and cattle without being taxed. Below I demonstrate how important this matter was to the villagers.

The politicians' interest in *garur* benefited the villagers in various ways, which was why the villagers welcomed the politicians and tried to strike a bargain. Aside from modifying the rules of admittance to the sacred forest, as in Sagna's case, the villagers showed a willingness to accommodate the politicians' needs in other respects as well. Undoubtedly the most striking example was the modification of the ritual calendar. Initially, 9 July had been set as the day of entry into the sacred forest. When this date appeared inconvenient to one particularly influential Jola politician the elders decided to reschedule the day of entry for 16 July. They made it possible for Saliou Sambou, Governor of Fatick and 'son of the village', to attend the most spectacular day of the entire celebration.[7] This sudden change in the ritual calendar obliged some migrants in the European diaspora to reschedule their holidays and flights if they were to attend the ceremony. The initiation accommodates the needs of migrants, but the presence of politicians is apparently deemed to be of even greater importance. In sum, the villagers had very clear objectives in their interaction with politicians. They knew how to manipulate the politicians, acknowledging that the politicians themselves had also set their own goals. The villagers readily recognised that the services were provided and the gifts were donated for a gift in return: electoral support. But the villagers' vote was not so easily won.

SEGMENTARY POLITICS

I have already mentioned that owing to a conflict about the appropriate moment for the initiation, Thionck Essyl was divided into two factions. More needs to be said about the causes and consequences of this conflict, since it provided the context for the political contest that was to occur in 1995. The population of Thionck Essyl had been preparing the initiation in unison in 1989 when three of Niaganan's sub-wards (Butem, Jiwat and Dyalil) decided that the initiation was to take place in 1990. Kafanta was the only Niaganan sub-ward that refused to go along with this decision – it

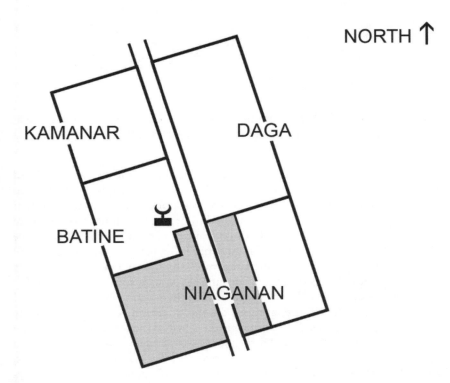

Map 4 *La commune* of Thionck Essyl showing the four wards

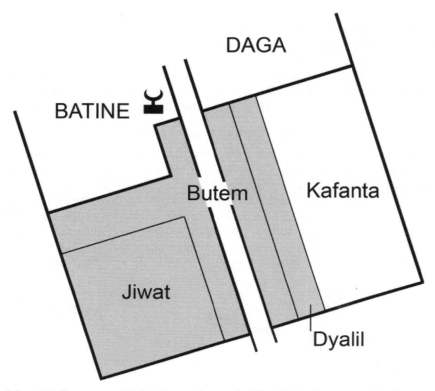

Map 5 Niaganan with its four sub-wards. The shaded area marks the part of the village ('Avance') that held its initiation in 1990

felt it was not ready at that time since some families had not accumulated enough funds to finance the ritual. The three sub-wards subsequently tried to mobilise the other wards of the village, but none of them approved their initiative. The three sub-wards continued to prepare without the support of the other wards, and indeed separated from the rest of Thionck Essyl (see Maps 4 and 5). The celebration of male initiation, formerly an expression of village unity, was to be performed separately by the two factions. This was an unprecedented step for the village, and it requires some explanation.[8]

Violations of the ritual order were seen as the reason why the 'the sacred forest' interfered in the preparations for the initiation. The mystical entity held responsible for the dissension was the spirit of the initiation shrine, still believed to reside in the sacred forest. One of the ritual violations mentioned by the villagers pertained to the sequence of entry into the sacred forests, which had been modified in 1940. In the past Niaganan ward had always entered its sacred forest a week before the other wards because Niaganan ward was thought to be an easy victim for attacks from the adjacent village of Tendouck, especially during the initiation period. Thionck's other wards would thus be on the alert during the first week of Niaganan's initiation and assist Niaganan in the event of an attack by Tendouck.[9] However, colonial pacification made attacks of this kind unlikely and in 1940 all Thionck's wards entered their sacred forests on the same day. But many believed that by changing the old order of initiation, the curse of the sacred forest had been invoked. The mystical sanctions materialised in the discord in the preparations for the 1990/1994 initiation, or so some believed. According to others, however, the mystical consequences of the violation of the sacred rules were to do with people's conversion to Islam or, vaguely, with *le modernisme*.

A specific and much more persuasive explanation for the dissension was that a conflict about a specific ritual responsibility had arisen. Specific individuals had run away from or, conversely, had unjustifiably assumed ritual responsibility. This argument focused on the family that was held responsible for the announcement of the initiation. In the entire ritual cycle, there is one particular rite where a man has to announce the initiation. This responsibility is charged with mystical danger and has always been the obligation of the Niassy family in Niaganan, which was said to be internally divided. This disagreement about whose responsibility it was to announce the initiation tore the family apart and led to Niaganan's and ultimately to Thionck Essyl's division. The reasons for the family's internal division remained obscure to me, since my informants kept giving different versions. Some people argued that this Niassy family actually consisted of two families, Niassy-*noir* (black) and Niassy-*teint clair* (white). Niassy-black was said to be an old family wielding the responsibility for annunciation. Niassy-white were 'strangers' who had been adopted by their Niassy-black hosts. Over the last century, the Niassy-black had declined and, though they had not died out, they had become the smallest family in Niaganan. The Niassy-white, on the other hand, had prospered. Some believed that the strangers had tried to usurp the ritual responsibility of their hosts.[10] Apparently, ritual responsibilities defined in terms of an ideology of descent were being contested. Yet, although the question of ritual responsibilities may explain why the Niassy family was torn apart, it does not explain why the entire village was divided. The true reason for the conflict is none of the above. All the explanations for the dissension in Thionck were invented *ex post facto*. The prosaic reality was that the conflict evolved out of a mere disagreement about when the initiation should be held. The inhabitants of Kafanta accused the urban migrants of the three sub-wards of having pressured their elders into announcing the initiation. Since migrants do have a significant say in village matters based on the financial support they offer, this accusation makes sense. Migrants living in Dakar were eager to initiate their sons and urged their village-based kin to announce the initiation. Whether or not the other wards would go along was viewed as being of minor importance. This once again corroborates my hypothesis that the initiation ritual has been transformed into a ritual that reinforces links between villagers and city-dwellers rather than the unity of the village as a whole (see Chapter 3). Most people nevertheless interpreted the dissension as a succession struggle within the Niassy family.

Thus, while the three sub-wards went on to prepare the 1990 initiation, Kafanta sub-ward allied itself with the other wards of Thionck Essyl and postponed the communal initiation. The Niassy family was torn apart in the process, since each of the two factions had tried to include at least part of this important family in its camp. However, while many unstable alliances were dissolved, other alliances were created. For instance, Batine ward increasingly allied itself with Kafanta. Due to a conflict about the election of the *chef de canton* back in the 1950s, Batine had always been opposed to Kafanta. The destruction of the central sacred forest and the relocation of Thionck's wards had contributed to their antagonism. Batine had actively opposed the Niaganan ward for almost half a century. Now Batine allied itself with Kafanta, one of Niaganan's factions. Marginalised for half a century, the members of Batine ward took this opportunity to drive a wedge between the opposing factions of Niaganan. Thus the political process was stimulated by the conflict about the celebration of male initiation.

Tensions rose between the factions throughout the period of preparations for the 1994 *garur*. Occasional fights broke out between the parties and one house burnt down after supposedly having been set on fire, resulting in two lawsuits. Relations had badly deteriorated when the 1994 initiation was finally performed. To avenge the allegedly unjust 1990 initiation, the elders of Thionck Essyl decided that the young men initiated in 1990 should not be allowed to enter the sacred forests where the 1994 initiation would be performed. They denied the young initiates of the three sub-wards their recently acquired status of adults, more or less negating the validity of the 1990 initiation. Their fathers declared their solidarity with their sons and boycotted the 1994 initiation. In the 1994 initiation, the men of the three sub-wards were not involved.

Interestingly, the parties used all means to legitimise their own points of view. When the national paper *Le Soleil* reported on the 1990 celebration, a member of the Niassy family was given ample space to present his claims on ritual responsibilities. No mention was made of the fact that three out of four of Thionck's wards were not participating in the celebration. Four years later, *Le Soleil* again devoted a couple of pages to Thionck's initiation. Again, nothing was said about the conflict. The partisans of each faction succeeded in having their celebration covered by the national newspaper, thus proclaiming the rightfulness of their celebration to the national public. But the role of the national media in this local conflict was not limited to the press. A documentary on Jola initiation, recorded during Thionck's 1990 initiation, was broadcast twice on national television. Again, the three sub-wards gave the impression that their celebration was the one and only male initiation of Thionck. The outraged inhabitants of the other wards watched the documentary and allegedly saw some 'secret' rituals, including the bathing of the novices, being broadcast nationwide. They swiftly accused the inhabitants of the three sub-wards of having disclosed secrets on national television. The local antagonism was increasingly expressed by means of the national media. Of course, the national public remained completely unaware of the source of the conflict. But the main purpose of using the media was to 'authorise' the political claims for a local public and the national media were effectively appropriated to this end.

THE SOCIALIST PARTY CAMPAIGN

After the 1990 and 1994 initiations, the new age sets were given names. The three sub-wards that had organised the early 1990 initiation called their new age set Avance, since their initiation had advanced the 1994 initiation. The thirteen remaining sub-wards that staged their initiation in 1994 called their new age set Matkane, a term that needs some explanation. In a fit of anger, one of the inhabitants of the three sub-wards had predicted that the 1994 initiation would never take place. Matkane means: 'That will never happen!' The expression was ironically adopted by the rest of Thionck as evidence of their ability to resist the various obstacles to the performance of their initiation. Other names were coined in the 1994 camp: Avance was also called Kaan Nooni ('They went on their own'), and Matkane was called Kaan Pehpeh ('They went together') or Diamoral ('Unity'), since they were a majority who had acted in union. In this divided community, local elections were to be held in 1995.

The fission resulting from the organisation of Thionck's *garur* was to play an important role in the political contest. The Socialist Party had scheduled its internal elections (*renouvellement des cartes*) for various levels of representation in the party. In May 1995, Thionck Essyl was divided in two factions, one that supported the SP faction Robert Sagna belonged to (*tendance A*), and one that supported the opposite faction (*tendance B*). Throughout Senegal, the Socialist Party is divided into two or more factions referred to as *tendances*. The system of antagonistic factions is essentially a system of vertical, clientelistic relationships.[11] Much of what follows should be understood as an expression of Senegalese political factionalism that is not specific to the political process in Thionck Essyl.

The irony of the electoral process in Thionck Essyl was, however, that the inhabitants of the sub-ward that had initiated Robert Sagna now supported his enemies within the Socialist Party (see Table 4.1). This shift in allegiance was related to the fact that Sagna's initiation contributed to

Table 4.1 Initiation factions in Thionck Essyl, their political alignment, and Socialist Party candidates at the village and regional level

Factions in initiation	Avance	Diamoral/Matkane (incl. Robert Sagna)
Year of initiation	1990	1994
SP factions	*Tendance A*	*Tendance B*
SP candidates (village level)	Baboucar Badji	Amadou Sadio *(ambaj)*
SP candidates (regional level)	Robert Sagna	Landing Sane

the bones of contention within a complicated process of segmentary opposition. The explanation is as follows. Thionck Essyl had been assigned the administrative status of *commune* in 1992. This administrative status gives the citizens the right to elect their own mayor. Since the winner of the SP internal elections at the *commune* level was to be the SP candidate in the mayoral elections, and since the Socialist Party usually gets a majority of the votes, the winner of the SP internal elections could reasonably be expected to become mayor. The mayoral election was thus viewed as the crux of the SP internal elections. In 1995, the mayor of Thionck Essyl, the lawyer Baboucar Badji, was a man born in one of the sub-wards of Avance, and many inhabitants of the remaining wards (Diamoral) were determined to oust him from office. What had he done wrong? First of all, he was born in the wrong sub-ward. Whether he did a good job or not, the people of Diamoral were unlikely to welcome a candidate from the opposite camp. There were, however, other objections to his candidature for prolonged office. First of all, he had never given a detailed account of the revenues and expenditures of Thionck's administration. Secondly, the management of the local tourist hotel, originally established by the community, had been appropriated by the mayor, and people feared that he himself was keeping the profits. Thirdly, the most important objection pertained to his supposed obstruction of the 1994 initiation. Quite unexpectedly, the *ressortissants* living in the Gambia had to face Customs, and the import of rice and cattle to Casamance had been problematic. Baboucar Badji, the mayor of Thionck Essyl, was blamed. On several occasions he stated emphatically that he should not be blamed, but to no avail. Moreover, the Diamoral members accused him of not showing any interest in the 1994 initiation save for the one moment when he accompanied Robert Sagna into the sacred forest. On that occasion, the initiated men of the Kafanta sub-ward had tried to prevent him from entering their sacred forest. The elders had had to calm the younger age set down.

The major problem during the SP election campaign, in terms of the segementary political process, was that Robert Sagna had been initiated in one of the wards that belonged to the Diamoral faction. Politically, however, Robert Sagna belonged to precisely the same SP faction as Baboucar Badji (*tendance A*), the mayor the entire Diamoral faction was opposed to (see Table 4.1). If Diamoral wanted to vote against the present mayor, their choice also implied a vote against the extremely popular Minister of Agriculture whom they themselves had initiated. However, even if Robert Sagna represented the surest channel of access to state resources, all the Diamoral members wanted was to vote the incumbent mayor out of office. In the Diamoral camp, long-time SP members were joined by long-time members of opposition parties, such as the PDS (Parti Démocratique Sénégalais) and And Jef, and even supporters of the separatist movement. All of them bought SP membership cards to vote against Baboucar Badji in the upcoming SP internal elections.

What about the Diamoral candidate? After all, ousting Baboucar Badji was one thing, proposing their own candidate for *tendance B* quite another. A good candidate was nominated, Amadou Sadio. He was born in the right place, one of the wards of the Diamoral camp. He had studied English and German and was a graduate of the Ecole Nationale d'Administration et de Magistrature. His career was splendid and he was working in the Senegalese national administration in Dakar. In 1995, he was forty-five years old, married, and the father of six children. Amadou Sadio seemed to be an excellent candidate. Yet his candidature was very awkward. When Amadou was still young his family had moved to Kaolack, a city in central Senegal. He had grown up in Kaolack and was a de facto stranger (*anaya*) in Thionck Essyl. Moreover, he was a non-initiate (*ambaj*). His father, a pious Muslim, had refused to initiate his son.[12] In an interview I had with Sadio, he stated that he was a Muslim by conviction and he questioned the usefulness of initiation. He expressed a wish for the initiation to be preserved (as a 'tradition') but refused to enter the sacred forest himself.

It is only logical that the issue of initiation should have entirely dominated the electoral campaign. Politicians of *tendance A* knew very well that the mayor of Thionck Essyl could not possibly win the SP internal elections. They opted for an alternative strategy, and emphasised the importance of the future project of regionalisation and the creation of a regional council. At this level, they observed, Robert Sagna stood for *tendance A*. They tried to induce the electorate to support Sagna, who was still very popular among the villagers because he had entered their sacred forest. The politicians of *tendance A* argued that even if the villagers strongly disliked the candidature of the present mayor, they would be wise to vote for *tendance A*. Their vote for Baboucar Badji would then be used to support Sagna's candidature in the indirect elections at the regional level.

The politicians of *tendance B* vehemently and correctly argued that the regionalisation project was not the issue in this campaign. They also contended that a vote for Amadou Sadio did not necessarily imply support for Landing Sane, Sagna's negligibly appreciated adversary at the regional level. Landing Sane was the most prominent man in *tendance B*, and although formerly quite popular, he had lost much of his support. People said Landing Sane 'can do nothing for the region'. Robert Sagna, in contrast, was considered a *travailleur* (worker). People felt that in his former capacity of Minister of Transport and Equipment, Robert Sagna had established more infrastructural works in the region than Landing Sane, who was the Minister of that department in 1995. If the choice was between Robert Sagna and Landing Sane, Sagna had a better chance of winning the elections.

As a matter of course, the politicians of *tendance A* also argued that Amadou Sadio could never be a proper mayor since he was a non-initiate (*ambaj*). Members of *tendance B*, however, didn't say a word about Amadou Sadio's status of non-initiate. This led to a paradoxical conceptualisation of *la politique* (politics). *Tendance A* argued that *la politique* and initiation should not be confused, but emphasised that Robert Sagna had been initiated in Thionck Essyl. *Tendance B* did not propagate an analytical distinction between politics and initiation. Of course, they could hardly do so, since their political unity was based on their unity in initiation. In practice, though, they did differentiate between politics and initiation, since their candidate was a non-initiate.[13] Thus initiation and local politics were confused and became intricately intertwined. The breach between Avance and Diamoral became the major dividing line between the SP factions. Initiation was a major issue in the election campaign.

MEETINGS POLITIQUES AND ELECTIONS

The electorate in Thionck Essyl was bitterly divided. Every conceivable effort was made to win the political contest. One of the strategies was of a procedural nature. In order to be eligible to vote in the SP elections, one had to be an SP member. Since most of the people who were interested in ousting Baboucar Badji from office were in fact members of the PDS and the other opposition parties, they had to join the SP to be able to vote. The strategy both factions used was to manipulate the distribution and sale of SP membership cards in order to prevent the sale of cards to sympathisers of the opposite faction. This strategy was not specific to the electoral process in Thionck Essyl: it is widespread in the SP internal elections throughout Senegal. Accusations of fraud with regard to the sale of membership cards are part and parcel of Socialist Party internal elections.

What was specific to Thionck's election campaign was that each of the factions developed its own distinct style of campaigning. The political rallies (*meetings politiques*) organised by the *tendances* to draw attention to their cause were quite different. Here, I describe two of these rallies. *Tendance A* organised its *meeting politique* for the entire electorate of Thionck Essyl on 2 July 1995. The village of Thionck Essyl, as I noted above, was relocated

in the 1970s. At the centre of the village, a large open square was designated to become the site of a market and bus station. But the village never
became the thriving commercial centre that was envisaged and the informal
locations remained in use. The modern buildings of concrete and corrugated iron were never used and testify to the unsuccessful modernisation of
Thionck Essyl. However, *tendance A* claimed a village-wide audience and
decided to hold its rally at Thionck's central square, the symbol of village
unity and modernisation.

A palm leaf fence closed off a rectangular space where the meeting was
to proceed. A reception committee of girls carrying flowers welcomed the
visitors and directed them to the meeting ground. High-ranking politicians from various towns in the region, all of whom belonged to *tendance A*,
had come to Thionck Essyl to attend the meeting. Their four-wheel-drive
vehicles were parked in front of the meeting ground. The meeting ground
itself was carefully parcelled up. The politicians were comfortably seated
on lounge chairs under a canopy of palm leafs, decorated with Senegalese
flags. A table with several bottles of mineral water stood in front of them.
Behind the first row of politicians, the elder *militants* of *tendance A* were
seated. Next to these notables was a row of women, wearing uniform dress
(*assoby*) who were there to enliven the meeting by dancing and singing.
The rank-and-file audience sat on the ground, facing the politicians. Three
categories of participants could thus be distinguished: the high-ranking
politicians and male elders, the female support act, and the rank-and-file
audience. In anticipation of things to come, the women danced while rhythmically accompanied by two drummers and a saxophonist. The rhythm
was *enyalenay*, a female fertility dance considered typical of Thionck Essyl.
The meeting began as soon as all the politicians had finally arrived and
started with a show by young girls. They performed a carefully choreo-
graphed dance to electronically amplified, modern Senegalese pop music
(*m'balakh*), but the audience hardly responded. More enthusiasm was
aroused by a wrestler who had recently won a wrestling match organised by
the SP-*tendance A*. He triumphantly made a victory round at the meeting
ground. But the serious part of the *meeting politique* started when a local
imam blessed the ensuing meeting. Then, one after the other, the politicians delivered their speeches. The women occasionally danced, either in
between the speeches or interrupting the speakers to emphasise their firm
statements. The meeting went on for about three hours and was concluded
with the recitation of a prayer.

In contrast to this well-organised and carefully orchestrated meeting,
the rallies of Diamoral (*tendance B*) were more relaxed and informal.
One of the meetings was held in Batine ward the day after the *tendance
A* meeting described above. The Diamoral meetings were not held at the
village central square but alternately at the various village wards. The most

striking difference with the *tendance A* meeting was the virtual absence of expensive consumer items. At this meeting there were no four-wheel drive vehicles, no flowers, no mineral water, no lounge chairs but popular deck-chairs instead, and no electronic equipment save a defunct amplifier. Many civil servants had attended the *tendance A* meeting, but here the audience consisted almost entirely of farmers. One of the spectators offered freshly carved wooden spades for sale. Even though the format of this meeting clearly resembled the official *tendance A* rally, people moved around freely and failed to adhere to the categories so rigidly defined at the *tendance A* rally. The politicians partook of the dancing and some of the female spectators delivered lengthy and humorous speeches. Instead of being entertained, people were expected to sing and dance themselves. For this purpose some traditional drums were carried to the meeting ground. Diamoral did not deliberately turn the spectators into a passive and submissive audience.

Since this *tendance B* meeting took place the day after the *tendance A* meeting, the speakers could react to the speeches delivered the day before. And some of them did so with great pleasure, be it with admittedly less professional skill. At the *tendance A* meeting, Baboucar Badji and other speakers had emphasised that he and Robert Sagna belonged to the same *tendance*. Badji had tried to get the audience to vote for him so that he could, in turn, support Robert Sagna in the indirect regional elections. At their meeting, in contrast, the *tendance B* speakers argued that Robert Sagna was trustworthy and accused Baboucar Badji of having abused his name. Baboucar Badji, they said, was a liar and Robert Sagna had wisely failed to attend the *tendance A* rally. *Tendance B* speakers also accused Baboucar Badji of having devoured the membership cards that had disappeared, which they said could be found in his toilet. The impressive number of political allies Baboucar Badji had mobilised for the *tendance A* rally also failed to intimidate the *tendance B* speakers. Most of these politicians were from Fogny. To be understood by his allies, Baboucar Badji had addressed his audience in Jola-Fogny, not the local dialect. 'Was this to show', asked one of the speakers, 'that he is a true polyglot?' Irony, dance and fun dominated the *tendance B* rally. Farmers addressed each other as 'Président de la République'. Ribald humour characterised the *tendance B* rally, while the *tendance A* rally had been very serious indeed. But resentment against the mayor and other politicians was also aired. At the *tendance B* rally, speakers accused politicians of being cheats and swindlers and argued that politics is just a dirty game.

The organisation and the contents of the speeches at the two meetings reveal some interesting contrasts. The *tendance A* rally was ambitiously modernist and professionally organised. The electorate was impressed by the presence of well-to-do political allies from other towns, which reinforced the distinction between politicians and the electorate. The message was one

Table 4.2 Results of the Socialist Party internal elections, 1995

	Tendance A	*Tendance B*
Thionck Essyl	1,355	1,548
Bignona Department	44,675	8,708

of a well-organised party machine led by a political class with access to the state and, by induction, access to the state for the client-voters. To the farmers, *tendance A* represented the state and its modernisation project. The *tendance B* rally, in contrast, expressed a suspicion of politicians, *la politique* and any of their projects. The farmers expressed their suspicion of both but simultaneously kept the option of access to state resources open. However, the farmers were primarily concerned with the rejection of their mayor, who had allegedly obstructed the celebration of their initiation. The Diamoral farmers also exhibited their distrust of the politicians invited by Baboucar Badji to his *meeting politique*. For sure, nearly all of the invited politicians were Jola but the Diamoral members did not assume their ethnicity to be any guarantee for sound political behaviour. Ethnic identity was patently irrelevant in that respect. The unity of Diamoral was based on the rejection of Mayor Baboucar Badji. Their cohesion was grounded in the collective celebration of their initiation.

The SP internal elections were finally held in all the administrative units of the Ziguinchor region in July 1995. In Thionck Essyl, *tendance B* won the elections and Baboucar Badji was defeated. In virtually all the other localities, *tendance A* (Robert Sagna) defeated *tendance B*. So Robert Sagna won the SP internal elections in all the villages of the region, with the exception of Thionck Essyl, the village where he had entered the sacred forest. This can be concluded from the election results I collected. The figures show that *tendance A* won the SP internal elections in the Bignona department, the administrative unit where Thionck Essyl is located. The results of the election (see Table 4.2)[14] also reveal that *tendance A* scored proportionally poorly in Thionck Essyl and lost the battle.

In the regional council elections in 1996, *tendance A* (Robert Sagna) won with an overwhelming majority. Sagna did not accept the chair of the regional council, which was considered incompatible with his other responsibilities, and passed on the office to a political ally. At the regional level his initiation had clearly contributed to electoral victory.

CONCLUSION

The ethnic discourse had turned the initiation into a resource for mediation. Robert Sagna had to enter the sacred grove and used the ritual to preserve his status of trustworthiness. Jola politicians, in need of voters, have to meet the demands set by their ethnic rank and file. Allegiance to 'tradition' was imposed on an elite that has not been dependent on popular support for its access to the state, but is increasingly forced to reckon with popular demands (cf. Osaghae 1991: 43). This might be considered a true *revanche de la société* (Bayart 1983a, 1983b). However, this allegiance to 'tradition' was a result of the pressure by the international donor community on the Senegalese government to render the political process transparent. The accountability the donor community demands of politicians indeed contributes to the expansion of the political space for local citizens. Surprisingly, the local discourse emphasises initiation as a requirement for proper political representation. One of the paradoxes of globalisation is that the IMF and the World Bank make Senegalese politicians accountable to their voters, and that the voters express their political preferences in unexpected local idioms (cf. Geschiere and Gugler 1998: 313). The case of Thionck's political process corroborates the hypothesis that globalisation contributes to the reinforcement of local specificity.

However, ethnicity was not the only strategy mobilised by the Jola population of Thionck Essyl. The villagers shifted their strategy over time. The initiation of the Minister of Agriculture certainly pleased Thionck's population, but this did not prevent the same population from nominating an uninitiated candidate. Whether he had been initiated or not was apparently not a criterion. What was more important was the villagers' wish to oust the incumbent mayor. Although entrenched in local antagonisms, the villagers kept an eye on the resources they might be able to acquire through the electoral process. When Diamoral had to select a candidate for the office of mayor it selected a qualified man with good relations in Dakar. Thus the villagers situationally changed their standards for qualified political representation. Elusive politicians now have to face an equally capricious electorate.

In various ways the initiation ritual was accommodated to the needs of politicians. This is quite striking, considering the general assumption that it was very difficult, if not impossible, for the Senegalese state to penetrate Jola society. Indeed, this assumption has been forwarded as one of the explanations for the making of a Jola separatist movement (Darbon 1988). Lower Casamance represents a clear anomaly in Senegalese state–society relations. In other Senegalese regions the Mouride brotherhood was instrumental in creating links between the administrative centre in Dakar and local society (Cruise O'Brien, 1971; Copans 1988; Coulon 1981; Villalón 1995). The state penetrated local societies by means of alliances with Muslim leaders. National politicians present themselves at important Mouride rituals to publicise their allegiance to the Mouride brotherhood (Coulon 1999). A striking resemblance now becomes apparent, because a similar tendency can now be observed in the Jola initiation ritual. This local practice is an occasion for politicians to manifest their allegiance to Jola 'tradition'. Although participation in the ritual is no guarantee of political success, the ritual does offer politicians a way of penetrating local society.[15] 'Tradition' increasingly becomes a resource in the way the state, or politicians, manage society (De Jong 2005). So the performance of the initiation ritual contributes to the integration of local society in the Senegalese political system. Providing villagers with leverage over politicians, the ritual offers an interface between local society and the state. Thus this secretive ritual plays a pivotal role in the politics of representation.

PART III

TRAJECTORIES

MANDINKO INITIATION: THE MAKING
OF AN URBAN LOCALITY

While the modernist reading of ritual and religion assumed that traditional rituals would vanish in the process of modernisation, the evidence shows that ritual and religion are in no way in decline. This invites us to critically review the assumptions of modernisation theory. One of these assumptions is that urbanisation equals modernisation and that urbanites no longer identify with the traditions associated with their ethnic identity. As Max Gluckman famously said, 'an African townsman is a townsman, an African miner is a miner'. The extent to which ethnicity continues to prevail in urban areas has been one of the research interests of the Manchester School, of which Gluckman was a prominent and outspoken proponent. But the persistence of ethnicity in African cities has been noted and explained in a variety of ways. In a classic essay, Mitchell (1956) suggested that ethnicity persists in urban areas as a system of classification. New dances are invented in order to perform this classification. Ethnicity here appears as an answer to the city's overwhelming complexity and, in fact, as part of cosmopolitan modernity. Along similar lines, Cohen (1969) suggested that ethnicity was reinvented in independent Nigeria in order to ascertain a particular ethnic group's monopoly in trade. In both cases ritual and performance served the purpose of defining boundaries between ethnic groups that are constructed in the city. A more recent study has argued that cosmopolitanism and localism on the Copperbelt are in fact urban styles, which one chooses to learn and perform (Ferguson 1999). 'Tradition', in a sense, becomes a matter of choice.

This chapter looks at the performance of a ritual in the city of Ziguinchor (see Map 2). It examines the urban trajectory of a rite of passage that was modelled after a rural initiation and transposed to the city. Most inhabitants of Ziguinchor – the largest city of the Casamance region – reckon this initiation ceremony is part of their cultural repertoire. Members of various ethnic groups have practised this initiation ever since its introduction in Ziguinchor and continue to perform the ritual to this day. The ritual has always been associated with a particular ethnic group, but members of various ethnic groups have participated in it. In contrast to the studies on the Copperbelt that suggested that 'tradition' is necessarily part of ethnic politics, the case presented here suggests that traditions persist for other reasons too. So questions arise regarding the salience of 'tradition' in the city. Why was a rural ritual introduced in the city? Why has this Mandinko rite of passage become the standard of urban initiation? And why is this ceremony performed up to this very day? In answer to these questions, this chapter will demonstrate that the ritual provided the population of Ziguinchor with a technique for the production of locality through its association with occult forces beyond the reach of the colonial government. The ritual initially enabled its participants to domesticate a colonial town, comparable to how performances on the Copperbelt enable migrants to make sense of the city.

The ritual under discussion did not reinforce ethnic boundaries. In fact, ethnicity seemed highly irrelevant in the organisation of the ceremony. Religious denomination, however, was critical in determining the participation in the ritual. I will therefore examine why few Catholics participated in the rite and why participation became almost compulsory for Muslims. We therefore need to assess why a particular ritual, the performance of which predated the arrival of the world religions, increasingly delineated a boundary between Catholics and Muslims. Part of the answer to the question why this ritual has persisted in the city is that it succeeded in accommodating Muslim precepts. Mediating and naturalising a sense of Muslim identity, the performance of this particular ritual enabled colonial subjects to domesticate a colonial city. In spite of the vibrancy of the ritual, the performance of initiation in the bush was increasingly incompatible with modern conditions of life and it declined in the 1960s. Surprisingly, it was subsequently revived in the 1980s as part of a distinctly national culture. This invites us to examine the ritual's potential to generate socialities and a sense of community in colonial and postcolonial contexts. This chapter suggests that practices of secrecy may thrive under colonial domination or the postcolonial construction of nationality, precisely because they provide the means for the production of locality 'from below'.

THE COLONIAL CITY

The ritual analysed in this chapter is performed in the entire Casamance region, but my account focuses on its history and contemporary performance in Ziguinchor. Before examining the initiation ritual, I present a short history of the city, focusing on the social dynamics that helped generate a sense of community among the inhabitants of this expanding city. In fact, the history of this city is still to be written and the present paragraph is but an initial attempt. Ziguinchor was probably a Bainunk township when Portuguese traders settled at this spot on the Casamance River in 1645. The trading post flourished for some time, but due to the decline of Portuguese trade, it was an insignificant port on the bank of the Casamance River when it was transferred to the French in 1886. However, the production of cash

crops and their marketing in Ziguinchor rapidly expanded after the 'pacification' of the Casamance region by the French colonial army. The dormant
comptoir became a flourishing trade town where several French trade houses
set up shop. Throughout the colonial period, the town was administered by
French expatriates. When Senegal was granted independence in 1960, the
French bureaucrats were replaced by Senegalese citizens. The Senegalese
who were appointed to positions in the city's bureaucracy were not of Casamance extraction, but came from other parts of Senegal. Wolof officials
replaced the Frenchmen (Bruneau 1979: 133; Trincaz 1984: 166). The
population perceived the Senegalese administration as a continuation of
colonial rule by *nordistes* ('northerners'). The expression of local discontent
with the Senegalese government in the early 1980s led to the introduction
of a new political line. The Senegalese government gradually replaced the
Wolof administrators with local clerks, a process stimulated by the nomination of Robert Sagna as Ziguinchor's mayor in 1984.

Throughout Ziguinchor's history, its population consistently grew and
its composition continuously changed. Let us briefly examine the historical
transformations in the population's composition, for this factor helped
shape the participation in the rite of passage under examination. In the
nineteenth century, Ziguinchor's population never exceeded three hundred.
Most of the inhabitants were Creoles, also designated as *gourmettes*. These
Creoles were descendants of mixed marriages between Portuguese traders
and indigenous women. Some of them were descendants of migrants from
other Portuguese trading posts south of Ziguinchor (São Domingo, Bissau).
They had Portuguese patronyms, professed Catholicism, at least nominally,
and spoke Creole. They probably were quite a homogeneous community.
When the French took over the town's administration in 1886, the *gourmettes*
were expelled from the city's centre, which was to become the 'European'
quarter. The *gourmettes* then founded the first 'African' quarter, Santhiaba.
They lost their prominent position in Ziguinchor's trade and administration,
since the French trade houses mainly relied on employees from other parts
of Senegal. Wolof and Tukulor from the four Senegalese *communes* settled in
Ziguinchor and worked for the expatriate elite. Throughout the first decades
of the twentieth century, the growing economic activities also attracted
migrant labourers out of the region. The first wave of migrants came from
Middle Casamance and included large numbers of Mandinko (Bruneau
1979: 131; Trincaz 1984). The Mandinko had always been active proselytisers of Islam in rural Casamance and their religious leaders founded
Koranic schools in the city. Owing to the arrival of these Muslims, the
religious composition of Ziguinchor's population, which had been predominantly Catholic in the nineteenth century, shifted to a Muslim majority
(Trincaz 1981: 47–8). This religious shift was accompanied by a linguistic
change: Mandinko competed with Creole as Ziguinchor's lingua franca. In

addition to the arrival of the Mandinko, there was an influx of significant numbers of Manjaku, Mancagne, Bainunk, Balanta, Fulani and Jola. The urban population rapidly expanded after 1945 and tripled within fifteen years (Bruneau 1979), a trend observed in many post-Second World War colonial cities. By the 1960s, the influx of migrants mainly consisted of Jola from lower Casamance and refugees from across the national borders. The bloody liberation war in neighbouring Portuguese Guinea (1960–75) drove many refugees across the border, and many of them settled in Ziguinchor. In the same period Fulani refugees arrived, fleeing Sékou Touré's oppressive regime in independent Guinea-Conakry. Changing migration patterns further contributed to urban population growth: seasonal labour migrants settled permanently in town. Today, Ziguinchor has approximately 200,000 inhabitants, the majority of whom have been born and bred in the city.

Some *ziguinchorois* claim their city is Senegal's most cosmopolitan town. Although Ziguinchor has a very provincial outlook – it is not uncommon to see farmers walk through the centre of town, carrying shovels – it is true that the composition of Ziguinchor's population is diverse in terms of ethnic extraction. The three largest ethnic groups in Ziguinchor are the Jola, the Mandinko and the Fulani.[1] The Wolof, the Manjaku and the Mancagne are numerically less important. All the other ethnic groups represent less than 5 per cent of the town's population. But mere numbers do not adequately reflect the lived reality of ethnic relations in Ziguinchor. Each ethnic group distinguishes itself through its specific cultural, economic and political position in the town's social structure. Although it would not be justified to suggest that social life in Ziguinchor is regimented by ethnicity, I will provide some examples of how ethnicity determines the social and spatial structuration of Ziguinchor.

Although the Bainunk do not figure in the national census, they are important in the city's ethnoscape as the original owners of the land. Ziguinchor was founded on Bainunk territory and the contemporary Bainunk vividly remember that the urban land once belonged to their ancestors.[2] Although these forebears 'lent' or sold most of their plots to urban migrants, the Bainunk continue to consider themselves the town's landlords. Nowadays, Jola claim that Ziguinchor is in fact situated in their territory. This claim is historically unjustified but results from their feeling that all of lower Casamance is their original territory. It goes without saying that these claims are part of the discourse on autochthony which has contributed to the making of the Jola rebellion and was subsequently exacerbated by the insurgency. However, all the Jola in Ziguinchor are immigrants, as is corroborated by the fact that most of them live in *quartiers spontanés* built after 1960 and constructed without administrative planning or consent. While many of the Jola live on the outskirts of town and practise urban farming (Linares 1996), the merchant elite lives in the centre of town.

Escale is the quarter where most formal trade is conducted, dominated by Lebanese traders. The local shrimp and groundnut processing industries are also located in this quarter that continues to be seen as the quarter of Whites, although few Europeans actually live in Escale. The popular quarter of Boucotte is the site of the city's largest market in cloth, food and utensils. The trade there is dominated by the Wolof. In short, the economic activities tend to be concentrated in specific quarters and each economic activity is dominated by one ethnic group, although none of the activities is totally monopolised by any of them. There is one exception: the small retail shops in all the residential quarters are invariably owned by Fulani from Guinea-Conakry. Their ethnically based cohesion enables them to keep prices artificially high in times of crisis. Consequently, their reputation for 'exploiting' the local population has given members of the MFDC an excuse to rob them. They have been the principal targets of the MFDC rebels in need of cash. The Wolof and other *nordistes* have also been subject to attacks by the MFDC. Many anxious Wolof decided to return to Central Senegal and their numbers among the population of Ziguinchor have dropped over the last decades. Thus the various ethnic groups occupy different niches in the economic and political landscape of Ziguinchor, resulting in an ethnic hierarchy. However, ethnic ranking does not fully determine individuals' social positions and some ethnic groups are internally highly stratified.

Other important variables that shape the social interaction in Ziguinchor are place of origin, school and workplace. The last two variables determine the interaction in formal spheres whereas place of origin is important in informal interaction such as leisure activities and life-cycle rituals. A common village of origin is very important for communal socialising, such as the organisation of parties at one of the city's nightclubs. Quite a few marriages are contracted among people from the same village. However, the place of actual residence is another important variable in shaping social interaction and most day-to-day interaction occurs in the quarter of residence. There are no quarters in Ziguinchor that are ethnically homogeneous although some quarters are known for the predominance of one particular ethnic group. The place of residence determines daily social interaction in residential associations and in more traditional associations such as *kanyalen*, a multi-ethnic women's association that treats barren women.[3] The quarter serves as the basis for recruitment in the quarter-based Association Culturelle et Sportive (ASC).[4] These associations form soccer teams that play against the teams of other quarters in a city-wide competition (a sub-competition within the nationwide competition, called *les navétanes*). To finance the team participation funds are raised by organising dance nights at fashionable night clubs. In addition to these leisure activities, associations also organise kindergartens and extra courses during the school holidays. The associations are a binding force among the residents of a quarter, especially among youth. More important in terms of interaction in day-to-day life, though, are the gatherings of young men and women around the brewing and drinking of tea. The composition of these gatherings change, but every young man is usually part of such a group of friends that discusses all manner of things around the tea pot. These 'gangs' carry names such as Pentagon, Black Pride and Berlin City, reflecting their deliberate assertion of global membership. Young women tend to stay at home instead, but their preoccupation with dress and make-up usually reflects a careful assessment and appreciation of the latest fashions in Paris.

In addition to the ethnic composition and residential pattern of Ziguinchor's population, its religious differentiation should be examined as religious affiliation is important for self-identification. The Creoles who constituted the bulk of Ziguinchor's population up to the time of French rule were all Catholics, at least nominally. But most of Ziguinchor's twentieth-century migrants were Muslims. Today, Muslims account for approximately 70 per cent of Ziguinchor's population, 24 per cent are Catholics and 6 per cent are of 'other religions', presumably local traditional beliefs (République du Sénégal 1992: 26).[5] Although quantitative data on the correlation between ethnic identity and religious beliefs are not available, it seems safe to state that the Catholic faith is predominantly professed by Ziguinchor's Creoles, Bainunk, Jola and Manjaku. Adherence to the Catholic faith is virtually non-existent among the Wolof, Mandinko, Balanta and Fulani. In many respects, religious beliefs are more clearly reflected in people's lifestyle than their ethnic identity. How people dress, what they eat and how they furnish their homes all testify to their religious identity. Religious denomination is therefore a more important outward sign of differentiation than ethnic identity. However, the Muslim community is itself divided into several sections. Most Muslims in Ziguinchor nominally adhere to the Tijaniyya and Qadiriyya brotherhoods. Mouridism, the Muslim brotherhood that has strong associations with 'colonisation' by *nordistes*, is not actively embraced by the *ziguinchorois* whose origins are in the Casamance region. The proselytising activities by Mouride disciples are rejected by many Muslims and Catholics alike.

Ziguinchor is known for its religious tolerance, as is exemplified by a graveyard where Catholics and Muslims are both buried. Indeed, religious cohabitation does not cause any major cleavages and often cuts across ethnic affiliation. In a few exceptional cases, however, the congregations of the mosques are ethnically homogeneous and it may be argued that ethnic and religious identity are sometimes mobilised simultaneously. In one case, ethnic oppositions have come to the fore in the management of a mosque. A mosque was built in the neighbourhood Soucoupapaye in the 1970s, but due to all manner of embezzlements, it was not completed until 2000. It was named Mosquée de la paix, as its religious services were meant to contribute to the peace process. However, its long-awaited inauguration never occurred as Jola and Mandinko disputed the nomination for the office of imam. The Jola insisted on having an imam originating in their community, but the Mandinko refused to accept a Jola imam. The conflict revolved around an office that generates considerable income for its officiant and was fought along ethnic lines. Apart from these material considerations, another issue was at play in the conflict: could Mandinko Muslims tolerate being led by a Jola imam? The attempt by the Jola to have a Jola imam was part of an ongoing struggle to emancipate themselves from Mandinko hegemony in Muslim matters. The conflict around the nomination of an imam took an ironic twist when one of the (Catholic) leaders of the separatist movement MFDC offered to negotiate in the conflict surrounding the Mosquée de la paix. Clearly, the politicisation of the nomination of an imam for the mosque goes well beyond the ethnic antagonism between Jola and Mandinko. In other cases, too, ethnicity seems to be 'politicised' for political reasons. With the nomination of Robert Sagna as mayor of Ziguinchor, a Jola was finally officiating as head of the city's administration. Jola were subsequently appointed to positions in the local administration, a policy which was initially experienced as redress for injustice. But when the regional council was won by the PDS in 2000, this regional body also came to be dominated by Jola civil servants. There is a shared sense that all political institutions are now dominated by the Jola. Clearly, competition for jobs and resources feeds ethnic tensions.

Ziguinchor has developed from a Portuguese trade post to a regional capital. While its harbour had introduced the city to international trade networks, the creation of the Transgambian highway in 1972 led to an increasing dependence on Dakar (Trincaz 1984). This direct connection to the capital also furthered Ziguinchor's integration in the Senegalese nation. The town's political elite has concomitantly shifted from being Creole-dominated to being predominantly Jola. While Ziguinchor is predominantly inhabited by ethnic groups originating in the Casamance region, the city is nonetheless a Senegalese city. The prevalence of Mouridism in Ziguinchor attests to the city's integration within Senegalese society. The presence of Wolof traders and pedlars is another token of this contested integration. The process of integration also resulted in the predominance of the Wolof language over local languages. Since independence, Wolof has replaced Creole and Mandinko as the city's lingua franca. But the plurilingual population of Ziguinchor has maintained its command of other languages. The dominant language therefore differs from one quarter to the next and from one family to the next.[6] Ethnic and linguistic antagonisms were and still are countered by the acceptance of a single lingua franca in each residential area. But a certain unification can be observed among Ziguinchor's youth, for whom Wolof helps to downplay their ethnic differences (Juillard 1994).

Moreover, a command of Wolof is a sign of modernity and urbanity. More than anything, Ziguinchor's youth identifies as urban and modern. Yet at certain moments in the year, especially during the school holidays, many young men suddenly show an interest in what they call 'tradition', the subject of the remainder of this chapter.

RELIGIOUS RIVALRY

In my research on the history of the male initiation ritual, I encountered two persistent problems. The first was how to determine the semantic connotations of the terms used to denote the ritual. All the inhabitants of Ziguinchor considered the initiation ritual a 'Mandinko circumcision'. Circumcision was indeed part of this initiation, but circumcision was also referred to by a number of terms such as *sunno*, *sunyaa*, *kuyango* or *kuyandingo*. This chapter is an effort to give more precise meanings to these terms, i.e. to unravel their semantic connotations that remained largely implicit to my interlocutors. This will show that the terms used by Ziguinchor's inhabitants actually do have diverse referents, but the historical contingency of initiation practices in Ziguinchor makes it hard for the practitioners to distinguish them. The second problem I encountered in my research on the history of the urban initiation ritual was the scarcity of sources. I interviewed a number of older men who had themselves been initiated in Ziguinchor or had officiated at these initiations later in their lives. There is no need to dwell on the various problems entailed in doing oral history and I will just mention that many of the accounts I collected were contradictory. Moreover, my interlocutors were often convinced that nothing had really changed in the history of initiation. In response to my inquiries about the history of the ritual, they frequently answered that 'it was exactly like today'. As I demonstrate, this certainly was not the case, but the contemporary inhabitants of Ziguinchor like to believe nothing has changed. On the other hand, other men suggested that the contemporary practice of initiation is in no way comparable to the initiation they themselves had gone through. They thus performed the masculinity produced in the initiation ceremony, evaluating their own initations as much more demanding than the contemporary practices. In addition to these contradictory oral sources, one detailed description of an initiation ritual is available. The fascinating article was written by Father Doutremépuich, a French missionary, and published in a 1939 issue of *Les Missions Catholiques* (Doutremépuich 1939). Father Doutremépuich was not a disinterested observer. His account reflects his partisan point of view but is still a valuable source of information. Much of the information in his article was not relevant to his effort to create a favourable public image for his activities, and probably gives a truthful account of his experiences. The information in this article by and large corroborates the information from oral sources, but my historical account of the initiation ritual nevertheless remains conjectural. However, most of the following account is based on observations I made myself during extended periods of fieldwork in 1990, 1994, 1995 and 2005.

The new immigrants of Ziguinchor performed their initiation in the face of fierce moral rejection by the Catholic Church and the colonial administration alike. Here I examine the attitudes of the Catholic Church and the colonial administration towards the initiation ceremony, relying predominantly on the fascinating account by Father Doutremépuich of an initiation ceremony he himself attended. A Catholic community had been present in Ziguinchor ever since its foundation by the Portuguese, but had been largely left to administer itself. After the French had taken over Ziguinchor, Catholic missionaries once again asserted their presence in the region and the principal city. The Casamance region offered the only opportunity for successful missionary work: the rest of the Senegalese colony was inhabited by Muslims who showed little interest in conversion to Christianity. The Fulani and the Mandinko of Casamance were practising Muslims too, so the missionaries concentrated their efforts on the Jola population in Lower Casamance (Foucher 2003a). While the colonial administration took an anti-clerical stance, the attitude of the administration towards the Muslim leaders was more positive. As elsewhere in Senegal, the colonial administration in Casamance relied on Muslim intermediaries in order to acquire legitimacy and it provided all manner of goods and services to Muslim leaders to obtain their support. In many Jola villages the administration appointed Mandinko Muslims as *chefs de village*. Yet, as Foucher (2003b) argues, their reliance on Muslim collaboration in Casamance was not as productive for the establishment of colonial rule as elsewhere in the Senegalese colony. But in spite of the anti-clerical attitude of the colonial administration, the missionaries established themselves in a number of Jola villages, as well as in Ziguinchor, where they founded the first public primary school in 1920 (Trincaz 1981: 36). In the 1950s and 1960s the Church established more than forty-five primary schools in the villages of Lower Casamance and another four in the town of Ziguinchor itself (Foucher 2003b: 18). The colonial administration heavily relied on the Catholic Church for its provision of education and other communal services. Although the Catholic Church refrained from legitimising the colonial administration and its 'civilising mission' (Trincaz 1981: 39–45), it shared with the colonial administrators an uncompromising rejection of local religious beliefs and practices as 'pagan idolatry'. It need not surprise us that Church and administration both rejected the initiation ceremony, although they did so for different reasons. The Catholic missionaries considered the initiation a 'pagan' practice in which idolatrous ideas were inculcated in the initiates. They considered initiation a pagan rite inspired by Satan and they punished participation in the rite by depriving the participants of taking communion

(Baum 1990: 387). The administration, for their part, rejected the initiation for its waste of economic resources – time and money – and the inculcation of gerontocratic values considered as potentially irreconcilable with colonial rule (Trincaz 1981: 94–5).

In 1939 the Holy Ghost Father Doutremépuich wrote an article about his visits to an initiation camp in the bush outside Ziguinchor. Published in the monthly journal *Les Missions Catholiques*, the article was part of the publicity the Holy Ghost Fathers gave to their activities in order to raise support for their missionary work among the French public. The article is a chronological account of the Father's visits to the initiation camp and his care for the Christian initiates, one of which he tried to 'rescue' from this 'devilry'. The article provides insight into the day-to-day proceedings in the initiation camp, the mindset of the Father and the interactions between him and the 'guardians' of the camp. Interestingly, in spite of his outright rejection of the immorality of the initiation practice, the Father also displayed a keen interest in it. His almost daily visits were not only meant to demonstrate his unfailing loyalty to the Christian initiates, but also to keep an eye on what was going on. As a dedicated student he even made notes of his observations. This did not go unnoticed, and the 'guardians' of the camp accused the priest of making notes. This, they assured him, was not allowed because they did not want anyone to know what was going on in the camp: 'We don't want you to go and tell what you have seen here!' (Doutremépuich 1939: 487). The guardians had to accept the Father's presence in the initiation camp but still strove towards preserving the secrecy surrounding initiation. In his article the Father did not address whether he should comply with their imposition of secrecy – it was presumably not a legitimate question. The Father pursued his ethnographic explorations for the benefit of informing the Catholic readership of the immorality of the initiation practice. The production of knowledge about the initiation practice eventually was to contribute to its eradication, but in order to eradicate the practice it first needed to be mapped.

When Father Doutremépuich noticed that most of the participants in the initiation were Muslims, he was concerned that the Christian initiates were forced to pray to Allah. However, the guardians reassured him that the initiates did not pray, which indicates that neither Islam nor Christianity was professed in the initiation camp. But the Father was not so easily satisfied. He did not accept that the Christians mingled with the Muslim initiates and he required that they had their meals apart from the others. But however much he insisted, the guardians simply ignored him. He represents the guardians, in particular their leader ('un vieux de 50 à 60 ans'), as inimical to his mission to rescue the Christian initiates. The old man, characterised by the Father as a persistent beggar, was firmly in charge of the entire initiation and allowed the guardians to chastise the initiates.

Father Doutremépuich thus relayed the initiation as a 'drilling exercise' ('école de dressage') and he emphasised the arbitrariness of the floggings and punishments meted out to the initiates, portraying his own interventions as benevolent. In his article the Father portrayed his interventions in a confident manner as morally upright, inspired by God, and dedicated to the propagation of Catholicism. In passing the Muslim guardians were portrayed as ignorant of Christian theology and too indolent to be bothered anyway. He portrayed the Christian initiates as victims of Muslim domination, exerted with indifference.

It is clear that the Father understood how a gerontocratic model was inculcated in the initiates through a variety of drilling exercises. He understood that the disciplinary regime in the initiation camp produced a subjectivity that socialised the initiates into an age set as part of an encompassing gerontocracy. He presented his interventions as legitimate attempts to undermine that very technique for the production of locality. The text portrayed the Muslim guardians as ignorant yet willing to receive his teachings on Christianity – as a result of his interventions. However, the old man in charge of the initiation was portrayed as beyond redemption. But the main message of the text was that the initiates could still be redeemed, if rescued from this diabolical milieu. At various moments the Father noticed among the initiates an interest in his presence, a willingness to confide and almost the beginnings of a mutiny (when one initiate made a face to the elder).

It need not surprise us that the elder and the guardians resisted the many visits by the Father. The priest tried to 'rescue' five Christian novices from the 'diabolical practices' (*diablerie*) they were allegedly exposed to in the bush. When he found out where the novices were secluded, he went there and encountered the guardians who told him, 'Whites need permission to enter the camp'. Father Doutremépuich persisted in his attempt to talk to the Christian novices and there were several disputes between him and the guardians. At one point the Father insisted that the Christians had their meal together, apart from the Muslims. One of the guardians then told him, 'Downtown you are in command, but here we are.' On another occasion, the priest invoked his sacred authority in order to have his way: 'God has sent me. He has ordered me to look after my sons. No man can prevent me from doing so.' The guardians did not acknowledge his authority and flatly stated, 'This is the bush!' Exhausted, the priest then threatened to call in the authorities. But the guardians acknowledged neither sacred nor secular authority and told the priest, 'Go and complain to the authorities in Dakar or in Paris!'

The conflict between Father Doutremépuich and the guardians of the initiation camp was fought with various means. Not only did the Father ally himself for the occasion to the *Commandant*, he also had recourse to spiritual support of God and the various charms the Catholic Church provided

Figure 5.1 Kankurang in the rice fields on the outskirts of Ziguinchor
(Photo: local photographer)

him with. So he took his crucifix into the initiation camp and made the sign of the cross on the initiates' foreheads, he sprinkled them with holy water and invoked exorcist formulas to drive the Devil away. The Devil nevertheless appeared to him. At one of his visits to the initiation camp, Father Doutremépuich met the Kankurang which he described as follows (see Figure 5.1):

> A masked figure, completely hidden in an ochre-coloured fibre costume, makes several gestures. His hands are completely covered, as well as his legs and feet. His face is hidden by a tuft of fibres that hang down from the top of his head. He holds in every hand a machete, a sort of cutlass, which makes his appearance even more terrifying, especially for the children. He jumps, advances and retreats, and strikes the ground with his cutlasses, either in front of him or in between the children. He extols a short and raw cry: 'Ee!' to which the children reply with a prolonged 'yo!' (Doutremépuich 1939: 490)

The Father had no trouble identifying the mask as 'the Devil, or at least a son of the Devil'. In this respect, there was a mutual agreement between the Father and the guardians who referred to the mask as a demon ('seytané'). The Father gave a long description of Kankurang's performance and how the mask demanded complete submission of the novices. He observed that 'Kankurang terrifies [the novices]. They are not allowed to watch him, remain crouched down and bow their heads' (Doutremépuich 1939: 490). The Father noticed that the children certainly held Kankurang to be a demon.

The Kankurang tried to provoke the priest and on several occasions attempted to make the priest flee. Acknowledging his fear of the mask, the priest nevertheless held his ground and even tried to expose the masquerade as a forgery. He proclaimed in public not to believe in this 'devilry', suggesting that the mask was in fact a man in disguise. These attempts to expose the secret were countered with denials by the guardians. The priest's attempts at exposure could have resulted in a serious conflict, and priest and mask indeed nearly came to blows.[7] In order to scare the guardians, the priest invoked his alliance with the *Commandant*. And when the guardians were not intimidated, the priest did indeed report the initiation ceremony to the administration. One of the Christian novices – a *métis* – was 'rescued' from the bush when it appeared that the mestizo's father was a French soldier. The administration removed the boy from the initiation camp. An occasional alliance between the colonial administration and the missionary led to an intrusion into the initiation camp. One can imagine how satisfied the priest was about his accomplishments. Indeed, it was reason enough for him to report this as a 'victory' over heathen practices. With a sense of drama, the priest reports how he removed the amulets from the boy's body and replaced them with a medallion of Jesus Christ. The boy was thus 'rescued' and his initiation completed through his reintegration within society as a Christian. The priest subsequently made him 'confess' his experiences in the initiation camp (acknowledging that this violated the obligation of secrecy the boy was under, presumably under threat of death in case of violation). He then took him to the church where he led the boy before the statue of the Virgin Mary. The priest reports that he subsequently took him to the *Commandant* and asked for the boy to be placed in an orphanage to prevent him from growing up in a Muslim milieu. The priest's article clearly invokes the metaphor of redemption offered to a young mestizo boy. Removed from the bush, the boy was taken to the Church and placed under French care. In alliance with the French administration, the Catholic Church prevailed over Kankurang, initiation and Islam. While the case was presented as exemplary, the other thirty-eight novices nonetheless remained in the initiation camp until their coming out two weeks later.

MANDINKO INITIATION

The migrants who settled in Ziguinchor introduced their circumcision and initiation practices into the city and regularly organised these rites (*kuyango*, plural *kuyangol*) in the bush outside Ziguinchor at intervals of five years. The initiation ritual was organised during the dry season and lasted from February to April. Circumcision was performed on the very first day of the ritual by a blacksmith, and in the months after the circumcision the novices (*niansingo*, plural *niansingol*) remained in the initiation camp. A lodge had been constructed in an open space in the bush where the novices slept while spending the day under some nearby trees. The ritual was organised by male elders, but the day-to-day supervision was delegated to the guardians (*kintango*, plural *kintangol*), who gave the novices a hard time. They made it impossible for them to sleep and forced them to observe utmost obedience. The novices were taught esoteric lore and instructed in a secret sign language (*passindiro*). If the novices made a mistake they were severely punished and they were regularly given a flogging. During the retreat the novices were not allowed to wash but the end of their retreat was marked by a ritual bath in the river, after which the novices were taken home (see Figure 5.2). A festive dance (*diambadong*) marked their re-entry into society. By means of their initiation, boys acquired the moral status of adult men.

Like many other ethnic groups in West Africa, the Mandinko ascribe special powers to the status group of blacksmiths. For example, among the Bamana in Mali blacksmiths are held to be experts in the handling of occult powers. It is one of their tasks to circumcise boys, a task deemed very dangerous not only to the circumcised but to the circumciser himself.[8] In Ziguinchor, too, circumcision was performed by a blacksmith, who also provided the protection that the circumcised boys needed, since they were held to be especially vulnerable to attacks by witches. The blacksmith

Figure 5.2 Initiates after their bath in the river, Ziguinchor (Photo: Roel Arendshorst)

was the appointed person to protect them because members of this status group were believed to have a 'wide head' (*kungfanunte*).[9] This 'wide head' comprised the spiritual capacity to recognise and combat witches.

The protection of the circumcised was not only ensured by the black-smith, but also by the Kankurang mask, which played various roles during the seclusion of the novices in the bush. First, the Kankurang's most important role was to protect the novices against the evil forces of witches. The costume of the mask was made of the bark of a special tree (*Fara*; Piliostigma thongii) that was thought to have special powers in itself (Weil 1995: 9–12). In addition, the masker who was to perform the Kankurang was selected from the age group of previously initiated 'guardians' and presumably possessed a 'wide head' (cf. Weil 1971: 282–3; Weil 1995: 29–35). Thus the mask was considered capable of fighting witches. Although the novices knew the Kankurang was supposed to protect them, they were not yet initiated into his secret. They ignored the fact that the Kankurang was a man in disguise and feared his appearance. While offering mystical protection to the novices, the mask ensured their submission. Second, the mask also articulated his power vis-à-vis the guardians who accompanied him in his wanderings around the initiation camp. During the performance, every now and then the mask ordered the guardians to lie down on the ground and the mask then danced on their backs. These young men were already initiated into his secret but they nevertheless acted subserviently and acknowledged the mask's authority. Third, the mask articulated his authority by demanding appropriate behaviour from women. If women accidentally encountered the Kankurang, they were not allowed to watch him and had to flee and hide. If a woman approached the initiation camp, she risked being beaten by the guardians of the mask. Male elders were the only people who were not disturbed by the mask. They used the masquerade to subjugate youngsters and women. In short, the inculcation of appropriate roles for the participants in the initiation ritual was reinforced by the masked figure.

The masquerade was also instrumental in mapping the categories produced in the initiation in space. The initiation was organised in the bush where women were denied access. The novices themselves were not allowed to leave their camp. Their ritual seclusion expressed their liminality and their formal separation from society. The guardians who were responsible for provisioning the novices often crossed the boundaries between the bush and the city. Unlike women and novices, they had the liberty to cross the boundary between the sacred space of the camp in the bush and the realm of the city. In the bush the male elders had access to another even more secret place where the mask was dressed. So the spatial organisation of male initiation produced categories based on gender and age, which were subsequently sacralised by the performance of the masked figure.

The performance of the initiation and the Kankurang mask expressed a rural cosmology that had been transposed to the city. I collected various oral traditions on Mandinko circumcision and initiation that reflect on the origin of the initiation ritual and the creation of the Kankurang. Collected in the 1990s, these oral traditions express a cosmology appropriate to the late twentieth century. However, as will be borne out by my analysis, they also seem to reflect cosmological categories that underpinned a much older worldview. One of these oral traditions holds that seven male elders decided to circumcise their sons. They took their sons to a bush where circumcision was performed by a blacksmith, Sinacho Kante.[10] We are told that the blacksmith, in order to perform the circumcision, used the power that men have (*kaya*). Once circumcision was accomplished, the elders and the circumcised boys remained in the bush. The boys were taught secret knowledge and were instructed in different forms of courtesy to be observed vis-à-vis the elders. However, during their seclusion in the bush the novices were susceptible to the attacks of witches. To protect the circumcised boys the seven elders produced all sorts of charms.[11] The Kankurang is presented as one of the techniques to protect the novices:

> Everyone wondered: 'Who will protect us while we stay in the bush?' Soukana Keita said, 'I will create something to protect you. It is called Kaywulo (another term for Kankurang).' 'How will you do this?' the

other men asked him. Like the others had done before him, Keita used his *kaya*. He went deep into the bush and shouted as never heard before. Then Kaywulo stepped out of an anthill and walked towards them. Everybody was scared, even the elders. But Tenen-buray Diambang stood up and said, 'Somebody should act, otherwise Kaywulo will hurt us.' He shouted, *'Cior mama, issabaree!'* (Mercy our Father, forgive us). Kaywulo approached the men gathered in a circle and roared once more. The men shouted in fear, *'Jeeboloo'* (Do not kill us). Kaywulo left and the six elders followed him. Every time he shouted, they replied, *'Cior Mama.'* In a remote place in the bush Kaywulo undressed and joined the elders.

The oral tradition also mentions that a curious woman tried to find out what was going on in the bush. She was beaten by Kaywulo and subsequently went blind.[12] After the seclusion in the bush, the elders and circumcised boys returned to the village. Kaywulo accompanied them into the village, chasing and beating all the bystanders.

This oral tradition was related to me by a Mandinko blacksmith who had been in charge of several initiation ceremonies in Ziguinchor. He claimed this story was part of the secret lore transmitted to the novices. What follows is an attempt to give an interpretation of this esoteric lore. The testimony claims that the elders created the circumcision cum initiation ritual as well as the means to protect the novices during their seclusion in the bush. They did so by using their power (*kaya*). *Kaya*, I was told, means 'manhood' and encompasses the male virtues of physical and mystical power, intelligence, virility, courage and endurance. *Kaya* is acquired throughout life. The story furthermore relates that one elder activated his *kaya* and transformed himself into Kaywulo (Kankurang). Once this transformation had come about, the Kankurang wielded powers superior to those of the elders. The elders associated themselves with this mysterious being by means of incantations that expressed their respect. The story thus conveys that the mask, if properly handled, provides the power to protect the novices against unknown danger. But the transformation required for the articulation of this power only comes about in the bush. The Kankurang is thus associated with the bush where the initiation is performed. Indeed, bush, initiation and Kankurang can be denoted with the same word, *Kaywulo*. The word is a compound of *kay* (male) and *wulo* (bush): 'the male bush'. Kaywulo refers to the construction of masculinity through initiation into the secrets associated with the bush. These secrets need to be protected from women who are supposedly trying to invade the bush of men, as demonstrated by the inquisitive woman who turned blind when she tried to pierce the male domain (through the use of their occult powers). The production of masculinity is thus symbolically threatened by occult, female incursions into the domain of men. However, the association with the bush empowers the men over the women and enables the men to rule over the women and non-initiates in town. So an entire cosmology is conveyed that expresses a structural opposition of bush versus town, whereby the association of men with the bush allows them to rule over women in town. This cosmology underpins the Mandinko male initiation.

Although little evidence is available, I suggest that Mandinko initiation has always expressed the cosmology outlined above. In his seventeenth-century travel account, Richard Jobson observed that circumcision ('The Cutting of Prickes') was practised in a community-wide ritual among the Mandinko on the bank of the Gambia River (Jobson 1968: 105 ff.). The young men were brought to a place in the bush and circumcised with a knife.[13] In the days afterwards, drums were played in a lodge in the bush where the circumcised boys were secluded and guarded by young men who had previously been circumcised. The elders denied Jobson and his fellows access to this lodge. The circumcised boys were also protected by 'a Devil'. The description of the seventeenth-century ritual practice is similar to the practice described for the early twentieth century. This same model structured twentieth-century conceptions of space in a Mandinko village in middle Casamance where Schaffer and Cooper found that the bush is associated with men, whereas women are linked with the village and the rice fields (Schaffer and Cooper 1980: 45). There is probably a strong historical continuity in the cosmology that underpins the spatial arrangement of initiation. Kankurang, male initiation and the sacred bush derive their meaning from a cosmology that structurally opposes town to bush. I assume this cosmology also underpinned the initiations of Ziguinchor which, until the 1970s, were performed in the bush.

COLONIAL LOCALITY

The inhabitants of Ziguinchor who performed this initiation considered the ritual a 'Mandinko' ceremony. This confirms my hypothesis that rural Mandinko male initiation provided the model for the urban male initiation.[14] Yet my informants assured me that Mandinko were certainly not the only ones to participate in this initiation. This is confirmed by Father Doutrémepuich who observed that Mandinko, Wolof and Jola were spoken at the initiation camp (1939: 475, 477, 486). The participation of members of various ethnic groups in this particular ritual can be explained by taking into account that the Mandinko had been active proselytisers of Islam in Casamance. In the 1840s, several revolutionary jihads had swept through the Mandinko kingdoms of the Senegambia (Leary 1971; Quinn 1972). Jihad leaders combined participation in the slave trade with the propagation of Islam and forcefully imposed their religion on those conquered. Substantial numbers of Balanta and Bainunk were converted to Islam by the Mandinko but the Jola resisted conversion by the sword. However, soon after the colonial pacification, Jola started migrating towards the Gambia to work on the Mandinko groundnut estates. Many of the young migrants converted to Islam during their stay among the Mandinko and returned as Muslims. As we have seen in Chapter 3, conversion to Islam was often coterminous with the assimilation of Mandinko practices (Linares 1992; Pélissier 1966). Muslims who recognised Mandinko spiritual authority participated in Mandinko-style initiations and they considered these rituals appropriate to their new religious faith. Hence, the Mandinko initiation became the standard rite of passage for urban male youth.

Clearly, the process of Islamic conversion has facilitated the acceptance of 'Mandinko' initiation among Muslims. As a consequence of this, Mandinko initiation produced a congregation encompassing not just Mandinko, but members of various ethnic groups. Remarkably, however, this congregation was so inclusive as to encompass Catholics as well. As we have seen, in the initiation ritual observed by Doutremépuich five Catholic boys participated. The rest of the thirty-nine novices were probably all Muslims, so the Catholics were a minority. Apparently, boys of various religious denominations were allowed to participate in a communal ritual that was open to all the immigrants arriving in Ziguinchor. Although Doutremépuich tried to prevent Catholics from participating, adherence to Catholicism was no reason for exclusion. My informants confirmed that Muslims and Catholics both participated in communal initiation rituals in Ziguinchor. The initiation provided for its participants a congregation to belong to, overlapping with but distinct from the Catholic and Muslim congregations. However, the Catholic Church has been successful in preventing congregation members from participating in the ritual. The Church has encouraged its members to practise circumcision at the hospital and today few Catholics participate in the Mandinko initiation.

It is remarkable that Mandinko male initiation was introduced in the city of Ziguinchor and regularly performed in the bush outside the town, because the cosmology that underpins male initiation justified male domination over women through association with 'the bush'. It could be argued that to the extent that male initiation reflected a rural cosmology, the performance had become virtual (cf. Van Binsbergen 1999). Why, then, was male initiation performed in the city? The performance of the ritual apparently provided the inhabitants of Ziguinchor with the symbolic means to structure the colonial city by means of an idiom that most shared. The categories produced through male initiation had been part of the cosmologies of the rural world the migrants originated in, and their reproduction in the Mandinko initiation had the reassuring effect of rendering the new urban environment their own. The ritual performance established an urban, ritual congregation that included all the 'mandinkised' ethnic groups. Inclusion or exclusion was based on no other criterion than initiation itself. Of course, the exclusion of women did not imply that they were not part of the ritual congregation. The very fact of the women's exclusion was an integral part of the initiation, since the principle of inclusion into the bond of initiated men depended upon women playing the role of non-initiates (see also Chapter 3). The same applied to the ways in which the urbanites interacted with the Kankurang masquerade. The congregation included everyone who played the game of secrecy and acknowledged the mask as their joint secret (that is, not the priest who threatened to expose the secret). Hence the cosmopolitan city was domesticated through the performance of a secretive ritual that reproduced gender categories. The migrants produced locality through a performance of secrecy whereby the reproduction of gender roles was at the basis of their appropriation of the urban space.

The initiation also enabled colonial subjects to 'colonise' the city in a metaphorical sense. Ziguinchor was a colonial city ruled by Frenchmen who were as a matter of course excluded from the sacred forest and classified as non-initiates. This is clearly demonstrated by Father Doutremépuich's experiences. The priest tried to 'rescue' five Christian novices from the 'diabolical practices' (*diablerie*) they were allegedly exposed to in the bush, but in the end succeeded in removing only one mestizo boy. The priest was denied any authority in the forest and it was only due to the military commander that the boy was removed from the initiation camp. The administration's intervention in the initiation practice must have been considered a grave violation by the performers of the initiation. Such interventions by the state occur even today (see Chapter 6). The colonial and postcolonial state do not encourage the production of a subjectivity that possibly goes counter to or even undermines the authority of the state. An alliance between the Catholic Church and the colonial administration was forged to reclaim the boy for French citizenship and Catholicism. The performers of the initiation were forced to recognise the colonial administration. The initiation nonetheless provided colonial subjects with a domain where they could exert authority, at least occasionally. By transposing the rural model of initiation to the city, the performers transposed their cosmological model which entitled male initiates to rule over the domesticated and feminised domain of the city. The performance of initiation symbolically transformed French rulers into non-initiates and colonial subjects into initiates, symbolically entitled to rule over the non-initiates in town (even though this symbolic reversal of colonial domination had very limited practical consequences). *Tubabokunda*, the town of Whites, was domesticated through initiation.

ISLAM AND INITIATION

Throughout the colonial period, initiations were regularly organised in Ziguinchor but from the 1970s onwards, male initiation was no longer performed in the bush. School schedules and the organisation of the urban economy made participation in the bush initiation for young men increasingly complicated. Since the initiations were held during the school year, pupils could only participate if they did not attend school. The production of 'traditional' manhood and 'modern' subjectivity were incompatible. Also, apprentices in workshops risked losing their job if they left their employer to join the initiation in the bush. It was increasingly difficult for the young men of Ziguinchor to participate in the initiation that lasted two months in the bush. Young men needed to invest their time elsewhere if they were to succeed in the urban economy. Moreover, initiation was increasingly seen as 'backward'. A modernist discourse rejected initiation as incompatible with contemporary standards of modernity. So fathers increasingly had their sons circumcised at a hospital. The act of circumcision was no longer performed by a blacksmith but by a medical doctor or qualified male nurse instead. Initiation into secret lore was no longer considered compulsory and many Muslims considered circumcision (*sunno*) the essential rite of passage for boys. Thus the practices of circumcision and initiation were disarticulated and the initiation of young men in the bush was given up. The demands of urban life, in combination with the increased prominence of a Muslim discourse on circumcision and initiation, led to the abandonment of initiation in the bush.

So we need to examine why the articulation of the old cosmology through the performance of initiation in the bush was no longer required. As a matter of course it can be argued that the cosmology that underpinned male initiation no longer accommodated the worldview of second- and third-generation migrants who had grown up in the city. Moreover, political independence had transformed the subjects into citizens, who legitimately exerted political authority in town through the secret ballot. The politics of representation replaced the politics of embodiment. Yet I think that another reason can be forwarded for the decline of male initiation in the bush: the progressive hegemony of a Muslim cosmology. This can be derived from evidence provided by oral traditions. In the oral tradition discussed above, no mention was made of Islam, but the relationship between circumcision and Islam is explicitly reflected upon in another oral tradition that a Bambara living in Ziguinchor told me. Like the other oral tradition, it explains the origin of the Kankurang but in this oral tradition Kankurang had allegedly been created by the Devil:

> When the time had come to circumcise his sons, the Prophet did not want to celebrate this.[15] He preferred circumcision as a sober event. He did not announce the event and circumcised his sons in austerity. In contrast to the Prophet, the Devil (*iblissa*)[16] wanted his sons' circumcision to become a spectacular celebration and he invited many guests and drummers. On the day of circumcision they left the village and

went to the bush. The Devil left the drummers behind and together with his friends and sons entered the bush. There, the Devil transformed himself into the Kankurang. Accompanied by his friends, the Kankurang left the bush and terrified the drummers. They had never seen such a thing before. The Kankurang beat them up and made them tremble with fear. Many people got injured. The Kankurang performed many miracles. Nobody has ever since equalled him. This is why the Kankurang is considered a Devil, even today. When the circumcised boys had recovered, they left the bush and for days and nights at a stretch people danced the dance of leaves (*diambadong*).

Many of the themes addressed here resemble the themes raised in the oral tradition discussed above. The association between bush, initiation and the Kankurang is maintained but the oral tradition also clearly departs from the other version in that it presents an alternative to the festive initiation. Austerity and celebration are presented as opposite alternatives, associated with a structural opposition with the Prophet and the Devil. The Prophet allegedly advocated circumcision in austerity. Celebration, in contrast, is presented as a 'pagan' aspect of the ritual. Clearly, this oral tradition is part of a local Muslim discourse and provides an interpretation of the ritual complex in Islamic terms. The emphasis on values presented as typically Muslim such as austerity probably helped bring about the major ritual transformations of the 1970s. Boys were increasingly circumcised at home and initiation in the bush was abandoned as a pagan practice. This need not surprise us, since 'the bush' had become a domain that, in the local Muslim cosmology, is defined as inimical to Islam. Note what Weil observes with regard to the meaning of the bush: 'In their syncretic Islamic religion, anything associated with the bush, with the sphere outside the Muslim community, is not Islamic, cannot be Islamic, and is thus evil' (Weil 1988: 160). The Kankurang is therefore considered an incarnation of the Devil. Hence, as Weil suggests, the bush and the Devil 'are increasingly understood as standing against the Muslim community and its members' close relationship with Allah' (ibid.). The transformation of the cosmological meaning of the bush was reflected in the abandonment of initiation in the bush.

The impact of conversion to Islam on Mandinko initiation has thus been twofold and contradictory, or at least productive in two different ways. Historically, conversion to Islam by non-Mandinko was usually understood to be equivalent to a 'conversion to Mandinko'. This process of mandinkisation led to the adoption of Mandinko initiation by part of Ziguinchor's urban population. On the one hand, conversion to Islam contributed to the diffusion of Mandinko initiation. On the other hand, however, the Muslim discourse appropriated circumcision as an Islamic precept while condemning initiation and the Kankurang as 'pagan' practices. This confirms that the Muslim discourse has never been mono-lithic. The perceived incompatibility between a particular Muslim and a particular Mandinko cosmology – which were at other times seen as iden-tical – provoked the abandonment of initiation in the bush. Islamisation has thus contributed to the diffusion of Mandinko initiation as part of mand-inkisation, as well as to the abandonment of initiation as a pagan practice. This demonstrates that Muslim beliefs were adapted to local practices, and that such adaptation was historically contingent (cf. Bravmann 1974). Of course, other factors have contributed to the abandonment of the bush initiation, like school schedules and other constraints imposed by state and market. These practical incompatibilities were reinforced by a modernist rejection of initiation as 'backward'. But the Muslim discourse has certainly been important in labelling initiation in the bush immoral. What emerged was a Muslim modernity, embodied in practices such as circumcision. Muslims increasingly circumcised their sons at home and communal, city-wide initiation ceremonies were no longer organised.

INITIATION AT HOME

While initiation in the bush (*kuyango*) had been abandoned, a new ritual emerged in the 1980s. This ritual was called *kuyandingo* ('minor initi-ation'), and circumcision was an essential element of it. However, the term *kuyandingo* does not so much refer to circumcision as to the practice of initiation (*kuyango*), which it is a concise version of. The word *kuyandingo* is a compound of *kuyango* (circumcision) and *dingo* (small). *Kuyandingo* is in fact a minor initiation adapted to modern urban conditions. While *kuyango* was a community-wide initiation performed in the bush, *kuyandingo* is organised at the nuclear lineage level and performed in town. From the 1980s onwards, many such 'minor initiations' were performed in all the quarters dominated by the Mandinko and 'mandinkised' ethnic groups (Boucotte, Peyrissac, Cité Balante, Soucoupapaye, Lyndiane and several other *quartiers spontanés*), usually during the school holidays. My observa-tions of many of these ritual performances in Ziguinchor serve as the basis for the following description.

As I noted above, circumcision is an essential element of the 'minor initiation' and is performed on the very first day of the ritual. Sometimes the novices are taken to a hospital or a male nurse comes to the compound where the novices are gathered. The operation itself is usually done without much ceremony. The boys are anaesthetised with modern narcotics. One by one, the boys are circumcised and immediately afterwards they are given a white hooded robe. They may also be given a stick, which is thought to keep witches at bay. The novices are subsequently taken to a room in their father's compound that serves as their 'camp' for the weeks to come. Women are not allowed to visit this room: contact between women and novices is said to be harmful to female fertility. During their seclusion at the 'camp' which lasts three or four weeks, the novices are supposed to refrain from quarreling and be cooperative. This is to socialise them into a formal age set ruled by solidarity. Any behaviour that is not in accordance with this explicit aim of initiation is likely to be sanctioned by corporal punishment, although everybody agrees that the disciplinary regime in *kuyandingo* is far less harsh than in the *kuyango* ritual it replaces. Yet secret lore is still transmitted in the minor initiation. In the weeks of seclusion, the novices are instructed by their guardians, young men previously initiated through either *kuyango* or *kuyandingo*. The secret lore consists of songs the novices have to learn by heart.[17] All the songs are in the Mandinko language. In addition to these songs, the novices are taught the rules to be observed vis-à-vis older persons, notably male elders. After three or four weeks, the novices have recovered from the operation and their period of seclusion is concluded with a ritual bath (*niansing kuwo*) in the Casamance River. Early in the morning the novices are taken to the river shore. Since many minor initiations are held simultaneously in different compounds of Ziguinchor, several of the rituals end on the same day and during each of the weekends in September up to ten groups of novices and guardians arrive at the river shore. At sunrise, the novices are taken into the river and each of them is washed by a guardian (see Figure 5.2). Each group that has come to wash the novices has usually managed to get the materials required for the fabrication of a Kankurang, which is dressed on the spot. The river shore is crowded with these masked figures, each shouting and slapping their machetes. With the drummers playing the rhythm of *diambadong*, the groups of novices go home one by one in festive processions. When they enter the town, the drumming attracts girls and women who start to participate in the procession, dancing the special steps of the *diambadong* rhythm. Women have to be careful though not to ignore the Kankurangs, since the masked figures circulate around the procession and threaten to beat the women. Every now and then the girls and women have to flee the masquerade and hide in nearby compounds. But the performance is not meant to send them away and women actually enjoy the play. Motorists, however, can be particularly annoyed by the masked figure since it may stop cars at will and the *diambadong* generally results in traffic jams. The *diambadong* is a ritual of inversion, since the participants dress in the apparel of the opposite sex (see Figure 5.3). The guardians often wear skirts or long dresses and wigs and make-up. Women, on the other hand, wear trousers and hats. The performance celebrates the liminality characteristic of this stage of rites of passage.

When the novices come home, their mothers walk out to greet them and dance towards them as they try to stem the flood of tears. The mothers are proud of their sons, who have almost accomplished their rite of passage. A special porridge is now served as a reward for the guardians who

Figure 5.3 Kankurang and one of his guardians dressed up like a woman, Ziguinchor (Photo: Ferdinand de Jong)

succeeded in taking their 'younger brothers' through this arduous ritual. After the meal, the novices and guardians are allowed to rest, while the guests continue the festivities. The father of the compound invites his kin, friends and the fathers of the other novices. Likewise, the novices' mothers invite their sisters and friends. They spend the late morning cooking a rich meal, and in the afternoon, the passage of the novices to their new status is formally concluded. While the men are seated in easy chairs and engage in more or less lively conversations, the women gather in the courtyard where the drummers play various rhythms. One particular rhythm is considered appropriate for this special occasion: *kindongo*. The new initiates, wearing a new colourful caftan, are then taken out of their 'camp' and led one by one into the circle of women. They then dance the *kin*, which they have supposedly learned during their seclusion.[18] However, since there usually has not been any training in dancing the initiates are just shown around the circle and ordered to sit down on a cloth in front of the drummers. Some of the initiates are given 500 CFA franc notes (approx. 50 US cents) attached with safety pins. Women dance up to them and throw coins over their heads. This dance marks the end of their seclusion and their re-entry into society (*niansing bondo*).

Since many practices in the *kuyandingo* ritual are now subject to monetisation, the less well-to-do inhabitants of Ziguinchor are not able to organise this kind of ritual. The *kuyandingo* is in many respects a commodified performance. Circumcision was formerly performed by a blacksmith who did the operation as a moral obligation of his status group.[19] Since the task is now often performed by male nurses, financial remuneration has come to play a role. Circumcision at a hospital costs 3,500 CFA (approximately US$7). A male nurse can also be hired to perform the circumcision in his spare time for only 1,500 francs. In addition to the medical costs of circumcision, initiation requires expenditure on the young men who actually perform the day-to-day tasks. If a father wants his sons to be instructed by guardians, he has to provide the guardians with meals. Other parts of the ritual, such as the Kankurang performance, are now also partially commodified. The father is also entirely responsible for the expenses on the 'coming out' day. Many guests have to be fed and meat is served. Moreover, the initiates are dressed in new garments that may cost up to 7,500 CFA each (US$15). Finally, the drummers have to be paid a sum of 6,000 CFA. The total costs of initiation through *kuyandingo* amount to at least 10,000 CFA for each novice (US$20). In 1995 this sum of money amounted to a quarter of the monthly pension of a low-ranking civil servant or twenty days' wages for an unskilled labourer. Today, many fathers can hardly afford to pay these costs. Yet every Muslim is obliged to have his sons circumcised. Moreover, the boys themselves often express a wish to be circumcised since social control exerted by their peers results in considerable pressure. Uncircumcised boys are considered inferior by their circumcised peers and this distinction is expressed in no uncertain terms (cf. Schaffer and Cooper 1980: 95). The term *solema*, uncircumcised person, is used as a term of abuse. Circumcision, however, can be performed in various ways. Some fathers are content with organising their sons' circumcision in austerity. Their circumcision does not resemble a traditional initiation, but is acknowledged as a fulfilment of the Muslim obligation.

This takes us back to the Muslim understanding of initiation as a pagan practice. The Muslims of Ziguinchor apparently do not unanimously condemn the initiation. How do they justify the performance of *kuyandingo*, a circumcision far more elaborate than is required by strict Muslim standards? The accommodation of these practices is, I suggest, made possible through a reclassification of the initiation. By contemporary Muslim standards, uncircumcised boys are considered impure (*seenya*, Mandinko) and circumcision is seen as a purifying act. This bodily transformation is considered an Islamic obligation, since circumcision was performed on the Prophet and the example should be followed. Thus, in the Mandinko tongue, circumcision is termed *sunno* after the Arabic *sunna*. Initiation, however, is classified as 'tradition' (*ado* after the Arabic *adat*). A Muslim inhabitant of Ziguinchor voiced his understanding of circumcision and initiation as follows: 'Circumcision is recommended by *Allah*. Initiation is our tradition.' Although not recommended, initiation is tolerated and usually seen as compatible with the Muslim faith. Most Muslims in Ziguinchor tolerate traditions as long as they remain compatible with Muslim obligations. Initiation has thus been incorporated into the local Islamic discourse as a 'tradition', as has the Kankurang masquerade. Although some Muslims prefer to define the Kankurang as a Devil opposed to Allah's powers, the mask is now always understood in Muslim categories. The Kankurang mask is no longer perceived as the transformation of an elder but as a *jino* (after the Arabic *jinn*) subordinate to Allah. Indeed, the category of *jinn* encompasses many spiritual forces that were incorporated into Islam during its long period of expansion. As Bravmann has demonstrated, the incorporation of traditional elements into an Islamic idiom is quite common in West Africa (Bravmann 1974: 32). In sum, the masculinity created through the 'minor initiation' is now fully compatible with Muslim standards.

Of course, the incorporation of *kuyandingo* into a Muslim cosmology required that the older cosmology that had underpinned the initiation was transformed. In this respect, it is significant that the minor initiation is now performed at home, in the city. In keeping with Muslim notions on the evil nature of the bush, the bush has been abandoned as the site of initiation. However, by performing the initiation at home the cosmological connection between male power and the bush is lost. This pertains especially to the Kankurang, the mask that embodies the powers of the bush.

The Kankurang is still performed at the occasion of the minor initiation, but the masks are increasingly made with materials that do not originate in the bush. Performers use rice sacks that are sewn into costumes and dyed with industrial paint. In addition to ochre-coloured masks clad in bark, artificially coloured masks have emerged in fancy colours such as purple. The rice-sack clad Kankurangs are called *Sisal*, a name that refers to the material used for their costumes. Power is now no longer obtained in the bush, but at the market.[20] The ways in which the Kankurangs are named, dressed and performed suggests that their occult function – the fighting of witches – is no longer considered as important as before (see Chapter 6).

In short, the performances of the minor initiation and the Kankurang masquerade have been incorporated into a Muslim worldview. Yet the transformations in the initiation ritual also testify to a reverse process: that the practice of initiation has accommodated Islam. The continuities and transformations in the ritual practice prove that *kuyandingo* is a syncretistic ritual that has incorporated Muslim obligations. But the minor initiation is not merely syncretistic in a religious sense; the ritual also incorporates other aspects of modernity. For example, a large part of the ritual is fully monetised, including the coming out ceremony. The drummers are hired, the guardians are often paid to initiate their 'younger brothers' and women express their respect for the new initiates by attaching banknotes to their caftans. All these acts illustrate how the initiation has been fully accommodated to the powers of Islam and the market economy, which are metonymically transferred to the initiates at the moment of their coming out through the deployment of Muslim caftans and banknotes. *Kuyandingo* is, in short, a ritual that initiates the novices into global powers and transfers them to the initiates, while simultaneously remaining elusive to their potentially homogenising effect.

AN URBAN HERITAGE

Many inhabitants of Ziguinchor have their sons circumcised through the minor initiation, *kuyandingo*. But the ritual that once expressed Mandinko hegemony has now been appropriated by non-Mandinko performers. This is corroborated by the participation of the Muslim Jola living in Ziguinchor who often have their sons circumcised through *kuyandingo*. The young Jola may be proud of their Muslim status achieved this way, but yet another male initiation awaits them in their father's village of birth (see preceding chapters). Jola boys consider the minor initiation of Ziguinchor inferior to the major initiation in their father's village of birth. The Jola participate in Mandinko *kuyandingo* to become circumcised, but it is at their proper initiation ceremony that they obtain full adulthood. Obviously, the value attributed to the Muslim circumcision is important, yet the participation in the Jola initiation is of overriding importance to the making of Jola masculinity. In that respect, it is clear that initiation in the sacred forests of Jola villages enjoys higher prestige, in terms of endured hardship and acquisition of secret lore, than the minor initiations of Ziguinchor. Initiation 'at home', although compatible with Muslim convictions, pales into insignificance in comparison with initiation into Jola manhood.

Kuyandingo produces Muslim manhood, but successful initiation through *kuyandingo* does *not* signal the acquisition of a Mandinko identity. In a context in which ethnicity has become increasingly important the minor initiation remains irrelevant to the acquisition of a particular ethnic identity. Members of various ethnic groups participate in the minor initiation which, although still referred to as 'Mandinko circumcision', does not produce Mandinko men. And although Balanta, Fulani and Jola living in Ziguinchor have their sons circumcised through this initiation, the performance of the ritual is not uniform. Apart from the standard core, there is considerable ethnic variation in the embellishments. For example, variation occurs in the sort of musicians invited on the closing day of *kuyandingo*. The coming out of the initiates in *kuyandingo* rituals organised by the Balanta or Fulani is celebrated with musical styles specific to these ethnic groups. In the Fulani compounds, musicians may be invited to play typical Fulani rhythms from the Futa Jalon. Balanta households may instead prefer xylophone rhythms claimed by the Balanta to be part of their cultural heritage. The minor initiation is organised by the members of one compound and allows them to choose a musical accompaniment specific to their ethnic group. The strongly 'mandinkised' Fulani and Balanta who live in Ziguinchor perceive *kuyandingo* as an appropriate rite of passage. The ritual reflects their 'mand-inkisation' and simultaneously enables them to express their proper ethnic identity.

It is clear that the performance of the minor initiation is increasingly valued for reasons that cannot be related to the Muslim identity of the performers. The contemporary understanding of the ritual implies a sepa-ration between circumcision as a Muslim prescription and initiation as a 'tradition'. The practices of circumcision and initiation are nonetheless fused in a circumcision cum initiation (*kuyandingo*). Under the influence of a renewed interest in ethnic heritage, the members of various ethnic groups perform what is still called 'Mandinko initiation' but they do so according to their own ethnic sensibilities. All performers of the *kuyandingo* ritual self-consciously assert the 'traditional' nature of *kuyandingo* – in spite of its obvious disjuncture and discontinuity with previous practices. The young men involved as 'guardians' take pride in their task and are encouraged by their mothers to take responsibility for initiating the novices. The youth of Ziguinchor have adopted *kuyandingo* and the performance of Kankurang as their 'traditions'. Their identification derives from a national ideology that posits that every ethnic group, city, region or country is supposed to have its proper cultural heritage. Ziguinchor's youth assumes ownership of *kuyandingo* as a way of claiming a cultural heritage which sets them apart from others in a national political economy of difference. Historically, the Senegalese state used to be a strong proponent of the modernisation discourse, rejecting the performance of what it considered resource-wasteful ceremonies.[21] But since the 1980s the Senegalese government has increasingly recognised the importance of tradition as part of a national heritage. The minor initiation and Kankurang are performed as 'traditions', part of an urban inter-ethnic heritage.

CONCLUSION

In Ziguinchor's early twentieth-century history, a specific form of secrecy made it possible to construct an urban community of migrants from widely divergent ethnic, linguistic and cultural backgrounds. The Mandinko initiation ritual (*kuyango*) provided the migrants in Ziguinchor with an idiom for the production of locality and enabled the performers to domesticate the colonial city. However, the importance of education and labour contracts as well as a modernist rejection of traditional ceremonies and an increased emphasis on Islamic precepts led to the abandonment of initiation in the bush. Circumcision was increasingly performed at home or at a hospital. But a new ritual emerged in the 1980s, the 'minor initiation'. Despite the popular perception of *kuyandingo* as a traditional custom, it is in fact a transformation of previous ritual practices, in a number of ways. First, the city-wide initiation gave way to an initiation organised at the compound level. In the city-wide *kuyango* the number of novices was unlimited, in *kuyandingo* it varies from five to fifteen. Second, place and duration of the initiation changed: instead of secluding the novices in the bush, they are set apart in a room at their father's compound. The two months of seclusion in the bush were brought down to three weeks of seclusion at home. Third, the moment of the ritual enactment shifted from the dry season consistent with the agricultural cycle to the school holiday consistent with the demands of the urban economy.

These transformations pertain to the form of ritual performance. However, the most important change occurred in the ritual's meaning. *Kuyandingo* reinforces the novice's Muslim identity. His circumcision amounts to an Islamic purification to enable him to pray and fast. But if the minor initiation primarily addresses an Islamic obligation, why does the ritual revive the ancient model of initiation into secrets? The ongoing performance of the ritual demonstrates that for Ziguinchor's inhabitants initiation into the Islamic *umma* still requires a measure of secrecy. But the secrecy surrounding initiation also sets the practice apart from Muslim circumcision at the hospital. I suggest that the performers of *kuyandingo* have cast the Muslim circumcision in a customary model of ritual secrecy because that model strongly suggests continuity with the past. The revitalisation of this tradition demonstrates that the urbanites believe that historical practices need to be preserved from the onslaught of modernisation. It represents what they conceive of as their heritage. As a form of ritual secrecy incorporating Muslim conviction, market economy and a national discourse on the value of tradition, *kuyandingo* is now performed as a 'tradition'. While the performance of initiation in the bush produced an urban, anti-colonial locality that asserted difference from the colonial administration, initiation at home expresses a local heritage in a national context.

6

SECRECY, SACRILEGE AND THE STATE

The masquerade is the public face of the secret society. In the past, numerous examples could be given of West African secret societies that operated masks. One of the questions raised in the research on these secret societies is how these secret societies related to public political structures. The intricacies of the debate focused on the extent of the competition between, or interdependence of, these structures. The Poro society, undoubtely the best researched secret society in West Africa, intervenes in many spheres of life, and its intricate political organisation has been amply discussed.[1] In large parts of the precolonial societies where it prevailed, the Poro society existed alongside the secular political chieftaincy, each acting as a balance to the other. The institutions of the Poro and the chieftaincy complemented rather than opposed each other in the management of the chiefdoms (Little 1966: 70). Under colonialism, this complementary relationship was redefined. Most secret societies resisted colonial rule and were consequently suppressed by the colonial administrations. The postcolonial governments, in turn, displayed a variety of responses to the Poro secret society. Depending on the country, the Poro society was either incorporated into the national political structure or declared illegal (Bellman 1984: 13–16). Recent studies suggest, however, that the Poro society provided the cultural model for the organisation of insurgencies against the postcolonial governments of Liberia and Sierra Leone (Ellis 1999; Richards 1996).

Secret societies continue to be important in the postcolony. What does the continuation of secret politics imply for our understanding of the postcolonial trajectory of the African state? The framework provided by Mamdani (1996) may be useful for our understanding of the incorporation of secretive politics in the postcolonial trajectory of the African state. The colonial legacy of Africa's postcolonial states, he says, consists of a bifurcation. Under colonialism, the subjects in the countryside were ruled through 'tradition', whereas citizens in towns were allowed to organise into civil society. This distinction, Mamdani argues, is fundamental for an understanding of the postcolonial trajectory of the African state. This observation is clearly relevant to Senegal, where colonial rule drew a distinction between the inhabitants of the four *communes*, who enjoyed full citizenship rights, and subjects of the hinterland who lived under *indigénat* or 'traditional' justice (Diouf 1999; Johnson 1971). The question is how this legal dualism has evolved in the postcolonial state. How have the institutions defined as 'traditions' by the colonial state been handled by the postcolonial state? Conversely, how have citizens used their 'traditions' in the context of the postcolonial state? Can we indeed apply the notion of bifurcation, as Mamdani proposes? Bayart (1993), in contrast, argues that the African state has been increasingly domesticated and by implication suggests that the new hegemony created by the state incorporates the domain of 'tradition'. In his view secret society politics has entered the domain of national politics through a process of assimilation. Indeed, illustrations of the interpenetration of secret society politics and democratic competition are provided by several authors (Cohen 1981; Ferme 1999; Ellis 1999; MacCormack 1979; see Chapter 3). It has also been demonstrated that the idiom of initiation and secrecy have been important in the making of insurgencies in the war-torn states of Liberia and Sierra Leone (Richards 1996; Ellis 1999).

In this chapter I examine the case of the Kankurang masquerade in Casamance. I demonstrate that legal dualism, if this ever existed in colonial Senegal, becomes increasingly blurred in the postcolonial performances of the Kankurang masquerade. Certainly, as the public face of a secret society, the masquerade continues to challenge the state's quest for hegemony. But the secret society penetrates the domain of public politics and is itself also increasingly penetrated by this domain. The masquerade is still used to contest state authority, but cultural brokers have also tried to make masked performances compatible with state hegemony. The masked performance should be understood as yet another domain subjected to state control, while simultaneously subverting the legitimacy of the state. Using a number of conflicts between the mask and the state, I delineate a historical trajectory.

THE KANKURANG MASQUERADE

The Kankurang masquerade is one of the cultural traditions of the Casamance region. The mask has an odd physical appearance. The Kankurang does not wear a wooden face mask, but a costume of multiple pieces of bark fixed in such a way as to render the identification of the masked individual impossible. The Kankurang carries cutlasses in both hands, adding a terrifying aspect to his mysterious appearance (see Figure 5.1). When the mask is brought out, it is usually accompanied by around ten young men who are fifteen to thirty years old. They carry sticks and threaten to beat the numerous spectators in the audience. These companions are usually more dangerous than the masked figure himself. Their acts are attributed to the mask, but the mask acts with impunity. Thus the companions can display licentious behaviour, which may have far-reaching consequences; the masked performance sometimes results in physical punishments. As Simmons observes: 'During the hours that the masked dancer roams through the village, the rules by which men normally govern themselves are temporarily suspended' (Simmons 1971: 161). Historically, the Kankurang mask was used to impose regulations issued by the secret society of male initiates. The mask was the disciplinary technique of the secret society and the mask was entitled to use violence.

The Kankurang has been studied by various authors, some of which situate the masked performance in a timeless tradition and overlook the contemporary contexts of its performance (Girard 1969; Kesteloot 1994; Schaffer and Cooper 1980). Mark (1985) has examined the history of the masquerade and interprets its diffusion as an indication of precolonial inter-ethnic contact.[2] A thoughtful anthropological analysis of Kankurang is provided by Simmons (1971). Among the Badyaranké of Upper Casamance the Kankurang is performed at circumcision, and whenever there is an emergency, to locate, humiliate, and sometimes to beat witches (Simmons 1971: 161). The Kankurang is directed against the anti-social elements of the village. The political meaning of the Kankurang is more fully addressed by Weil (1971), who considers the masquerade a form of social control at the village level.[3] His analysis of the social structure of the Mandinko village and the role of the Kankurang secret society in the maintenance of that order is very much indebted to the structural-functionalist paradigm. Here, I propose to situate Kankurang performances in historical contexts and demonstrate how historically contingent performances question the place given to 'tradition' by precolonial structures of authority and the post-colonial state.

Most authors hold that Kankurang originated among the Mandinko, or more precisely in Kabu.[4] Mandinko tend to attribute the origin of many of their customs to this former polity. They believe that circumcision, Kankurang and the art of forging originated in Kabu. This testifies to the symbolic meaning of Kabu as the 'origin' of the Mandinko. This claim is, however, never contradicted by members of other ethnic groups which have, to some extent, been subject to 'mandinkisation', a process examined in detail in Chapter 5. The process of mandinkisation also accounts for the contemporary distribution of the Kankurang masquerade from western Senegal throughout the Gambia and Casamance to Guinea-Bissau. The Kankurang is considered a Mandinko tradition in all these regions. Many male Muslims, converted to Islam by the Mandinko, have gone through Mandinko initiation and are initiated into the secret of Mandinko masquerade.

The Kankurang masquerade is the ultimate secret of the Mandinko initiation. The knowledge that the mask is a man in disguise is marked as 'secret'. Every initiate is morally obliged to preserve secrecy with regard to the nature of the mask and is committed to this secret. Confrontations occasionally occur between the community defined by its commitment to the secret of initiation and the agents who defy this secret. These confrontations are a recurrent theme in popular stories about Kankurang performances. Many examples are cited of violent confrontations between the mask and its opponents who presumably violate the rules set by the mask. Although some of the violations are eventually settled by the payment of a fine, other such clashes result in more serious punishments. But whatever the outcome, popular stories always claim a moral victory for the Kankurang.

MASK AND *MANSA*

The secret society of initiated men uses the masquerade to assert itself in the public domain. There is some evidence that the Kankurang performance has always been a mode of political action. To examine its historical roots, I would like to use a description of the masquerade in precolonial Mandinko society, from an eighteenth-century travel account by Francis Moore. Relating his travels along the Gambia River, Moore gave a description of a 'bugbear' which, among the Mandinko, 'is what keeps the women in awe' (Moore 1738: 40). His description of this 'cunning mystery' corresponds to today's Kankurang. Moore elaborated on the mask's role in Mandinko society, and subsequently presented an account entitled 'Tragical story':

> On the 6th of May, at night, I was visited by a *Mumbo Jumbo*, an idol, which is among the *Mundingoes* a kind of a cunning mystery. It is dressed in a long coat made of the bark of trees, with a tuft of fine straw on top of it, and when the person wears it, it is about eight or nine foot high. This is a thing invented by the men to keep their wives in awe, who are so ignorant (or at least are obliged to pretend to be so) as to take it for a wild man; and indeed no one but what knows it, would take it to be a man, by reason of the dismal noise it makes, and which but few of the natives can manage. It never comes abroad but in the night-time, which makes it have the better effect. Whenever the men have any dispute with the women, this *Mumbo Jumbo* is sent for to determine it; which is, I may say, always in favour of the men. Whoever is in the coat, can order the others to do what he pleases, either fight, kill, or make prisoner; but it must be observed, that no one is allowed to come armed into its presence. When the women hear it coming, they run away and hide themselves; but if you are acquainted with the person that has the coat on, he will send for them all to come and sit down, and sing or dance, as he pleases to order them; and if any refuse to come, he will send the people for them, and then whip them. Whenever any one enters into this society, they swear in the most solemn manner never to divulge it to any woman, or any person that is not enter'd into it, which they never allow to boys under sixteen years of age. This thing the people swear by, and the oath is so much observed by them, that they reckon as irrevocable, as the *Grecians* thought *Jove* did of old, when he swore by the River *Styx*.

About the year 1727, the king of *Jagra*, having a very inquisitive woman to his wife, was so weak as to disclose to her the whole secrets of this mystery, and she, being a gossip, revealed it to some other women of her acquaintance, which at last came to the ears of some who were no friends to the king. They consulted upon it, and fearing that if the thing once took vent, they should not be able to govern their wives so well as they otherwise would, they took the coat, put a man into it, went to the king's town, sent for him out, taxed him with it; he not denying it, they sent for his wife, and upon the spot killed them both: so the poor man died for obliging his wife, and the poor woman for her curiosity. (Moore 1738: 116–17)

If this really happened, then the Kankurang has for long been a secret that was not to be disclosed. Violation of the mask's secret was punished by death, a fate even the king could not escape. Similar cases in other African societies demonstrate that masks were often used by secret societies to exert power, sometimes even superior to that of the king.[5] Masks were perceived as supernatural agents that acted with impartiality. These observations were probably also valid with regard to the precolonial Kankurang masquerade. Transformed into a supernatural being, the secret society could even legitimately kill the king. This opposition between the king and the mask was probably profoundly embedded in local cosmology. Although my data are scanty, I submit the following hypothesis. In the circumcision ritual, both mask and blacksmith play important roles as guardians of the circumcised. As seers they have access to the world of the witches they combat. Thus the Kankurang and the blacksmith represent the occult powers society can mobilise against the destructive force of witches. These powers are cosmologically associated with the 'bush', in particular with the male forest. Since they are capable of mobilising such vital powers and transposing these powers towards the town, the mask and the blacksmith are both liminal figures. Blacksmiths are excluded from chieftainship, but they do enjoy a certain licence (Simmons 1971: 82–4; McNaughton 1988: 130). Likewise, the Kankurang always transgresses the laws of the town and imposes his laws of the bush. Both Kankurang and the blacksmith are elevated above the power of rulers. Thus in Mandinko cosmology the Kankurang and the blacksmith represent occult powers from the bush that can be mobilised to oppose the power of the king (*mansa*), who rules in town.

In his study on Bamana blacksmiths in Mali, McNaughton observes that the Komo secret society is also directed by blacksmiths. Not only is the Komo association extremely influential in a spiritual sense, but political leaders have close relations with the association because they depend on spiritual alliances (McNaughton 1988: 130). The Komo secret society apparently wields considerable influence over political leaders. Likewise, the Mandinko blacksmiths of Casamance may have used the Kankurang to direct their political leaders. Historically, the Kankurang has probably been the voice of the blacksmiths in their interaction with the king. The late black-smith Salif Touré, who organised several initiations in Ziguinchor, explicitly referred to this relationship when he stated, 'Kankurang and king should mutually respect each other.' The relationship between the Kankurang and the political leaders is inscribed in a collective memory that allows each of the agents autonomy of action. The king and the mask should 'respect each other' and not interfere in each other's domains. This notion is still part of the contemporary Mandinko conception of state–society relations. Today, the Mandinko perceive the postcolonial state as the contemporary successor to the precolonial kings and refer to the contemporary state with the same word they use for their former kings (*mansa*). They also feel the Kankurang may still be used to oppose the state.

THE MASK IN COURT

Marsassoum is a town in the *département* of Sédhiou and has approximately 7,000 inhabitants (République du Sénégal 1988a: 45; see Map 2). A majority of the population is reported to be Mandinko, but there are other ethnic groups as well, whose cultural practices have long been subject to 'mand-inkisation'. In 1987, a number of foreigners were living in Marsassoum. The devastating liberation war in the Portuguese colony of Guinea-Bissau, leading to independence in 1974, resulted in a huge inflow of refugees in the Casamance region. These refugees settled in the villages and towns of Casamance and some of them lived in Marsassoum, including Solo Thiouda with his family of three wives and seven children. Solo Thiouda belonged to the Manodj, a Balanta subcategory of which most members live in Guinea-Bissau.

The following account of Solo's violation of a Kankurang is based on an article published in the national paper *Le Soleil* and several testimonies I collected in Marsassoum.[6] According to the newspaper, Solo Thiouda was forty-five years old, industriously worked the land and did his utmost to feed his family. He always made contributions to the festivities organised by Marsassoum's community. He was, in short, an exemplary member of his community. This evaluation differs from the oral testimonies that hold that Solo was in fact a lazy good-for-nothing who persistently refused to take part in public work. According to my informants, Solo's behaviour corresponded with the prejudices against his ethnic group. The Manodj are generally thought of as great lovers of palm wine and cattle thieves, with an inclination to settle disputes by using violence. The oral testimonies have it that Solo was a true Manodj and that he himself was responsible for the strong dislike the local population felt towards him. Moreover, Solo dared to challenge the Kankurang.

In April 1987, an initiation was organised in the bush near Marsassoum. A Kankurang was performed on the occasion. Solo encountered this Kankurang when he was walking down the street in Marsassoum. No one knows why, but the two came to blows and Solo, who was a strong man, partially undressed the mask and took one of his sleeves to the local administrator, the *sous-préfet*. On his way home from the *sous-préfecture*, Solo met Diato Djiba and told him about his encounter with the Kankurang. Diato perceived Solo's act as a grave violation and was seriously annoyed. A fight started between the men, which was easily won by Solo despite the fact that 'Diato' means lion, and this name is not given to just anybody. Djiba subsequently ran to the initiation camp in the bush, where he informed the guardians of the matter. A meeting was immediately held in the bush and it was decided that Solo's act called for revenge.

The next morning, the guardians came to Solo's compound. Each of them was armed with a club and the young men were accompanied by two Kankurangs. Solo locked himself in his house with his family. The men set fire to his house and waited for him to come out. Solo and his family could not stand the heat, left their refuge and tried to escape the crowd. But the men held Solo back and beat him up. Solo's uncle was alarmed by the noise and came to rescue him. However, Solo and his uncle were both beaten to death. Solo's corpse was subsequently burned. Some of Solo's children were beaten and one of his wives was robbed. The police intervened and arrested 26 people who were taken to Ziguinchor and incarcerated.

Some of these men were tried in 1996. From an account given at the trial, it can be inferred that Diato Djiba himself was the masker and that Solo Thiouda did not take the mask's sleeve but his machete. That may indeed be a more accurate version than the one in the newspaper. The journalist was probably misled so as not to reveal that Diato Djiba was the masker and quite possibly involved in provoking Solo Thiouda. This means that right from the start, secrecy was used to conceal the facts about the confrontation between Solo and the Kankurang. Secrecy has also limited my own reconstruction of the event. While I was doing fieldwork in Marsassoum, some young men threatened to kill anyone who agreed to talk to me. As the violation of secrecy had led to the execution of Solo Thiouda and his uncle, I had no choice but to leave the village.

The trial eventually took place on 6 March 1996, nine years after the crime, in the court of Ziguinchor. I have no way of knowing why the trial took place after such a long delay. When I talked to the court coroner in 1991, he suggested that the case had been strongly delayed because, in his opinion, it had been 'cursed'. He suggested that the Marsassoum suspects had used occult means to obstruct the progress of the judicial process. Was this the reason for the delay? Or was it a justification for an unacceptable bureaucratic delay? In the Senegalese judicial process, delays of several years are not uncommon. It seems to me though that in this particular case, the court was not so much afraid of the trial because of the occult powers associated with it but because of its political consequences. The culprits had wide support among the Casamance population. Below is an account of the hearings:

> There was overwhelming public attention and the court was packed with interested observers. Of the twenty-six men arrested in 1987, only five were brought to trial. All of them were natives of Marsassoum. They belonged to various ethnic groups and two of them were over sixty years old. All five defendants denied the accusation of murder. In their defence, they said that Kankurang is a sacred being (transcribed in the court minutes as *le Sacré, être surnaturel, personnage sacré, esprit surnaturel*, etc.). Moreover, they argued that the Kankurang is part of Mandinko tradition. The judge invited several dignitaries from the Mandinko community to give their opinion on the events in Marsassoum. Some of them suggested that it was not the individual suspects but the Kankurang itself that had killed the victims. As a supernatural being, they argued, the Kankurang could not be tried. One of the lawyers elaborated on this issue and said, 'Before we pass sentence we need to face the question of responsibility. Who killed? Who set fire to the house? Does anyone know?'[7] This basic uncertainty, he felt, supported his request for the release of the suspects. Another speaker suggested that Solo Thiouda had in fact deserved his death: 'By undressing the Kankurang, Solo Thiouda shook the pillars of Mandinko culture and therefore he deserved to be sanctioned.'[8] Another lawyer placed the case in a much wider context, and compared Solo Thiouda's fate to that of Jesus Christ and Salman Rushdie. Both, he argued, were sentenced to death because they had desecrated the Sacred, thus implying that Solo's fate was the universal consequence of deliberate desecration. The public clearly favoured the release of the suspects on the grounds that they were either innocent or rightful defenders of Mandinko culture. Eventually, two suspects were given suspended sentences of seven years, one suspect was given a suspended sentence of five years, and two were discharged.

At this point I would like to briefly analyse the execution of Solo Thiouda and the subsequent trial. It seems that the immediate cause for Solo's execution was his desecration of the Kankurang. But it is conceivable that the Kankurang provoked Solo up to the point that he felt compelled to react. In this case, the sacrilege was probably provoked by the mask himself and resulted in the execution of a social deviant. Solo's act of sacrilege was the last straw that broke the camel's back. Some informants stated that Solo's behaviour had long since annoyed the inhabitants of Marsassoum. He was lazy, refused to take part in public work and messed around with other men's wives. Complaints about Solo's behaviour had been repeatedly made to the local authorities but requests to deport Solo to Guinea-Bissau were never taken into consideration. Thus the local population ultimately took recourse to their proper form of social control and bypassed the state. When the state remained negligent, the Kankurang performance provided a way to solve the problem. An accumulation of anger came to a climax with the apocalyptic death penalty. The sacrilege of the mask triggered a reaction in keeping with the demands of ritual secrecy, and accompanied by the Kankurang the men executed Solo and his uncle. Yet, even though their impunity was thus assured in the culprits' eyes, the state could not but accept its juridical responsibility.

Who were the people who attacked and executed Solo and his uncle? The question is difficult to answer. One particularly dramatic account of the 1987 event holds that even the women wanted the men to seek revenge for Solo's violation of the local tradition. According to this version, all the men gathered at the sacred forest and discussed the wrong Solo had done to the people of Marsassoum. They decided that Solo's sacrilege had to be avenged. According to this oral account, the decision to execute Solo might well have been made with the consent of all Marsassoum elders. Considering the age of two of the suspects, at least some of the elders were indeed implicated in Solo's execution. Whether they represented the entire community or merely a faction of it is something we have no way of knowing.

This brings to mind Weil's analysis of how the Kankurang serves as an instrument of social control for the benefit of the entire community. Weil (1971) argues that the secret of the mask provides the village elders with a device to control public life. The Kankurang should thus be conceptualised as the sacred and indispensable face of the secret political structure. Weil's analysis is convincing, but the events in Marsassoum suggest a different interpretation of the Kankurang organisation. We do not know whether the elders actually operated as a steering committee and sent the young men into town to inflict the punishment. Were the young men indeed acting in the community's best interests as defined by the lineage elders? It is true that once the perpetrators were held responsible by the state, the Kankurang was defined as a sacred entity. Yet the definition of the Kankurang as a sacred entity was certainly not shared by everyone. The stranger Solo Thiouda perceived the masquerade as an institution he did not have to acknowledge. The masquerade was not an expression of an integrated society, but an instrument that part of the local population used against an immigrant. In this case, the Kankurang masquerade defined the boundaries of a community. The violation of the community's secret resulted in the stranger's death. An analysis of the Kankurang as an instrument of social control should not conceptualise the village as a closed, integrated social unit as a structural-functionalist analysis does.

The execution of the strangers was a violation of the state's monopoly on the use of violence. The perpetrators were arrested and brought to trial. However, in the popular perception the Kankurang can act with impunity. The deeds and misdeeds of his guards are attributed to the mask. During their trial, the defendants made references to this generally recognised discourse on the masquerade. Accused of killing Solo, all the suspects denied doing so. They said Solo was executed by the Kankurang, which they considered a sacred being. Invoking the mask thus absolved them of any responsibility. The lawyers' defence of the suspects was basically ambiguous. They suggested that the evidence of their clients' role in the homicide was weak. One of the lawyers argued that individual implication in the homicide had to be demonstrated for each of the suspects. The suspects should not be tried collectively. However, the same lawyer suggested that the Kankurang had played an important role in the execution. 'We do not know who beat whom. Who is this Kankurang, what is it? Can you tell us, members of the court?'[9] The lawyer thus presented the Kankurang as the principal actor, and he actually seemed to challenge the members of the court to deny this. The lawyer challenged the court to violate the mask's secret and to state openly that the mask was in fact a man in disguise. This, of course, was impossible. The lawyers played this game quite well. As quoted above, one of them asked, 'Who killed? Who set fire to the house? Does anyone know?' While this question was apparently phrased in the court's idiom, asking for the presentation of legally binding evidence, it also implied the possibility that the Kankurang had been responsible for the killings. The mask thus became a suspect in the homicide case. Of course the mask could not be summoned, and this impossibility was deliberately emphasised by the lawyers. The mask's impunity remained uncontested and was almost celebrated at the court. With a huge audience of initiates, no one dared to publicly divulge the secret of the mask. The mask's authority as sacred judge remained uncontested at the court.

The court did acknowledge the mask's secret but somehow had to deal with this sacred figure. In other postcolonial African countries, similar problems exist with regard to the persecution of occult powers. In Cameroon, the state openly acts on witchcraft accusations. The courts of justice rely on the opinion of witchfinders in dealing with these witchcraft accusations and often condemn the witches (Fisiy and Geschiere 1990 and 1996; Geschiere 1997). In contrast to Cameroon the court case here did not involve 'experts' as the Kankurang has no equal and cannot be represented. This resulted in a situation in which the ambiguity of secrecy was maintained at the court. The Public Prosecutor suggested that the Kankurang had been implicated in the execution of the Manodj, but he did not dare to go all the way and state that the Kankurang performance had provided a pretext for the homicide. Nor did he argue that the maskers should be tried.[10] On the other hand, the court did not concede to the defenders of Kankurang that he was a legitimate means of social control. Recognising the Kankurang as a means of social control intrinsic to Mandinko society would be tantamount to recognising the use of violence by an institution outside the control of the state. The court was not prepared to recognise the Kankurang as an autonomous domain of ethnic self-rule. However, the court could not withstand the pressure from the population. The allegiance to the secret of male initiation and the widespread hatred of the Manodj strangers resulted in considerable pressure on the court to release the suspects. The suspects, although found guilty, were given very mild sentences. Nevertheless, no one dared state that the masquerade was an unacceptable form of legal dualism. Although the case amounted to a trial of Mandinko 'tradition', the mask's impunity remained unaddressed. So even though the trial kept up an appearance of a viable state judiciary, the court tacitly acknowledged a 'traditional' practice of social control. The Kankurang remained immune.

SACRILEGE AND THE STATE

As a means of social control, the Kankurang masked performance may challenge the state monopoly on the use of violence. The next example demonstrates a clash between the population of a town and the state's armed forces, triggered by the mask's desecration by police officers. The bond of secrecy was the determining principle of organisation in the conflict that unfolded. The conflict occurred in Sédhiou, a town of approximately 13,000 inhabitants on the Casamance River (République du Sénégal 1988a: 45; see Map 2). The town grew from a trade post founded in 1836 by the French, who made it the administrative centre of their expanding territory. However, at the end of the nineteenth century the regional administration was transferred to Ziguinchor, leaving Sédhiou with only a commercial function. By the mid-twentieth century, the town had also lost much of its commercial significance. During the period of my research, all the roads to Sédhiou were in disrepair. The streets were littered with filth and the municipality was bankrupt. The population's only hope consisted of the projects financed by the European Union. Sédhiou was a gloomy town, and although it has long been a stronghold of the Socialist Party, the national administration clearly lacked legitimacy. The case described below testifies to Sédhiou's problematic integration in the national state. This account of the event is based on articles in the national newspapers complemented by information from oral testimonies provided by witnesses.[11]

During the school holiday of 1988, several initiations were held in Sédhiou. On Sunday, 18 September, a *diambadong* dance was held to celebrate the coming out of the initiates. A Kankurang accompanied the dancing crowd. The mask probably created some disturbance which offended the Assistant Prefect. He made a call to the police station and ordered the Kankurang arrested. Police officers arrested the mask and took it to the police station. There, the officers took the unprecedented step of undressing the mask and interrogating the masker.

The news about the desecration of the mask rapidly spread throughout the town. The following night the males of Sédhiou held a meeting at the local soccer field. They decided that a committee of elders would go and inform the Prefect of the high esteem in which the Mandinko hold their Kankurang. The Prefect would be summoned to release the masker and prevent a recurrence of the violation. The young men decided to demonstrate their indignation by performing a Kankurang in front of the prefecture.

The next morning, the young men went to the prefecture accompanied by a Kankurang. The elders met with the Prefect in his office and the young men waited outside. At that very moment, the Assistant Prefect responsible for the mask's violation passed by in his car. To make his way through the crowd of about four hundred men, he honked his horn loudly. This was interpreted as yet another provocation. The young men pulled the Assistant Prefect out of his car, beat him up and set fire to the car. Police officers who came to rescue him were stoned by the crowd. Things got completely out of hand. The policemen threw hand grenades. (They did not explode because, according to the testimonies, the crowd was protected by charms.) But one young rioter was shot in the arm by a police officer. The crowd then attacked the homes of the police officers and set fire to their furniture. In an effort to restore law and order, an anti-riot squad was brought in from Kaolack by plane. They restored order and arrested forty men, who were transferred to Ziguinchor and incarcerated.

Before discussing the follow-up to these events, I would first like to analyse the desecration and the ensuing riot. As usual, the coming out of the initiates was celebrated with a Kankurang performance. The Kankurang was arrested because the mask disturbed the Assistant Prefect. There is no way of knowing how and why the Assistant Prefect was annoyed by the mask. Public disturbances are, however, quite common during Kankurang performances and any masquerade creates a sufficient pretext for police intervention. But the police do not usually interfere, which is why the undressing of the mask was an unprecedented sacrilege. Moreover, according to the oral testimonies, the police officers asked two girls to identify the masker. The involvement of girls in the identification of the masker was perceived by the population as an outright provocation. As in the Marsassoum case, the violation of the mask was the critical event that triggered the subsequent actions. Informed about the violation, Sédhiou's male population was quickly mobilised and organised a meeting at the soccer field. The meeting was only open to initiated men. Secrecy was to be observed with regard to anything discussed in the meeting. In the demonstration in town as well, all the demonstrators were initiated men armed with amulets and clubs. Thus the practical preparations for the demonstration were entirely embedded in the practice and discourse of initiation. First, the events were triggered by the mask's desecration. Second, the site of the meeting was denoted as 'forest' (*wulo*). Third, the meeting was only accessible to initiated men and secrecy was to be observed with regard to its proceedings. Some of the men present at the meeting did pass on information about its proceedings to the local police and were subsequently branded as 'traitors'. Finally, the demonstrators were all bare-chested. This important detail was mentioned in the newspaper and in the oral accounts. It is quite common for men to appear bare-chested when participating in the processions related to the initiation ritual. By appearing bare-chested in this protest march, the demonstrators expressed their commitment to the secret of initiation (*kuyanto kulo*). The violation of the secret by the local police had to be avenged by the initiated men. In short, the entire event can be interpreted as determined by the principle of initiation. As in the Marsassoum case, the presence of Kankurang during the demonstration licensed the demonstrators to act with impunity.

In oral testimonies collected two years later, my informants repeatedly referred to the ethnic identities of the actors involved. Most of the informants knew exactly how to identify the Prefect, his Assistant and the police officers. But no one found it appropriate to indicate that the Assistant Prefect, a Mandinko, was implicated in the desecration. In contrast, the only police officer who was not initiated into the Mandinko secret, the Wolof Birame N'Diaye, was accused of having tried to discover the mask's secret. My informants identified Birame N'Diaye as the main culprit, although he had merely executed an order given by the Assistant Prefect. A Wolof thus became a scapegoat. The informants explained the event in an idiom related to initiation. They also believed that all the people of Sédhiou had taken part in the riot against the administration, and that all the policemen of local extraction had respected the mask's secret. In line with their regionalist reading of the event, the Wolof violator was identified as a *nordiste*, denoting his origin in central Senegal. The local understanding of the revolt expressed a regionalist opposition to the state, which many in Casamance view as dominated by the Wolof ethnic group. These feelings are quite widespread and are not restricted to supporters of the separatist movement. So it is no wonder the Wolof police officer Birame N'Diaye was singled out as the main culprit and accused of wanting to discover the secret of the mask. While the different actors were identified in terms of their ethnic extraction, the idiom of initiation was chosen so as to delegitimise the interference of the police and to legitimise the actions undertaken by the rioters.

Although the rioters pursued what they perceived as a sacred obligation, the jailed suspects still had to appear in court. They were quickly brought before a judge and the sentences were immediately pronounced. All the suspects were found guilty and given probation. Some of them were given a suspended six-month sentence, and most of them a suspended three-month sentence. The rapidity of the judicial process and the mild sentences are only understandable if the context is taken in consideration. Many of the people of Casamance were indignant about the mask's desecration and many of them had aired their grievances. Some of Ziguinchor's dignitaries had pressured the local police commander and the court magistrates to pronounce a lenient verdict: after all, the suspects had merely met their obligation to protect the Kankurang. According to an officer of the court, the leniency of the sentences was intended to appease the population. Moreover, the prefect, his assistant and police officer N'Diaye were transferred to other towns. In the Sédhiou case, the local population literally avenged itself on a state that desecrated the Kankurang. Again, the Senegalese judiciary gave way to the power of a local mode of political action that appeared to most Casamançais as more legitimate than the state.

The cases discussed above suggest that the mask continues to be used as a check on the presence and policies of the postcolonial state. Unconditional loyalty to the secret of initiation can serve as an organising principle for political action. The Kankurang – as the secret of initiates – operates as a mode of political action in the contemporary context of the postcolonial state (Bayart 1983a, 1983b, 1986). However, we should be careful to situate the secret in a domain inaccessible to the state as administrative policies have been developed to penetrate this domain, not unlike the regulations imposed on masquerading in Sierra Leone (Nunley 1987). The state permits the production of a local subjectivity through initiation, but it does not tolerate the violence that is an intrinsic part of its performance. The state has not accepted violations of the law, although it has had to give in to the pressure from the population. While apparently losing ground to the Kankurang masquerade, the state has introduced a policy to domesticate the performance. After the Marssassoum execution, the prefect of Sédhiou issued a decree (*arrêté préfectoral no 047/D.S. du 30 Avril 1987*) to regulate further Kankurang performances. From April 1987 onwards, an official licence that had to be obtained from the local administration was required to perform a Kankurang. The duration of the performance and the route the mask was to take had to be specified on the application form. In addition, prior to the performance four men had to accept responsibility in case the Kankurang created a nuisance or destroyed private property. However, since this legislation was introduced it has been consistently ignored by the population and no one has ever bothered to apply for an official licence. The arrested Kankurang of Sédhiou, for instance, was an unlicensed masquerade. People in Sédhiou had never applied for a licence, nor were they compelled to do so by the local police. Things suddenly changed, though, after the Sédhiou revolt. People did not start to apply for licences but an awareness of the risks entailed by 'unregulated' Kankurang performances led to increased self-regulation. A committee of elders was appointed to control any further Kankurang performances in their respective residential districts. The population recognised the risks of uncontrolled masquerading and readily accepted this self-imposed regulation. The masked performance was brought under the control of the town's community.

After the revolt in Sédhiou, the Kankurang was increasingly drawn into the domain of political society as the revolt became subject to local political competition in Sédhiou. Socialist Party politicians assisted the insurgents who had to appear in court. The politicians propagated mild sentences and thus supported the men involved in a revolt against the local administration. Moreover, two factions within the Socialist Party accused each other's members of having passed on information about the secret meeting in the bush to Sédhiou police officers.[12] The revolt became subject to political contestation and it seems that some Socialist Party politicians wanted to convey their loyalty to the secret of initiation rather than their affiliation to the state. The politicians thus tried to win an electoral advantage and made the revolt itself subject to a political contest. The politicians apparently felt compelled to express their allegiance to their electorate and overtly recognised the rioters as legitimate performers of a licentious 'tradition'. They even adopted the task of defending the suspects' collective conduct in the legal process. *La politique* entered the domain of this mode of political action. The boundaries between loyalty to the secret of initiation and political representation became blurred. Just like in the Jola initiation of Thionck Essyl, where initiation and political representation became increasingly entangled issues, the Kankurang revolt in Sédhiou became entirely 'politicised'. Nowadays the Kankurang's domain of action is not always as clearly separated from the domain of the state, as they assimilate each other. The occult has entered the domain of modern politics, as it does elsewhere in postcolonial Africa (cf. Geschiere 1997).

TRUE AND FALSE KANKURANGS

In the 1980s, the Kankurang operated as a mode of political action, in correspondence with how its historical script defines its role. In spite of that, the masquerade was increasingly seen as deviating from that role: elders in Ziguinchor felt the Kankurang performance was subject to 'secularisation'. Signs of the secularisation of Kankurang have also been reported by Weil who observed that in some Gambian villages, small uncircumcised boys were allowed to watch the masker put on his costume (Weil 1971: 291). But the fierce reactions to the violations of the mask in Marsassoum and Sédhiou suggest that secularisation was not what was at stake. There, dese- cration still triggered the appropriate reaction from the population if the political context required it. Before addressing the changing evaluation of Kankurang performances, I would first like to present the transformations that are considered signs of the performance's 'secularisation'.

In the past the performance of the mask was considered dangerous and people who were beaten by the mask were thought to experience the mystical consequences afterwards. The masker himself might be hurt if he failed to obey the strict rules of the masked performance. When the mask roamed the streets at night, cooking fires were extinguished, lights were switched off, and women would close the doors and hide themselves inside their homes. However, by the 1980s none of these rules were observed in Ziguinchor. At that time an increasing number of city-dwellers had their sons circumcised and initiated in a 'minor initiation' (*kuyandingo*). Novices in *kuyandingo* did not retreat to the bush but were secluded in a room in their father's compound instead (see Chapter 5). This transformation in the initiation practice was to have serious implications for the Kankurang performance. The Kankurang was now dressed in the novices' rooms and the secrecy formerly observed so carefully was now ignored. Moreover, whereas the initiations in the bush were subject to surveillance by male elders, often ritual specialists, the day-to-day supervision of the 'minor initiation' was often left to teenagers who did not have the authority to make women subservient. Increasingly, boys who before would have been considered too young to stage a mask were now performing the Kankurang (see Figure 6.1). Moreover, young maskers boasted about their Kankurang performances to their girlfriends. The Kankurang performance lost much of its fearsome character and was increasingly appreciated for its playful character. Kankurang performances in Ziguinchor started attracting large crowds of children who were delighted to participate in the play. During its performances, the children came as close to the mask as they dared and as soon as the mask lunged in their direction, they ran away laughing and sought refuge around the nearest corner. The Kankurang was no longer feared in the same way.

Another transformation of the performance was that it came to provide a means to earn pocket money (cf. Weil and Saho 2005). The guardians accompanying the mask have started begging for money or cigarettes, pretending the gifts are for the novices.

In 1994 I heard a Kankurang roam through my neighbourhood, and decided to go and watch his performance. A young man introduced me to the guardians who immediately started begging for money. After a while, the Kankurang himself appeared. I was a little afraid as

Figure 6.1 Boys playing with their Kankurang, Ziguinchor (Courtesy Royal Tropical Institute, Amsterdam)

> it was pitch dark and the mask was carrying two machetes. However, the masker took the bark away from his face and looked at me. Then he held up his other hand with a familiar gesture and demanded a handout.

While this may remind the reader of the confrontation between Father Doutremépuich and the Kankurang in the 1930s (see Chapter 5), the difference is that not only the guardians beg for money – historically part of their role – but that the Kankurang himself has started begging. Many adult men lamented these developments. They also accused the guardians of using the masquerade as a pretext for theft. However, stealing is an act that has long been permissible for the initiation participants. In the seventeenth century, Jobson observed that Mandinko novices were licensed to steal.[13] Licentious behaviour has probably always been part of the initiation ritual and masked performance. Kankurang performances have probably always had a transgressive aspect, and indeed have to have, as they convey the mystical powers associated with the bush. Nevertheless, in the 1980s the people of Ziguinchor considered the behaviour of the mask performers evidence of the masquerade's 'degeneration'.

The transformation of the masked performance also involves innovations in the costume. With the bark of the *Fara* tree increasingly hard to find, the mask performers started using industrially produced material for the costume (see Chapter 5). These masks were considered mystically less dangerous. A new classification of masks emerged to account for this transformation. Today, the people of Ziguinchor draw a distinction between Ziguinchor masks and the ones performed elsewhere. The 'real' Kankurang is supposed to wield powers his urban counterpart does not possess. For instance, the real Kankurang is believed to be able to fly and jump from one roof to another. He is presumed capable of splitting and being in two places at once. He combats witches and remains invulnerable to their powers. But this real Kankurang is only found in the countryside, not in Ziguinchor. In addition to this spatial dichotomy, a temporal contrast is invented to account for today's 'false' masks. Thus most urban dwellers project the 'real' Kankurang either onto the past or onto faraway places in the bush. These spatial and temporal oppositions allow incredulous people to maintain their belief in the mystical powers of the mask. The distinction between true and false Kankurangs reinforces beliefs in the venerated qualities of Kankurang even where many mundane Kankurangs let that belief down. Thus it would be incorrect to assume that the prevalence of 'false' Kankurangs implies secularisation in a linear and irreversible way. It would be equally wrong to assume that the Kankurang performance has evolved from a ritual into a play. According to Kasfir the transformation from serious ritual into playful pastime can be observed in many African masked performances (Kasfir 1988a). However, as Huizinga (1985) states, play and seriousness do not necessarily contradict each other. I presume that playful masquerades can indeed turn into serious business, as can be deduced from the cases discussed above. A 'false' Kankurang may at any time transform into a 'true' one. However, in the 1980s many men felt the masquerade had lost its terrifying power and potential to instil fear in women and novices. They attributed this decline to the fact that everyone had become familiar with the secret of the mask.

RESTORATION OF THE SECRET

The view that contemporary mask performers violate the secrecy required for its efficacy motivated a number of Ziguinchor dignitaries to regulate the Kankurang performances in their town. In 1988, some of the elders in Ziguinchor – usually referred to as the city's dignitaries (*notables*) – made a first effort to regulate the masked performance. They went to see the governor and the chief constable and asked them to cooperate in preventing the further 'secularisation' of the mask by regulating its performance. The dignitaries proposed making it mandatory for mask performers to apply for a licence that was to be distributed by the authorities. The licences would only be given to the people who organised initiations in the bush of Ziguinchor. With the violent conflicts of Marsassoum and Sédhiou still fresh in their minds, the governor and chief constable were pleased with the proposition. In subsequent years, Kankurang performances were indeed rare. However, people generally did not bother to apply for a licence, nor did the administration strictly implement the policy. If Kankurang performances were infrequent after 1988, it was mainly because young men were afraid to go into the forest and strip a *Fara* tree of its bark. The young men feared the MFDC rebels hiding in the bush around Ziguinchor.

A couple of years later Kankurangs were being performed again. In 1994, Sana Diolo, a spokesman of the Mandinko community in Ziguinchor, made another effort to regulate the Kankurang performances. Diolo was in charge of two programmes on Mandinko culture at the local broadcasting station. During the circumcision period of 1994, he regularly discussed the virtues and vices of Kankurang performances in the broadcasts. Upon the positive response to his ideas from the public, he decided to resume the work done by his predecessors and introduce a regulation of the masked performance. Since he was unemployed himself – he was not paid for his radio work – and badly in need of funds, Diolo accepted the help of Souleymane Seydi, a successful Mandinko merchant. The two of them went to numerous mosques in Ziguinchor to inform the assembled congregations about their efforts. They invited a number of the city's dignitaries to a meeting, including representatives of four ethnic groups: Mandinko, Jola, Balanta and Bainunk. In addition, the chiefs of several quarters (*chefs du quartier*) were invited. The governor, the mayor and the chief constable were not at the meeting but they had been informed about it beforehand and encouraged the men in their efforts.

At the first meeting, all the dignitaries expressed their grievances about the 'abuse' of the masked performance and its use as a pretext for theft and the settlement of old scores. The men loathed the dissipation that supposedly accompanied the performances of the mask. One elder informant pointedly described the performers as 'thieves, offenders, minors and gangsters'. Everyone agreed that interference with the 'degenerate' tradition was necessary. A second meeting was held at the city hall and the local dignitaries were invited again, together with representatives from Sédhiou, Marsassoum and other towns in the region where Kankurangs are regularly performed. At a third meeting, a resolution was adopted prohibiting Kankurang performances in Ziguinchor for a period of five years. It was decided that after this five-year period, Kankurang performances would only be allowed during initiations in the bush of Ziguinchor that were to be organised at five-year intervals, 'in correspondence with the customs of the various communities.'[14] The site of the ritual's enactment was to be stipulated by the dignitaries. People were still allowed to circumcise their sons by means of a 'minor initiation' (*kuyandingo*) as long as they did not perform the mask. The resolution was signed by three representatives of each ethnic group (Bainunk, Jola, Mandinko and Balanta) and contained an article requesting the administration to implement this decision and see to its observance. The mayor and the *chefs du quartier* were asked to appoint vigilantes in all the town's districts. The results of the meetings were widely publicised on Diolo's radio programmes as well as in special broadcasts in various local languages. The public response to the decisions was favourable, although there were incidental expressions of discontent from the town's young men. For a few years no Kankurangs were performed in Ziguinchor. This is quite surprising since the administration did not set up a structure to implement the decisions, nor did the dignitaries appoint any vigilantes.

The dignitaries designed the regulation to 'preserve a tradition'. They were especially concerned about the preservation of Kankurang's secret. The town's dignitaries wanted the mask to be a terrifying secret that was held in awe by everyone. Interestingly, the elders decided Kankurang masks would only be allowed in the bush. Their initiative to confine the masked performance to initiations in the bush was designed to exclude women from the ritual space where the mask is dressed. By redefining the appropriate context for the masked performances, the dignitaries also denied young men any authority in the matter. In that sense, the elders' intervention was part of ongoing generational conflict. Young men and women did not welcome this, but certainly did not publicly contradict the elders. The elders succeeded in transforming the model for ritual enactment and successfully reasserted their authority over the young men and women (cf. Rea 1998). Their intervention was a deliberate effort to renegotiate their position in the organisation of circumcision, initiation and masked performance. They did so by reclaiming the secrecy surrounding the masked performance. Bringing the mask back to the bush meant resituating the mask in the domain that, cosmologically, legitimises male authority over women and youth. The dignitaries tried to restore a gendered gerontocracy, which is unviable and obsolete in Senegal today.

Surprisingly, the dignitaries and the self-proclaimed spokesmen for the various ethnic communities turned to the administration to impose their decisions. They admitted that they no longer controlled the young men involved in the mask's performance and needed the state to intervene. Thus the administration was solicited in an attempt to restore a gerontocracy. The *chefs du quartier* were invited to attend the meetings and the dignitaries repeatedly stressed that they were acting according to law and justice. The dignitaries asked the local authorities to assist in implementing their decisions. In view of Kankurang's historical role vis-à-vis the state, this attitude is very surprising indeed. In fact, some young men reproached the dignitaries for discussing the mask's regulation at the town hall. They argued that the meeting should have been held in the bush instead. In terms of

Figure 6.2 Cartoon published in national journal *Le Soleil*: the man beaten up by the Kankurang is shouting: 'This is not a real Kankurang! It's Modou, whose brother I recently punished!'

the proclaimed aim to restore the secret of initiation, that would indeed have been a proper place to discuss matters regarding the masquerade. The strategy chosen by the dignitaries and their close collaboration with the administration testifies to the overwhelming presence of the Senegalese state. It is ironic that male elders should have required the assistance of the administration in the management of the secret of initiation. But it also shows that the dignitaries have started to reconceptualise the Kankurang performance as a tradition that should be subservient to the rule of law. They viewed the masked performances in Ziguinchor as too playful and conducive to uncontrolled acts that defied the authorities – both the elders and the state. Thus the regulation introduced by them was an effort to transform the masquerade and make it compatible with the state monopoly on the means of violence. The secret that was to be saved was simultaneously subordinated to the Senegalese state.

Yet there was still more at stake. The intervention was also designed to reappropriate the masquerade. The Mandinko dignitaries did not publicly say so, but they believed that members of other ethnic groups were not as

seriously committed to keeping the mask's secret. In other words, their imposition of a regulation was also a subtle effort to claim Mandinko 'ownership'.
Indeed, the Mandinko involved in the restoration of the mask's secret envi-
ously perceived Jola initiations as carefully managed expressions of Jola
'culture'. Jola initiations usually got a good press as authentic 'traditions'.[15]
In contrast, the Kankurang was often portrayed in the national newspapers
as a troublesome tradition that caused conflicts and fatal accidents (see
Figure 6.2).[16] In line with this perception, the Mandinko managers of the
Kankurang started to interpret the licence of the Kankurang as incompatible with the close cohabitation of various ethnic groups in an urban
context. They interpreted the violent conflicts at Marsassoum and Sédhiou
as accidents that do not properly belong to the Kankurang performance.
The Mandinko elders therefore proposed that Kankurangs would only be
performed at initiations in the bush, which they termed 'major initiation'
(*kuyangbaa*), as distinct from the 'minor initiation' (*kuyandingo*) practised
by members of all the ethnic groups (see Chapter 5). The dignitaries wanted
everyone to value this ceremony as much as the Jola initiation is valued. In
short, the regulation of the Kankurang masked performance was designed
to increase the respectability of a Mandinko ritual. As I noted above, in
Senegal cultural practices are increasingly reified as 'traditions' or 'cultural
heritage' (*patrimoine culturel*). In combination with an ethnic discourse that
ascribes each ethnic group its proper 'traditions', this leads to a competition for ethnic 'heritage'. In Ziguinchor, the Mandinko cultural entrepre-
neurs transformed the Kankurang into part of their ethnic 'heritage'. The
reification of the Kankurang into a key symbol of Mandinko identity has
primarily served to assert a Mandinko presence in a national context. And
indeed, in 2005 the Mandinko initiation rite and Kankurang performance
have been recognised by UNESCO as a 'masterpiece' of intangible heritage.
Kankurang is turned into a symbol of Mandinko identity, as part of a
national culture.

CONCLUSION

One might wonder whether the Mandinko dignitaries, in their effort to
preserve the Kankurang performance, adopted the right policy. Their redef-
inition of the masquerade as a practice that properly belongs to the bush
may restore the secrecy surrounding its performance. However, the young
men who performed the unlicensed masquerades have a real taste for the
performance and are more motivated to stage the mask than their elders.
Defining the masquerade as 'heritage' in order to restore an imagined authenticity might alienate the young men from playfully performing the mask. In
their own way, Ziguinchor's young men have accommodated the Kankurang
performance to the urban context. However, the dignitaries consider their
performances as conducive to conflict and ribaldry. Their regulation of the

Kankurang masquerade is an effort to control this vibrant practice and turn it into a respectable 'tradition'. Bausinger once argued that folklorisation means 'freezing' dynamic rituals: 'While earlier folk traditions often merely insisted on a few elements as fixed formulas and therefore allowed for a playful rearranging of the remaining parts, now the whole form became fixed and was valued precisely because of its frozen state' (Bausinger 1990: 78). The regulation of the Kankurang masquerade by the urban dignitaries clearly involved this kind of fixing, but the stakes were high. In a region where a separatist movement is striving for political independence, the competition for ritual control is yet another means of political competition. As the insurgency was supported primarily by members of the Jola ethnic group, the Mandinko clearly preferred to steer clear of the rebellion. It was not accidental that most members of the committee were *chefs de quartier* or otherwise affiliated with the local administration. The folklorisation of the masquerade was an effort to reclaim authority over the performance and establish ethnic ownership, with the unarticulated but obvious aim of pacifying the masquerade. The Mandinko cultural managers transformed the Kankurang into part of an ethnic 'heritage' that is meant to abide by the law instead of triggering riots and rebellion. However, after a few years Kankurangs were being performed again and one wonders whether the elders will ever succeed in domesticating the masquerade.

The masked performance should be understood as a practice that is situated in a variety of contexts. Mystical protection for the participants in circumcision and initiation rituals is one of the aims of the masked performance. Embodying the powers of the bush, Kankurang establishes the ritual separation between the sexes and participates in the production of masculinity and a generational structure. The society of initiates relies on its symbolic association with the bush and the performance of the mystically dangerous mask, to impose order in town. In precolonial times, the rulers in town had to abide by the authority of the masked figure. Even in postcolonial Senegal, the state and the masquerade have acted as balances to each other. The cases in this chapter point out that the state may have violated the secrecy surrounding the mask, but it has also been forced to acknowledge the secret in court. For several reasons, the most important of which is the elders' loss of control over the masquerade, the contemporary masquerades of urban Casamance are losing their authority. In an attempt to restore the secrecy surrounding the masked performance, the elders have tried to regulate the performance. This regulation is an attempt to redefine gender relations and address generational tensions, a claim to ethnic ownership of the Kankurang, as well as an intervention in the relationship between the state and the mask. The transformation of Kankurang into 'heritage' amounts to the transformation of what formerly was the ultimate authority in Mandinko society into a national 'tradition'. While not entirely losing its association with the bush, the mask becomes increasingly associated with the state.

A brief comparison with a similar attempt at domestication in The Gambia may be interesting. In The Gambia, the Mandinko constitute about fifty per cent of the population, so it is not surprising that the national People's Progressive Party has attempted to please its electorate by creating an alliance with the mask of Mandinko initiation. Weil observed that during a particular election campaign in the 1970s, some Kankurang masks had a 'PPP' symbol added to their costume (Weil 1971: 291; 1995: 22–3). The most important political party at the time clearly sought to ally itself with the dangerous masked figure. But the state itself had also made a move towards the Kankurang in an attempt to legitimise itself. Masks are increasingly performed at National Youth Day and Independence Day celebrations (Weil and Saho 2005: 165). The Gambian National Museum presents Mandinko traditions as part of the national cultural heritage. The ethnographic department of this small museum displays a Kankurang miniature and drawings of various Kankurang types. By displaying the mask at the National Museum, the Gambian state is incorporating this tradition into the national cultural heritage and furthering its own nationalist project. The Gambian Kankurang is made into a national symbol and used by the state to create a national culture and enhance its legitimacy (cf. Ebron 2002). There is a photograph at the Gambian National Museum of several eminent political figures meeting a Kankurang. What does the photograph tell the museum visitor? Does this picture portray an unstable alliance of modern rulers and a spirit of the bush, or does it convey the successful domestication of the masquerade as a 'tradition'?

PART IV

TRACES

7

MASQUERADE OF MIGRATION

The Kumpo masquerade is one of the cultural traditions of the Casamance region that is regularly performed in a variety of settings. In many Jola villages, Kumpo is performed by the Kumpo secret society at the village square. However, the Kumpo is today also performed at cultural festivals and hotels, for audiences quite different from those in the villages. The troupes that perform the masquerade in these settings are paid for their performance, which is thus commodified. So far studies on commodification have focused on the social life of objects, which either acquire the status of a commodity and become an exchangeable object or lose that status and become decommodified. This chapter does not aim to describe the social life of objects (Appadurai 1986b). Instead, by focusing on the Kumpo masquerade, it describes the divergent trajectories of a masquerade. Interestingly, although the masks used in the Kumpo performance never became commodities themselves, the performance did.

This chapter may seem to tell a familiar meta-narrative of the progressive incorporation of a pristine society into the global market economy, resulting in the inevitable commodification of its relations of production and exchange. In this process, the cultural practices peculiar to that society prior to its incorporation are commodified and lose their authenticity. However, this chapter proposes a different narrative, one in which the cultural practices accommodate to the global market economy. I show how the meaning of the mask and the modalities of masking depend on the context of performance as it is shaped by, and as it shapes, the impact of the market economy. I hope to show that performances of secrecy do not necessarily disintegrate as a result of the incorporation in the market economy. Rather, a part of the population uses the performance to reinforce their successful participation in that economy. Although the commodification of the masked performance has resulted in a radical transformation of the masquerade, it also mediates participation in the global capitalist economy. The masquerade provides a means of moderating the migration of villagers. In other words, the masquerade is not a remnant of tradition that has so far survived modernisation but is the other side of a Janus-faced modernity.

Figure 7.1 Kumpo and Jarrimamma pose for the photographer, Diatock
(Courtesy Royal Tropical Institute, Amsterdam)

THE POWER OF THE MASK

Kumpo does not wear a carved wooden face and may be classified among
the leaf and fibre masks. The figure looks very much like a haystack, since
it is made of the leaves of palm trees that extend from the head to cover the
entire body, including the arms, legs and feet (see Figures 7.1 and 7.2). A
pole projects upward from the head.[1] Kumpo is usually performed in the
village square. The day set for a Kumpo performance is announced by the
mask itself. At dusk, the mask comes out of a sacred forest and walks through
the village to inform young men and women that their presence is required
at the performance. The mask does not usually speak to the bystanders, his
presence in the village being enough to indicate that a performance will be
held that evening. At nightfall the young women gather and line up at the
central square. They then begin to sing and dance, using old spades for
rhythmical accompaniment, and are later joined by the young men. After
some time Kumpo appears, stalking around and frightening the children.
Three drummers then heat their drums at a bonfire and start playing,
encouraging the young men and women to dance (see Figures 7.3 and 7.4).
Every now and then Kumpo intervenes and corrects the dancers. Kumpo
admonishes the youths to take the dance seriously, participating in the
dance himself. He sticks his pole in the ground and whirls in circles around
it, displaying great speed and agility. The pattern of Kumpo participating

Figure 7.2 Kumpo, dancing with the women, Diatock (Courtesy Royal Tropical Institute, Amsterdam)

on and off in the dance continues well into the night. Towards the close of the performance Kumpo addresses the audience. He speaks with a strange nasal voice and his words therefore require 'translation' by a member of the audience. The translation is usually done by one of the young men present (cf. Girard 1965: 70). Kumpo's message is invariably an order or a warning of one sort or another. Kumpo then returns to the sacred forest and the villagers go home.

The case outlined above of the Kumpo masquerade cannot be generalised across all African masked performances. It does, however, contain features which do occur in other masquerades. It has been firmly established that a masked performance involves an impersonation, the coming into being of a *persona* (Napier 1988: 232; Tonkin 1979: 240). The transformation of a human being into a *persona* does not merely consist of disguising the performer, but involves the multiple activities that masks display. The mask comes to life by running around, speaking or shouting and often threatening the audience. A mask cannot exist without an audience, and without playing its part in the performance which establishes a complex series of interactions between itself and the audience (Tonkin 1979: 243; Kasfir 1988a: 2–3). The form and aesthetic qualities of a mask are essential in seducing the audience into the delightful and frightening interaction with the mask (Kasfir 1988a).

Figure 7.3 Young men and women dancing, Diatock (Photo: Maarten Bavinck)

In some societies masks are regarded as reincarnated ancestors, in others as incarnations of forest spirits. However, not all masks are regarded as ancestors or spirits by their audiences. Sometimes the identity of the mask remains a mystery. This is apparent from one of Achebe's novels which provides us with a dialogue between a man and a mask. The man is asked to identify the mask, and replies: 'How can a man know you who are beyond human knowledge?' (Achebe 1971: 250). Yet, even when the mask is regarded as beyond human knowledge, the mask performer may well be recognised by members of the audience. Mask performers are nearly always male and their identity is kept a secret from women.[2] Most women know much more about the masks and their performers than they are willing to admit. But even if women recognise their son or brother, the mask nevertheless instils fear. The ambiguity of the mask actually delights both the performers and the audience (Ottenberg 1975: 211). Thus masks are by their very nature ambiguous, and yet they are frequently used to exert unambiguous coercive power. The mask manipulates the behaviour of its audience, both during and after the performance. One difficulty clearly lies in trying to resolve the ambiguous quality of masking so as to account for its unambiguous social effects.

In a seminal essay, Tonkin (1979) argued that the explanation for the coercive power of masks lies in the fact that the audience generally believes

Figure 7.4 Young men and women dancing, Diatock (Photo: Maarten Bavinck)

that power resides in the mask. She argued that this can only be accounted for by the particular paradoxes involved in masking. Although the audience may attribute a particular meaning to the mask, such as the incarnation of an ancestor or bush spirit, its exercise of coercive power cannot be explained by this subordinate aspect since power is attributed to *all* masks regardless of the indigenous meaning given to them. I take that as a valid assertion, yet one should not ignore the multiple meanings attributed to the mask by the members of the audience.[3] Women know far less about the mask than the men who are initiated into its secret. The perception of the mask is differential, depending on the social position of the observer, resulting in differential behaviour vis-à-vis the mask (Weil 1988). In view of the fact that women are not supposed to question the mask's identity and often constitute the audience, one might argue that the performance involves only the male half of the community. The very act of excluding the women, however, is itself an integral part of the performance, since the power of illusion and secrecy depend upon women playing the role of the non-initiated (Kasfir 1988a: 7). Hence, the masked performance should be analysed as a form of secrecy that prohibits the audience from questioning the mask's identity, while simultaneously incorporating the audience in the performance.

Secrecy of course plays a crucial role in the mask–audience relationship. When examining the social dynamics of a masked performance, the following question therefore has to be asked: 'Who has the right to present a mask and to turn others into an audience?' (Tonkin 1988: 246). The performer–audience relationship is, according to Tonkin, an index of a socio-political relationship. Taking her argument one step further, I will argue that a masked performance, like any other ritual, does not merely reflect or legitimise social relationships but produces them. The right to present a mask and to turn others into an audience is itself subject to negotiation. The masked performance serves very well the purpose of exerting coercive power, but needs to be imposed. The rules of secrecy consequently prevent an open discussion of the objectives of the mask performers. Henceforth the audience is in the disadvantaged position of being unable to contest the mask–audience relationship. The performance will then 'mask' those hidden social relationships.

THE SPREAD OF KUMPO

Most scholars agree about the origin of Kumpo. According to Girard (1965), Kumpo originated among the Bainunk ethnic group, a point of view that he thinks is supported by the fact that Kumpo has a firmly established meaning in Bainunk cosmology whereas among the Jola the mask remains a 'mystery' (1965: 46–60). However, Mark argues that it is both difficult and misleading to consider the Bainunk and the Jola as completely distinct groups (Mark 1985: 50). To attribute distinct cultural features to either Bainunk or Jola is a haphazard enterprise considering they have a shared history of more than four centuries. Yet informants consistently attributed the Kumpo mask to the Bainunk ethnic group. I think, however, that this was part of a continuous process of boundary construction in which each ethnic group is attributed its own masquerade, although the practice is actually shared by all (see Chapter 6). The ethnic discourse in Casamance maintains ethnic boundaries while cultural interaction is the day-to-day practice.

In the 1930s Kumpo became very popular in Jola villages.[4] The performance was probably organised once or twice a week in every village ward. The mask would come out at night and entertain all participants in the performance. The character of the performance has probably remained unchanged throughout this century and must have been similar to the performance described above. How can the sudden spread of the Kumpo masked performance to so many other Jola villages during the 1930s be explained? Girard (1965) suggested that the introduction of Kumpo into the Jola villages was a response to the Jola's conversion to Islam. In order to counter the individualising effect of Islam, he believed the masked performance had been introduced and directed by the elders to reinforce the cohesion of village society. However, Girard's point of view must be questioned on the grounds of being too glibly functionalist. Van der Klei has suggested that the mask was used by a specific category of the village popu- lation to promote their own particular interests. He supposes that Kumpo was introduced by the elders in order to control their sons who had started to participate in labour migration, thereby temporarily escaping paternal control (Van der Klei 1989: 218). Although the spread of Kumpo was without a doubt related to labour migration, I will argue below that it was not the elders but the young men themselves who introduced Kumpo to their villages.

Mark claims that '[t]he key to understanding kumpo's wide geographical range lies in the universal appeal of a figure that could combat the ever- present danger of witchcraft' (1985: 48). According to him, the Jola had traditionally relied on the ordeal by poison to try those accused of witch- craft. With the suppression of the ordeal by the French administration at the beginning of the twentieth century, the Jola were forced to find other ways to combat witchcraft. However, although Kumpo may have been used to identify witches, I found no evidence that affirmed that the mask was used to pass sentence on them. It seems gratuitous to argue that the masquerade is to be seen as a substitute for the poison ordeal. This chapter suggests another explanation for Kumpo's rapid spread during the years of increased labour migration.

LABOUR MIGRATION AND SOCIAL CONTROL

As a play the Kumpo masquerade certainly provided its audience with enter- tainment, and any explanation for its spread should take this into account. Along with the traditional wrestling matches the performance provided an amusing pastime which came into fashion during the 1930s.[5] The fash- ionable masked performance, however, served not simply to entertain the youth, but also to play a distinct role in social control. Unmarried men and women were not allowed to mock Kumpo or transgress the rules he made. Girls were warned not to forget to sweep the family yard as negligence would always be detected by the omniscient Kumpo. Quarrels between young men or young women also warranted his intervention. There was no subject in which Kumpo could not involve himself. In the course of his performance Kumpo reprimanded anyone who had displayed unruly behaviour. If the mask itself did not correct anti-social behaviour then a person's faults were mentioned in the songs that the audience sang during the performance.[6] In addition Kumpo imposed a penalty (*alaman*) several times a year, which was always collectively imposed and usually consisted of a goat or a pig. The penalty had to be presented to Kumpo, after which a two- or three-day feast was held consisting of endless dancing, singing and eating (cf. Girard 1965: 80) (see Figure 7.5).

The obvious question to be addressed here is: who directed the perfor-

Figure 7.5 Yaya offering chickens to Kumpo, Kandhiou (Photo: Ferdinand de Jong)

mance? The organisation of the masked performance was in the hands of the Kumpo society, a secret society whose members belonged in one ward to the age group of initiated but unmarried young men (cf. Girard 1965: 77–80; Mark 1985: 46). These young men were familiar with Kumpo's secret. They knew that one of them was dressed with the mask, how he was dressed and where this took place, normally in a sacred forest of the ward. The young women, who were excluded from Kumpo's secret, were to pretend that the mask was a mystery to them. The Kumpo society itself held its meetings in a sacred forest where matters were discussed pertaining to the Kumpo performance. As I demonstrated before, sacred forests were and still are the most important Jola sanctuaries. The most important sacred forest was the one associated with male initiation but other forests of secondary importance existed alongside. The Kumpo society held its meetings in such a forest of secondary importance. This forest was also believed to be the dwelling place of Kumpo. This suggests that the young men were able to create their own sacred forest which did not derive its sacredness from a shrine but simply from Kumpo's secret. Nor was its management a matter for the elders, but only for the young men of the Kumpo society. In view of the fact that a sacred forest was an important symbol of the elders' authority, one wonders how the young men were allowed to establish a sacred forest of their own.

As I noted before, the pacification of the Casamance region had led to the seasonal labour migration of young men to the areas of groundnut culti-vation. Young unmarried men were thus able to earn a monetary income, and as the first converts to Islam they expressed their independence at home by rejecting their ancestral religion (Mark 1985: 112). In their villages this change led to alternative sources of authority, namely cash and Islam (cf. Snyder 1978: 241–2). The young men nevertheless remained dependent on their elders for other reasons such as the initiation, inheritance of rice paddies and to receive a wife. But the young men were able to renegotiate their relationship with the elders. To express their newly found indepen-dence, the young men had recourse to a well-established source of authority: the sacred forest. The prevailing sense of secrecy with regard to everything related to the forest was elaborated to incorporate the Kumpo mask. Since the mask was believed to originate in the sacred forest, those not initiated into its secret were not allowed to talk about Kumpo and had to conform to his commands.

The changed status of the young men was not confined to a renego-tiation of their relationship with the elders but was equally expressed in a transformation of their relationship with young women. Their attendance at the masked performance came to be compulsory from the moment they reached marriageable age up to the day they were married. The young women were subject to the mask's surveillance and rules. Secrecy prevented open discussion of the mask, and his commands were accepted by the young women even when unfavourable to them. The young men thus turned young women into the audience of their masked performance. By means of an expansion of secrecy, the category of young men renegotiated the relations between age and gender categories, empowered by the new possibilities of the market economy.

CONTROLLING FEMALE MIGRATION

The introduction of the Kumpo performance in Jola villages attested to the changing social relationships between gender and age categories in the villages. From the 1950s onwards, however, despite the introduction of new masks (Jarimamma – see Figure 7.6) in the performance, Kumpo began to lose ground to other forms of entertainment that had made their way into village life.[7] From the 1950s on, young men also started to migrate to the cities in the region or to the national capital, Dakar. The migration which formerly used to be focused on the production of groundnuts in rural areas was now directed towards the urban economy that was far less dependent on seasonal supply and demand. Most of the migrants no longer returned to their villages on a regular basis (cf. Snyder 1978: 241). Consequently a lack of interest in the masked performance led to its abandonment.

Towards the end of the 1960s fewer and fewer young men returned to the village to help with the rice cultivation. The elders approved of this

Figure 7.6 Jarimamma threatening the photographer, Diatock (Photo: Maarten Bavinck)

development as they thought their sons would make a better living by holding jobs in the urban economy (and consequently would be better able to support their parents). Van der Klei convincingly showed that the young men's involvement in rice cultivation was detrimental to 'young farmers', those adult men living in the village who had founded their own households but did not yet have children old enough to contribute to household production. Since the labour force of migrants had formerly been used in rice cultivation, their absence confronted these farmers with a labour shortage. Elders faced the same problem but were still capable of hiring work groups with the money provided by their sons working in the urban economy (Van der Klei 1989: 43–84). The young farmers began to protest against the labour migration of young men. In 1969, this resulted in open disagreement between the young farmers and the elders in the village of Diatock (see Map 2). The young farmers forced the young men residing in the cities to return to the village in defiance of the express wishes of the elders to the contrary. Initially, their initiative was successful, but eventually the conflict was concluded in favour of the elders. Nevertheless, the young farmers' protest had been voiced and henceforth any future labour migration involving the young men was subject to negotiation between the elders and young farmers (Van der Klei 1989: 219–42).

In 1974 Diatock held its male initiation, a decision prompted by the young farmers. All members of the community returned to the village. The young farmers used the occasion to found a village association of young men and women that merged the associations of all the village wards. As young women increasingly participated in labour migration, the association set itself the target of regulating the migration of both the young men and the young women. Its committee (*assemblée générale*) decided that young women were to return to the village every year by 15 July (the start of the rainy season) in order to assist in the planting of the rice seedlings. In the event of a young woman returning late, a fine was to be imposed (7,500 CFA francs, then approx. US$25). If a woman failed to turn up at all, then the fine was doubled. The labour migration of young men was not regulated to the same extent, as returning home could result in them losing their jobs. The association purposely sought to regulate the labour migration and organised several new events to make life in the village more pleasant during the rainy season, such as a soccer competition and dance nights in the village dance hall.[8] Encouraged by a Dutch anthropologist working in the village the young farmers of two wards of Diatock also decided to revitalise the Kumpo performance. In addition to the association regulating the labour migration, Kumpo also helped by ensuring that young women arrived in time for the planting of the rice seedlings. If after the rainy season the village association permitted the girls to leave for Dakar, then girls living in one of the Kumpo-ruled wards also required the mask's permission, which could be withheld. Whose interests were served by the mask's new role? First, young farmers profited by the young women working on the rice fields. Kumpo not only saw to their return but also admonished the girls to unite themselves into labour associations and offer their labour to farmers. Secondly, the young unmarried men also had their interests promoted by the Kumpo. Their aim was to discipline the girls to ensure appropriately submissive behaviour.

By the 1980s the young men's migration proved less and less rewarding (cf. Reboussin 1995: 178). The general decline in economic growth led to increased unemployment and young men who had spent several years in the towns eventually returned to their villages and settled down as farmers. The young female migrants, on the other hand, were not so much concerned about their job careers but about the selection of their future spouses. The girls primarily sought marriage with a civil servant, certainly not with a farmer which would entail a life of hard labour in the village. The young men jealously watching their female peers seeking out better opportunities fell back on the Kumpo performance in the hope of controlling the girls' behaviour. The most obvious collective strategy was to force them to return to the village. Kumpo obliged them to take up labour in the fields and to keep up the skills which would eventually enable them to make good wives in an agrarian household. In collaboration with the village association, Kumpo therefore entreated the girls to return to the village during the rainy season, and imposed fines when anyone failed to obey. Since fines are always collectively imposed, Kumpo reinforced social control among the young female migrants by making them responsible for each other's transgressions (see Figure 7.5). This new policy of the Kumpo performance has been pursued up until the present day. In addition to disciplining the girls, Kumpo also regularly imposes penalties and organises feasts. This enables young men to keep close contact with the girls. The importance of these occasions is probably on the increase since young men find it increasingly difficult to get a job in the city whereas the girls can more easily find employment as maids. As more young men prefer to stay in the village the regulation of the girls' labour migration is the only way to assure that they make contact with potential wives from their generation.

Not surprisingly, since Kumpo's rules reflect the interests of young men and young farmers, the Kumpo society that revitalised the masked performance comprised members of both categories. Whereas the Kumpo society had formerly been directed by initiated, unmarried men, from 1974 onwards it was directed by the young farmers (young men with their own households). The elders are still excluded from the Kumpo society, even those who formerly as young men had been full-time members. Interestingly, while young men and young farmers never revealed to me that Kumpo and other masks were actually created and directed by them, the elders did not keep this a secret. Those who had their interests promoted by Kumpo maintained the secret, while those whose interests were not at stake were on the whole indifferent about it. Young women, however, were not allowed to express doubts about the nature of the mask, or even to suggest that Kumpo served the interests of young men. In Kandiou, a village located near Diatock, women were fined twice for whispering that Kumpo had unjustly imposed a penalty unfavourable to the young women.

A TOURIST ATTRACTION

Tourists intent on a holiday in the Gambian sun are very likely to be welcomed by a Kumpo at the airport. Today it is not uncommon for tour operators to hire a local dance troupe to perform a Kumpo at the very moment that tourists disembark from the aircraft. The performance is accompanied by dancing and singing, and the young men and women performing are dressed in 'authentic' raffia skirts. In this way tourists are introduced to the local 'culture'. Occasionally, other masks are also performed, and it is interesting that some of them are not rooted in local traditions. Since the tourists in general have no idea of the local cultural repertoire, the dance troupes can easily include performances and dances from other regions or countries. The performances anyway are likely to be thought of by the tourists as 'typically African'.

Most tourists, from Scandinavia, Britain or the Netherlands, normally spend two or three weeks lounging on the beach. Some indulge in the sexual services offered by their Gambian hosts while others may make tours around the region. Tours offered by travel agencies last from a couple of hours to up to eight days. The latter option includes a visit to Casamance's regional capital, Ziguinchor. The hotel where the tourists stay overnight puts on a folklore show performed by one of the local dance troupes (*troupe théâtrale*). The show lasts for one hour and is usually staged next to the hotel swimming pool. The show consists of four or five plays each comprising music, choreographic dance and singing. Each play is usually inspired by a dance, feast or ritual from the local cultural repertoire. The Kumpo performance is presented as a part of this show. The dance troupe is paid a small sum of 18,000 devalued West African francs (US$26).

The masks used in the Kumpo masquerade are made specifically for that purpose by local artisans. These masks cannot be bought at the local market nor at tourist art shops. The commodification of the masks used in the Kumpo performance would inevitably be tantamount to a public scandal. This would amount to sacrilege, the disclosure of the mask's secret. Thus, whereas the individual masks used in the Kumpo performance have not yet been commodified, the performance itself has. Fierce competition among the different dance troupes may have triggered the initiative. Appadurai (1986a: 23–7) and Kopytoff (1986: 73) claim that in every society objects or traditions exist – in particular *sacra* – that are not allowed to function as commodities. Sometimes, these things nevertheless enter the commodity phase, a turn in their social life that Appadurai has termed a 'diversion'. Diversions always carry a risky and morally ambiguous aura (Appadurai 1986a: 27). Steiner, for instance, argues that the traders in African art often are outsiders, which he sees as a precondition for their participation in the art trade (Steiner 1994: 88). This may be the reason why the dance troupe that performs the Kumpo performance for tourists consists predominantly of Mandinko, an ethnic group of which the members do not reckon Kumpo to be part of their cultural heritage.

Kumpo is performed on hotel premises and the mask is never undressed. It has been possible to commodify the performance without disclosing the secret of the mask. The disclosure of the mask's secret would make its performance far less interesting for the tourist audience anyway. After all, the tourists too delight in the mystery of the mask. The performance does nevertheless result in 'diversion' of Kumpo. In the village context the mask emerges from the sacred forest, while in the hotel setting it comes out of the swimming pool changing room.

FOLKLORISATION OF KUMPO

The commodification of the Kumpo performance may be categorised as a form of folklore, a category of cultural expression which often is considered to be inauthentic. However, in the last decade a process of folklorisation has been witnessed in Jola villages that is triggered not only by commodification. Some village communities organise cultural festivals during which all sorts of traditional dances and plays are performed. In this context the dances are no longer enacted in a way to make the audience participate but rather deliberately turn the audience into passive onlookers (Mark 1994). The audience witnesses their traditions being performed as 'culture'. The Kumpo mask was recently performed in this way at a cultural festival in Ziguinchor organised by the village association of Tendouck. A programme consisting of a rain-dance, initiation dances and the Kumpo performance was put on to entertain the youth, their male and female elders and invited officials (see Figure 7.7). As usual during these performances a couple of young men recorded the songs and dances with video cameras and cassette recorders. This produced the somewhat strange scene of old men watching a Kumpo performance (though not very attentively) which they would normally consider a 'childish' amusement for younger age sets. While salvage paradigm anthropology might make short shrift of the matter, relegating the performance to the realm of 'inauthentic' culture, the performers and their audience clearly considered their performance an authentic expression of local culture.

Such performances may serve a political goal. High-ranking civil servants

Figure 7.7 Kumpo at a cultural festival in Ziguinchor (Photo: Ferdinand de Jong)

and politicians are usually invited to attend the festivities. Although not compelled to do so, these visitors are requested to make a financial contribution to the festival's association. When, for instance, Robert Sagna visited the village of Diatock in December 1994, he was treated to the performance of several dances including a Kumpo masquerade.[9] The show was intended to establish a reciprocal relation with the politician that might benefit the village community. The Minister for his part was seeking to enlarge his electoral support. The villagers' political foresight was proven right when the Minister donated 1,000,000 francs (US$1,750) to the village association, to be used for the village sewing workshop. The Kumpo performance is clearly used by the village community to cement relations with high-ranking officials in the hope of receiving financial or other benefits.

Patronage for the Kumpo masquerade is not only offered by Senegalese politicians. While the Kumpo mask performance is considered the 'cultural heritage' of the Bainunk ethnic group in Senegal, it has recently acquired the status of a national heritage in the Gambia. This development is related to a change in the Gambian government. For several decades The Gambia was governed by Dawda Jawara, a Mandinko. However, in 1994 he was ousted from power by the young military man Yaya Jammeh, a Jola. While the status of the Jola had been low under Jawara's regime, the Jola ethnic group now regained confidence and asserted its presence in the national public sphere. The Kankurang, generally associated with the Mandinko, had always enjoyed the patronage of Dawda Jawara (see Chapter 6). But since Jammeh came to power the Kumpo masquerade has acquired national recognition as yet another 'ethnic heritage'.[10] This shows that masquerades are increasingly being turned into 'heritage' thereby validating the national politics of ethnic recognition, whereby each masquerade is made to stand for an ethnic group.

As the masquerade is performed in new settings, one would assume that its meanings would radically shift. The Kumpo mask indeed acquires new meaning when it is performed for tourists. Before the start of the play, the tourists are informed about the mask. A commentator explains to the tourists the meaning which Kumpo has in local society. Usually Kumpo is said to be a 'demon' which is part of the 'tradition' of the Bainunk 'tribe'. This reflects the notion that both tourists and performers have of Africa as made up of distinct tribes, each with a distinct culture of its own. Ironically, the members of the dance troupe do not belong to the ethnic group to which Kumpo is attributed. The performance is commodified as a reified form of culture, typical of an equally reified notion of bounded, a-historical ethnic groups. Clearly, the meaning that the Kumpo performance acquires for tourists does not adequately reflect the mask's actual use in the regulation of labour migration. Moreover, the fact that Kumpo is performed in a hotel testifies to the multifarious contemporary trajectories of the mask, a fact that is lost on the audience. The meaning Kumpo acquires for tourists does nevertheless largely coincide with the meaning that it is given in local cultural festivals, in which the audience conceives of the performance as a 'tradition' that may not necessarily be particular to 'our tribe' but which is certainly conceived of as being 'ours'. It also indicates a heightened awareness of their 'modernisation', in as much as the population of Casamance has started to conceive of its customs in terms of 'tradition' and 'culture'. This way of conceptualising local practices is a result of the experience of modernity and the subsequent labelling of local practices as 'tradition'. In Casamance, 'tradition' is referred to by various terms today: *coutume* (introduced by the colonial administration), other French terms such as *tradition, folklore* or *culture,* or *thiossane* ('roots', a Wolof term used by the Senegalese government in promoting the preservation of local culture). Nowadays the Kumpo performance is referred to with terms that all denote the same substance: culture as reified tradition. Tradition is defined broadly and encompasses the performances for tourists and officials (cf. Errington and Gewertz 1996: 116).

In the global context of identity politics, reified culture can be attributed different meanings. When performed in the context of local cultural festivals with an audience of villagers, the Kumpo masquerade becomes an expression of authentic local culture. The performers are thus involved in the process of articulating a cultural identity (cf. Mark 1994). In the case of the Kumpo performance organised for Robert Sagna, the performers deliberately tried to create a sense of shared identity with the state official, himself a Jola. The performance was used to gain access to state resources. The same observation applies when the masquerade is performed in the Gambia. There, the performance of Kumpo also symbolises an ethnic boundary with the Mandinko. When performed for tourists the Kumpo mask is also used to symbolise a local cultural tradition, not however to create identity, but to create difference between Africa and Europe. In the context of a hotel performance Kumpo acquires meaning as the authentic expression of the Other. In fact the performers are deliberately 'othering' themselves (cf. Crain 1998). The mask is then used by its performers to gain access to the resources of the global tourist industry.

The masked performance is part of the worldwide production of images of authenticity. A website meant to promote tourism to Casamance displays various pictures of local 'traditions', including a picture of Kumpo.[11] A dance troupe from Dakar consisting of migrants from Casamance has toured around the world performing Casamance dances which included the Kumpo masquerade. The troupe has had various audiences. In France the troupe was intended to promote tourism in Senegal. It has also been invited to participate in international cultural festivals including carnivals in Paris and Japan and a festival in Washington with an audience of predominantly African-Americans. Kumpo generates identity and difference on a global stage.

CONCLUSION

Masked performances can be subject to multifarious trajectories. The Kumpo mask was introduced to Jola villages by young men, thus enabling them to articulate a change in their status within the local social structure brought about by their participation in capitalist relations of production. At a later stage Kumpo helped regulate the participation of young women in the capitalist economy. From its inception the Kumpo performance was intricately linked to the dynamics of the market economy. Recently, the masked performance began to serve other objectives such as the expression of authenticity, for both tourist audiences as well as for locals in cultural festivals. All of these performance contexts are contemporaneous. Kumpo simultaneously functions as a disciplining device and an expression of 'authentic' culture. Paradoxically some trajectories of the Kumpo performance have developed due to the appropriation of a discourse on modernity which always denied tradition a future. Some performances, in their transformation of local traditions, testify to the life, not the death, of tradition. However, the performances are embedded in systems of increasingly unequal relations, of young men marginalised by capitalist relations of production trying to regulate the labour migration of young women, of local communities striving for access to the resources of a volatile state and of dance troupes trying hard to access the prizes of a very competitive and equally volatile global tourist market. The mask is used in various ways to manage the impact of capitalism.

While it is not being argued here that all traditions will be subject to commodification, the fact that some local dances are transformed into plays for tourists and are thus commodified has the effect of transforming *all* local traditions into a cultural repertoire, thereby paving the way for further commodification. In the Gambia the Kankurang is increasingly performed for tourists (Weil and Saho 2005). However, in Casamance the Kankurang masquerade is not yet commodified as a tourist performance. While performers do get paid for Kankurang performances in ritual contexts, the mask is not staged at hotels, since the cultural values contained in its performance prevent the local dance troupes from doing so. We should therefore refrain from assuming linearity in commodification processes. The commodification of the Kumpo performance need not be the future of other masked performances.

The performance of a mask as an expression of authentic culture for an audience of villagers, tourists or officials highlights a crucial change in a local tradition. We noted earlier that the act of masking enables certain groups to exert coercive power on condition that the audience participates in the performance and subjects itself to the capricious behaviour of the mask. This is certainly not the case when the mask is performed for foreign tourists or a Minister. The official watches the mask while comfortably seated under a canopy, engaged in a conversation with his hosts. Likewise, the tourists are seated in front of a stage on which the mask dances while the tourists themselves sip cocktails. The tourists are even allowed to video the performance without being reprimanded or disturbed by the mask. The relationship between the mask and his audience has been substantially transformed in an attempt to remodel the performance in a way to lend it a new instrumentality. Examining the performance for tourists and officials, it turns out that the social relationship between players and audience is very different from the one within the village context. Tourists and officials are allowed to attend the masked performance without being subjected to his authority. Although the secret is not violated, it has lost its coercive potential. In such performances the secret is instead staged as a local form of authenticity.

8

THE ART OF TRADITION

The Casamance cultural repertoire is not restricted to the performances discussed so far but also encompasses cultural forms commonly understood as popular culture. High culture – to use a controversial term to denote the cultural expressions usually associated with it, without suggesting a hierarchy – is far less disseminated. Yet in some middle-class interiors, one may find modern paintings, some of them made by Casamance artists. Although they cater to an audience consisting of the local middle class, the expatriate community and tourists, these artists are inspired by local traditions. In their representations of traditional culture, the artists focus on masquerades and initiation rites. In fact, they represent the secretive performances discussed in the previous chapters. This presents us with a conundrum. How can these performances of secrecy be represented in art? Why does their representation in art not amount to desecration? As paintings are forms of visual communication, one wonders why these representations are not equivalent to the disclosure of secrets? Judging from the favourable reception of these works of art, I would say that they are not. Why not? Taussig gives us a clue: 'It is the task and life force of the public secret to maintain that verge where the secret is not destroyed through exposure, but subject to a quite different sort of revelation that does justice to it' (Taussig 1999: 3). So how do these works of art do justice to the secret? In this chapter I examine the situational meanings attributed to a set of artworks which in one way or another represent circumcision, initiation and masquerading.

PAINTERS OF TRADITION

Living and working in Casamance, Badji and Camara operate within the regional as well as the national art world. They both spend most of their time in Casamance and are the region's most renowned painters. Malang Badji is of Jola extraction. He was born around 1943 in Yabone (*département* of Ziguinchor) and raised in a predominantly Mandinko environment. He spent a couple of years at the Ecole Nationale des Beaux Arts in Dakar (1961–63) and had his first exhibition in 1966 at the Festival des Arts Nègres de Dakar. Badji has had a successful career with many shows in Senegal and some in France. He currently lives at Carabane, a picturesque small island in the Casamance estuary predominantly populated by fish-

Figure 8.1 The painter Omar Camara with one of his paintings of a Jola initiate (Photo: Ferdinand de Jong)

ermen and hotel personnel. Badji usually works in a cabin near the beach. While Badji is nearing the end of his working career, Omar Camara has just become successful. Camara was born in Ziguinchor in 1963. He is of mixed ethnic extraction (Bambara and Fulani). After secondary school, he moved to Dakar and graduated from the Ecole Nationale des Beaux Arts in 1986. After his education he returned to Ziguinchor, where he started working on the depiction of tradition. By 1994 he had acquired local fame and took his first trip to France in 1996. Camara had exhibitions in Ziguinchor, Dakar and France. The theme of his work closely resembles my research interest in practices of secrecy and we have regularly discussed our work. In contrast to Malang Badji, a well-to-do laid-back philosopher, Omar Camara is actively exploring his future options (see Figure 8.1). He is very eloquent about his work and he is a good salesman. He lives in Ziguinchor and regularly travels to Dakar to exhibit his paintings and explore the market for commissions.

What themes do these artists address? Malang Badji was around fifty when I met him, and has made so many paintings that it is hard to pick out a few themes without doing an injustice to his work as a whole. Since he sold all the works and never kept any record of them, it is also hard to know what his former work consisted of. In his current work, there are a few types of paintings that can be specified. Badji has made numerous paintings of women. His women command respect and are often depicted with children. Maternity is a prominent theme in his work. He also made landscapes which convey the idea of a Senegalese Eden or, perhaps more precisely, a pastoral Casamance. Badji also produced a series depicting agriculture in all its local varieties of labour division, exemplifying the mandinkisation of rice cultivation. However, most of Badji's works depict ceremonies. They portray Jola rituals, including initiation ceremonies, in which men tend to dominate, with attitudes that men typically embrace in these performances. Badji makes them appear strong and courageous.

When I met him Omar Camara had not yet established a style of his own and was experimenting with form and content. A series of his paintings represents children's rights, women's liberation and the life of the handicapped. These themes reflect a connection with the international aid organisations that finance artistic activities that publicise their programmes. Other paintings that reflect Camara's pragmatic attitude and market orientation depict the Casamance region as a tourist destination. He painted them as part of a campaign to publicise tourist facilities in Casamance. Finally, the sort of painting that interests us most here is referred to by Camara as *retour aux sources* ('return to one's roots') and corresponds to what Malang Badji represents in his ceremony works. In Senegal the term *retour aux sources* refers to the participation in traditional rites and has connotations of linking people to their collective past, which is thought to have a healing effect on the alienation produced by modern urban life. Whether or not *retour aux sources* can be considered a genre of painting, it is clear that the term denotes a central theme in Senegal's national culture. As we will see, this discourse articulates a sense of nostalgia and a need to recover the past by at least preserving a memory of tradition.

If we classify these artists according to the model proposed by Vogel and Ebong (1991), both of them can be considered 'international' artists. Unlike traditional artists such as woodworkers or blacksmiths, they do not belong to historical status groups and have acquired their position by personal achievement, not by birth (ibid.: 50–2). They both have had formal training. They paint on paper, since canvas is not on sale in Ziguinchor and is too expensive anyway. They travel widely and exhibit their work at banks, hotels and branches of foreign cultural institutes where they sell their work to expatriates and tourists. Badji and Camara both make a relatively comfortable living although Badji charges higher prices for his work than Camara, a reflection of the fact that his work is in high demand. The work produced by these artists is not a contemporary transformation of traditional art (Graburn 1976). Nor is it intended for the local tourist market. Although the artists do sell their work to tourists, their art is not tourist art (Jules-Rosette 1984; Steiner 1994). Considering their educational background and the materials they use, their art might be categorised as 'academic art' (Vogel and Ebong 1991), a form that is well developed in Senegal and has led to the renowned École de Dakar (Harney 2004). The elitist nature of the art prevents the consumption of Casamance art by the vast majority of the population. However, although it manifestly addresses popular issues, Casamance art is not popular art (cf. Szombati-Fabian and Fabian 1976; Jewsiewicki 1991). Unlike popular painting in Zaire, its consumption remains restricted to the wealthy middle class. Nor does it claim a public place, as the popular art of the Mourides does (Roberts and Roberts 2003). Casamance art therefore does not seem to fit the genres of academic, popular, tourist, airport or traditional art. The system of classification that orders the bewildering hybridity of artistic production in the African postcolony and legitimises the formation of separate canons does little to enhance our understanding of how art functions in several contexts. This system, which distributes value in a discriminative way, may be useful to the collectors of African art but one wonders whether the classification has much use value for academic purposes. The mediums, messages and markets of African art combine in unexpected ways that defy our expectations. Classifications that result from the European history of art (art/craft, high/low, etc.) clearly cannot be transposed to the African postcolony. This chapter therefore starts from the premise that art should be understood in context and that works of art acquire their meaning situationally. Which meaning prevails, however, does to a large extent depend on the social and political context in which they are exhibited and on the interpretations provided by the artists.

MEMORY OF TRADITION

It goes without saying that the representation of secretive rituals is hazardous. Only under certain conditions can the secret be depicted. The problem inherent in the representation of secrets is a parallel to the issue of the commodification of *sacra*. Generally speaking, moral ambiguity prevails if sacred objects are made to serve a non-religious purpose (Appadurai 1986a: 27). Taboos are invoked to prevent commodification but once the secret has been commodified, it loses its awesome nature. This having been said, it is very surprising that local painters should have selected secret practices as their principal theme. To what extent is their work at odds with prevailing prohibitions? Malang Badji's paintings only depict the public celebrations of secret ceremonies. His paintings do not portray anything that might be defined as taboo (*nyau-nyau*). The paintings by Omar Camara, however, do reveal scenes that women and other non-initiates are not supposed to witness. His paintings of Jola initiations depict scenes at the sacred forest. They portray the novices secluded at the forest, facing an officiant who

Figure 8.2 'Detail' by Omar Camara, representing the mystery of the Kankurang (Photo: Ferdinand de Jong)

sprinkles consecrated water over them. Camara also made numerous paintings of the Kankurang masquerade (see Figure 8.2). Camara legitimises his depiction of the secret with an academic discourse on art, claiming to represent the transfiguration of the Kankurang mask. In much the same way as European Christian art represents Jesus as transfigured, Camara glorifies sacred places and performances. Although this line of reasoning may make sense in the art world, I doubt that it is acceptable to those inhabitants of Casamance who are not initiated in art-historical discourse. So what popular discourse do Badji and Camara invoke to legitimise their depictions of the sacred?

Both painters are versatile in articulating their points of view on the meaning of their work. Despite the differences in their age, ethnic extraction, styles and techniques, the discourses they produce are strikingly similar. This seems to indicate a more general and widespread discourse on the ritual practices they both depict. Both artists articulate an anti-modernisation discourse. They regret the effect modernity has on tradition, which are considered irreconcilable. This is manifest in their paintings that tend to portray either traditional or modern scenes. The paintings depicting modern life contain many signs associated with modernity. The urban scenes show crowded streets teeming with cyclists, cars and buses, and there are no trees.

The traditional images, however, are usually set in a rural environment without traces of modernity. I once noticed that Omar Camara used a photograph for his portrayal of an initiation camp, and the photograph had been taken in the city of Ziguinchor. The painting was a literal reproduction of the image except for the brick wall in the background, which had been replaced by a vista of lush greenery. This was no exception. All the paintings focusing on 'tradition' depict uncontaminated village life (cf. Svašek 1997: 40). The artists produce a dichotomous imagery of *la tradition* versus *le modernisme*.[1]

By now, it should be clear why these artists produce images of tradition. They fear that traditional ceremonies are bound to vanish in the process of modernisation. Badji represents them on canvas to preserve 'traces'. Badji considers it his responsibility to preserve the ancient rites in art. Omar Camara articulates his responsibility in an even more pronounced way. He too firmly believes that initiation rituals and the Kankurang masquerade will vanish in the process of modernisation and feels that 'today's youth simply amuses itself with sacred ritual'. Like his fellow townsmen, Camara welcomes the policy of the town dignitaries in prohibiting any more Kankurang performances in town. His commitment to this policy originates in his concern with preserving tradition. This same commitment is what motivates him to depict the masquerade. He has set himself the goal of creating a legacy for future generations: 'Il faut laisser une mémoire' ('We have to keep a memory'). On several occasions, Camara has invited secondary school classes to come and see his exhibitions and discuss the paintings. He also exhibits his work at secondary schools in Ziguinchor. His aim is to induce students to reflect upon their 'cultural heritage'. Apparently, Casamance artists have embraced the salvage paradigm. This paradigm, as defined by Clifford, 'reflects a desire to rescue something "authentic" out of destructive historical changes' (1989: 73). Both artists situate themselves within this paradigm and have accepted their responsibilities to save traditions. Their art is functional and plays a social role. Salvation is intricately related to the conceptualisation of cultural practices as 'tradition' (Clifford 1989). So the artists store traces of tradition to stimulate their remembrance and prevent their erasure by modernisation. An interesting contrast with popular art in Zaire becomes palpable. There, artists neither define their art against tradition nor toward modernisation (Szombati-Fabian and Fabian 1976: 18). In Casamance, however, painters define their art against the predicament of modernity and toward the conservation of tradition, if only through remembrance. The memory produced by these artists is restorative, rather than progressive (cf. Fabian 1996).

In producing traces of tradition, the painters cannot help but select some traditions as more valuable than others, and they thus construct a corpus of 'traditions' they identify with. Malang Badji considers himself a Jola artist and focuses on Jola traditions in his work, although he was raised in a Mandinko milieu and is fluent in Mandinko. He recognises that Jola and Mandinko have certain cultural practices in common: 'We live in community. We share our customs.' But in his art, he concentrates on Jola ritual. A similar avoidance of the representation of cultural interaction is evident in Camara's works of art and self-identification. Camara identifies as either Bambara or Mandinko, and admits to having undergone Wolof transculturation in Dakar. He considers himself uprooted (*déraciné*). After his return from Dakar to Ziguinchor, he decided to portray his presumed cultural background in order to recover his self: 'pour se reconnaître, pour se retrouver'. Instead of thematising cultural hybridity, his art reflects a strategic preference for the selective presentation of 'pure' cultural traditions. All the rituals represented in his paintings can be classified as either Jola or Mandinko. Wolof or Western 'influences' on local rituals do not figure in his portrayals of Casamance ritual. Hybridity is negated.

In an article on the performance by Aboriginal painters for an American audience, Myers suggests that painting is an event of performing oneself for others (Myers 1994). Painting enables artists to construct an identity and in doing so, they tend to select from and transform their own experiences. The question arises as to what induced our artists to present themselves in this and not in any other way. Why do their works of art negate hybridity? I suggest that the answers should be sought in the prevalence of several connected popular discourses. First, the discourse on ethnicity emphasises a need for ethnic purity. As already noted, among Muslim Jola this discourse focuses on the pre-Islamic past. But not only Muslims are interested in an imagined authenticity, presumably found in a pristine, precolonial society. Catholics, too, have become increasingly interested in their 'roots'. The Catholic Church, in particular after the Second Vatican Council, has made sustained efforts to reconcile its dogma with local practices, encouraging the production of a discourse on Casamance and Jola particularity (Foucher 2005). Although the discourse on ethnic purity is not limited to Casamance – *retour aux sources* is a national Senegalese discourse – the quest for authenticity is particularly strong in Casamance. As a matter of course, this quest is connected to the salvage discourse, which qualifies contemporary traditions as 'polluted' by modernity. Thus the works of art depict traditions that need to be salvaged.

THE ART MARKET

Malang Badji and Omar Camara consider it a social obligation to leave traces and construct a cultural heritage for future generations. Yet what they proclaim to be social responsibilities may also be construed as instances of salesmanship. After all, they need to sell their paintings to make a living and their themes need to appeal to consumers. Tourists constitute one category of potential buyers. Here I would briefly like to examine the Casamance art market and the destination of art works once they have been sold.

At the start of the era of mass tourism to the Third World in the 1970s, the Casamance region was immediately presented as one of the major attractions of Senegal. A great deal of attention was devoted to the region in French travel guides, only surpassed by the attention devoted to Dakar and Gorée (Copans 1978: 121). The Casamance region has indeed become one of the principal tourist destinations in Senegal and tourist facilities greatly expanded in the 1970s and 1980s. Tourism has been a mixed blessing to the inhabitants of Casamance, since land was sometimes expropriated for the construction of hotels. The first anthropological studies on tourism indeed focused on the disruptive impact tourism would have on the host communities (Smith 1977). It was felt that tourism would be detrimental to the cohesion of the host communities. Anthropologists feared that tourism would contribute to the commodification of local culture, which did indeed occur (Graburn 1976; Greenwood 1977). In recent decades, however, a great deal has changed in tourism studies and earlier assumptions have been replaced by research grounded in a much more complex reality. Tourism can be appropriated by locals to further their own goals (Tilley 1997). Indeed, the Casamance artists clearly benefit from tourism since the tourists are their customers.

Like much of twentieth-century African art, Casamance art is partially market driven. Malang Badji likes to proclaim his artistic freedom and social independence – in much the same way Western painters do. Yet, in addition to his large canvases, he produces small paintings – A4 size – that are more attractive to travelling tourists. The size is adjusted to suit the customers' convenience. It is also significant that Badji's cabin is strategically located at Carabane beach, a tourist resort. Omar Camara depends less on tourism, but he is equally dependent on foreigners, especially development aid workers. Both artists also sell their work to expatriates with a taste for the arts. This is why they regularly exhibit their paintings at shows in Ziguinchor, where the expatriate community lives. Thus the situation is very similar to the one in Ghana, where Svašek observes that Ghanaian artists 'like to believe that their work is free from commercial constraints, [yet they] do adapt at times to consumer demands' (Svašek 1997: 42).

These consumers are not so much interested in preserving traces of tradition. They wish to purchase a souvenir that reminds them of the Casamance region and provides them with a competitive means of distinction at home. What better suits their need than a painting depicting a local tradition? The paintings are unique status markers and signs of local colour. Representations of tradition become signs collected by the postmodern tourist (Urry 1990). The fact that the paintings represent local colour is their most important selling point. Camara has exhibited his work several times in

Dakar, but was less successful at selling his paintings to Dakar-based expatriates and conference delegates. Representations of ceremonies do not sell well beyond the confines of their place of performance.

The artists produce auto-ethnographic representations to preserve traces of tradition. The discourse on salvage inspires the artists in their artistic production but their own need to survive obliges them to sell their works of art. The commodification of their works leads to their geographic dispersal to expatriate and European living rooms, including my own. The paintings lose their specific local use value as soon as they are successfully marketed. Yet there is this striking convergence in the discursive positions of the artist, the tourist and the anthropologist: they are all interested in signs of locality. The representations of local rituals become commodities in a global industry of ethnic specificity (cf. Steiner 1994: 93; Van Binsbergen 1995: 34). Studies on African art often deny that ethnicity is an important determinant in its production and consumption (Vogel and Ebong 1991: 26; Fabian 1998: 2), but the paintings by Casamance artists are clearly signs of 'ethnic traditions' in a global sign economy.

THE POLITICS OF ART

Casamance works of art have various destinations. But the works of art become subject to a third trajectory in yet another context that gives yet another meaning to Camara's oeuvre. In this section, I examine the politicisation of Camara's art in an exhibition at the Alliance Française in Ziguinchor. The Alliance Française is one of the cultural institutes financed by the French government to support its worldwide policy of 'francophonie'. As such, the institute promotes the French language in particular and French culture in general. Although this goal is still of primary relevance, the Alliance now also explicitly aims to promote cultural expressions of the population in the host country. The Alliance promotes the production and consumption of plays and other cultural performances of originally Western design in locally appropriated ways. In Ziguinchor the Alliance is one of the two formal institutions to promote the diffusion of 'high' culture.[2]

The exhibition at the Alliance was staged in 1995, under the heading of 'Cultural Dialogue: Initiation in Jola and Mandinko Milieu'. Camara exhibited thirty-seven paintings related in one way or another to the overall theme. A brief overview of the paintings should suffice to give an impression. There was *Retour Exilé*, a key work in Camara's career because it addresses his return from Dakar to Casamance. Then there was a series of paintings portraying novices and scenes from initiation practices, including paintings of the Kankurang mask. Prices varied from 30,000 CFA to 300,000 CFA (US$50 to US$500). The catalogue, written by Omar Camara, contained a brief introduction on the theme of the exhibition, saying that social diversity and mutual respect all depend on cultural dialogue.[3] The catalogue also argued that cultural dialogue contributes to 'development'. But in contemporary Casamance, such general concepts easily acquire very specific connotations. Every Casamançais recognises that the economic development of the Casamance region depends on the ending of the armed conflict that opposes the separatist movement MFDC to the Senegalese state. The exhibition at the Alliance could not help being situated in that political context.

Ziguinchor's cultural elite and a number of politicians attended the opening. The Minister of Culture and the governor of Ziguinchor were represented by delegates, and the French director of the Alliance and the mayor of Ziguinchor gave speeches. In his opening address, the director of the Alliance said, 'Jola and Mandinko culture are two pillars of Casamance culture, *therefore* of Senegalese culture [my italics].'[4] This statement clearly situated the exhibition in the political context of the struggle for regional independence and the regime's attempt to contain that struggle. Local and national media covered the event and publicised the exhibition as a political statement. One national newspaper said, 'If peace in Casamance depends on a dialogue, it should primarily be a cultural dialogue.'[5] The exhibition thus acquired a political meaning that was so clear that Camara started feeling uneasy. Camara had never claimed that his work contributed to the political peace process. Since he knew any political commitment could be dangerous, he refrained from taking political sides. He was afraid that the MFDC would interpret any support of the peace process as a rejection of their armed struggle for Casamance independence.[6] But Omar Camara could not keep his art from acquiring a political meaning. In the end, he accepted Socialist Party patronage. A year after the exhibition I met Camara at a Socialist Party rally. Apparently, he had accepted his co-optation by the dominating political party and fulfilled his role as party member. Several exhibitions resulted from his new political connections.

Camara's paintings on Jola and Mandinko traditions acquired explicit political meaning. This was a rather remarkable development, as Camara's works at the exhibition consisted of paintings of 'ethnic traditions'. Ever since independence the Senegalese government has refused formally to recognise ethnicity as a field of political identification (Gellar 1995: 119). The first president, Léopold Sédar Senghor, inaugurated a prudent management of ethnicity. He himself belonged to an ethnic and religious minority – Senghor was a Catholic of Serer extraction – and he introduced a number of laws to curb ethnic tension in Senegal (Makhtar Diouf 1994: 109). French was adopted as the official language so as not to privilege any of the country's indigenous languages. Senghor's thoughts on *Négritude* provided the Senegalese state with a theoretical basis for the creation of a national identity that supposedly superseded ethnic particularities (Skurnik 1965: 366). But in the shadow of this official policy, Wolof became the dominant language and Mouride Islam the dominant religion (Cruise O'Brien 1998). The Senegalese state tacitly accepted and reinforced this Wolof–Mouride hegemony. This led some authors to argue that the Senegalese state has never been able to cope with ethnicity except in a clandestine way (Diaw and Diouf 1992: 30). Moreover, Senegal's national ideology completely failed in Casamance (Mamadou Diouf 1994; Faye 1994). In the 1990s, the crisis forced the Senegalese regime to look for an alternative to its unsuccessful strategy of nation-building. The regime then encouraged reflexion on how ethnic and cultural differences could be made subservient to Senegal's national development (de Jong 2005).

Senghor's cultural discourse emphasised the need for *métissage* and *convergences culturelles*. His ambitious ideals of *Négritude* have been translated into a policy that was to create a Senegalese unity based on a cultural dialogue between ethnic groups. These ideals were also implemented in Senegal's art policy (M'Bengue 1973; Ebong 1991; Snipe 1998). Omar Camara adopted the idea of *convergences culturelles* as the motto for his exhibition at the Alliance. His art was co-opted to serve the imagination of a national community of *métis*. Obviously, the political meaning attributed to Camara's art is completely at odds with the meaning he gave it on other occasions. In his effort to store traces of tradition, Camara reified traditional practices into uncontaminated 'traditions'. However, by way of his strategic choice of the exhibition's motto, he made his work relevant to the political project of nation-building. His success was a result of his discursive competence, i.e. his capacity to adapt and shift his ideological stance. Paintings that portrayed different Jola and Mandinko traditions were interpreted as representing different aspects of a single tradition shared by Casamance's various ethnic groups.

CONCLUSION

Casamance art may acquire various meanings depending on the context where its signification occurs. Interestingly, the meanings attached to the works of art sometimes contradict each other and which meaning prevails depends on the signifying context. However, the art's multivocality ultimately depends on the artist's competence to switch his discursive position and emphasise a specific aspect of his identity, painting or the process of painting. Omar Camara's energetic attitude and his eloquent academic art talk qualify him better for this type of versatility than the established and introverted Malang Badji. Moreover, Camara paints Jola as well as Mandinko traditions, whereas Badji only focuses on Jola traditions. Camara successfully plays various cards. In situating their art in divergent contexts, the Casamance artists do not construct a single and stable identity, but multiple and shifting ones (cf. Svašek 1997: 50–2). When they present their works of art as traces of tradition, the artists situate themselves in a discourse on modernity. In this discourse, modernity is thought to progress at the expense of tradition. Then, the artists present themselves as the heirs and preservers of specific ethnic traditions. In the words of Omar Camara, 'La tradition est une carte d'identité.'

Self-representation through traditions has become an integral part of Senegalese modernity. The initiation ceremonies and masked performances that the artists have selected to represent in paintings are not selected for their secretive nature. They are selected by the painters because they can be made to stand for 'tradition'. It is remarkable, however, that the secretive nature of some of these performances has not prevented Camara from depicting them. Some of the scenes represented in the paintings could indeed be marked as 'secret' by Jola or Mandinko initiates. However, Camara has never met any opposition to the exposition of his works on the grounds that they 'divulge' secrets. The reason for this, I suppose, is that all those who are initiated in the secrets of initiation and masked performances tend to share Camara's discourse on the loss of tradition and the obligation to restore it. The salvage paradigm is widely spread in Casamance society and the artists' argument that their work contributes to the preservation of tradition is shared by the viewers of their work. This discourse thus legitimises the representation of secrets, justifying their revelation. Secrets are nowadays represented in order to be restored.

9

WRITING SECRECY

Concealment and revelation are part and parcel of the fieldwork experience. Secrecy is performed not only between Casamançais: they often performed secrecy in interaction with me. Secrets and their revelation are often ambiguous, or deliberately meant to produce ambiguity (Piot 1993). I was often at a loss as to what was secret and what not. Often, it was hard to tell whether secrecy was performed for all or just for me. Yet the ambiguity of this fieldwork experience is usually not represented in the ethnographic text. In ethnographic texts fieldwork is often made to appear as the gradual penetration of hitherto hidden knowledge (Clifford 1988; Gable 1997). Ethnographic authority is built upon mastery of the secret. This raises the question how secrecy is represented in ethnographic texts, as the question of ethnographic authority remains relevant (Clifford and Marcus 1986; Clifford 1988; Geertz 1988; James et al. 1997; Sanjek 1990). We need to re-examine every aspect of the way in which we make representations. Here, I would like to conclude by examining how the rhetoric of secrecy has contributed to a particular ethnographic understanding of culture and how it has sustained the positivist distinction between subject and object in ethnographic writing. This chapter therefore deals with the politics and poetics of secrecy. Rather than assuming that a focus on the poetics of ethnography leads us away from its politics (Said 1989), this final chapter works with the assumption that poetics and politics are intricately intertwined.

SECRETS AS BOUNDARIES

Secrecy as a metaphor in the construction of ethnographic authority contributes to our paradigmatic belief that cultures are bounded. The metaphor of secrecy allegorically creates cores of culture that are set apart, and therefore require revelation through ethnography. The metaphor of secrecy therefore needs to be exposed as instrumental in the production of boundaries. That alterity should be spatially distributed is problematic, and it becomes even more problematic in an age of globalisation. If we can no longer think of culture as territorialised (Gupta and Ferguson 1992; Malkki 1995), then we need to acknowledge that the anthropological 'field', in Africa or elsewhere, can no longer be spatially defined. It is no

longer productive to posit impermeable cultural boundaries. Here, I hope
to demonstrate that secrecy is in fact an intersubjective performance that
includes the ethnographer in the 'field'.

It is not hard to establish that secrecy serves to establish boundaries (cf.
Barth 1969). In fact, in the previous chapters numerous occasions have been
provided where the secret is performed to establish a boundary, notably
between the sexes, between ethnic groups or between political subjects
and the state. In the most general sense, a secret establishes a boundary
between those 'in the know' and those excluded from the secret knowledge.
To what effect secrecy is used, however, depends very much on the context.
For instance, it can be argued that Jola male initiation primarily serves to
demarcate a realm of male ritual activity from which women are excluded.
Such a realm allows the construction of a particular masculinity, based
on ritual separation and instruction in male esoteric lore. Arguably, male
initiation not only structures the male population into a hierarchy of age
sets, but also the entire population into separate genders.

The male initiates are instructed into the secret knowledge transmitted
in the ritual process. While they become fully entitled to this knowledge by
virtue of their initiation, women are deliberately excluded from it. Women
would never expect to be initiated into male secret lore, just as men would
never expect to be initiated into the female secret lore as transmitted
through female initiation rites. In other words, the performance of secrecy
should not be understood as a power struggle between those 'in the know'
and those who want to know. The excluded are expected to play the role of
non-initiates and they usually do so. In that sense, secrecy is a performance
that requires the cooperation of the members of the excluded group. Here,
we can see that secrecy not only excludes, but even includes those who are
de facto excluded. The excluded become complicit in the performance of
secrecy that excludes them. The construction of boundaries through secrecy
is therefore a highly complex form of interaction in which the excluded are
fully aware of their necessary presence.

In the light of this, it is not surprising that the actual secret lore is often
known to the excluded. As mothers, wives or girlfriends, women do access
parts of the secret lore from which they are actively excluded in ritual
contexts. Even researchers like myself can sometimes access the secret lore
denied in other contexts. The boundary of the secret can be permeable.
While conducting fieldwork in the Mandinko initiation, I had several
conversations with a blacksmith who had been organising a number of these
events. In one of our meetings he told me the origin myth of circumcision
and the Kankurang mask and he solemnly concluded his story by saying:
'This is the story I tell the initiates in the sacred forest,' implying that this
was the secret knowledge transmitted to the novices in the sacred forest.
Secret knowledge can apparently be transmitted without the formal initi-

ation of the anthropologist. The blacksmith did not explicitly refer to me as a non-initiate, and thereby defined the knowledge as accessible to me. Secrecy does not depend on the contents of the secret, but on the 'speech environment' that defines the status of knowledge (Bellman 1984).

At other times, however, I was deliberately excluded from what was then defined as secret. The most salient example relates to an embarrassing moment in my fieldwork when I wanted to explore the social drama that had led to the execution of two men by the Kankurang mask and its companions in Marsassoum (Chapter 6). When my assistant and I settled in the town with the intention of examining this event, the prosecution of the perpetrators was still under way and the judicial process had not yet been concluded. We were not aware of this. But our inquiries into the matter were quickly noticed and our presence was identified as being of possible harm to the perpetrators. At one point, a young man came to see us and explained to us the delicacy of our research topic, adding that any person willing to inform us faced a similar verdict to those men who had disclosed the mask's secret. We had no alternative but to leave the town. Imposed silence prevented us from producing the knowledge that, the culprits imagined, might have had an impact on the judicial process.

Mandinko men consider the secret of the Kankurang masquerade the core secret of male initiation. This is why they can be swiftly mobilised to defend the secret, or when it has been divulged, to avenge its desecration. However, in the case of my obstructed research in Marsassoum, secrecy did not pertain so much to the masquerade itself, but to the executions allegedly perpetrated by the masquerade. The secrecy with regard to the executions hardly pertained to the core of Mandinko culture. It was performed to protect the culprits from persecution. This performance of secrecy was part of an established mode of cultural performance, but the conditions under which it was re-enacted were not those of a pristine, bounded culture. Secrecy was performed in order to create an impermeable boundary vis-à-vis the court. And therefore the inquiring anthropologist was excluded. Indeed, what can be conceived as the core of culture is in fact a cultural mode of performance to negotiate relations to the world at large. The preceding chapters demonstrate that secrecy is the cultural performance by means of which men and women in Casamance negotiate their place in the world. Secrecy enables them to domesticate a colonial city, to regulate international migration and their participation in the market economy, to incorporate Islam and consumer culture. In short, it enables the Casamançais to be modern on their own terms.

THE CORE OF CULTURE

Anthropologists use a variety of metaphors to establish ethnographic authority. One of the best known of textual strategies describes the arrival of the anthropologist among the people to be studied, his or her initial confusion, the separation between the ethnographer and the Other, and the gradual rapprochement through the establishment of rapport. Geertz's arrival among the Balinese is the most often quoted example (Geertz 1973). Another textual strategy relates to the anthropologist's initiation. The initiation of the anthropologist into the secrets of the tribe authorises the ethnographic text. Clifford (1988: 53) has made this argument with regard to the work of Marcel Griaule. What was to become a classic ethnography (Griaule 1948) was entirely framed in terms of an initiation. Griaule's magnum opus *Dieu d'eau* is allegedly based on revelations made to the author, and whether Griaule was indeed initiated into secret cultural knowledge or had simply been told a number of intricate improvisations by his principal informant, Ogotemmêli, is beside the point. What matters is the rhetoric used by Griaule. His ethnographic authority rests upon his alleged initiation into the deep cultural knowledge of the Dogon. Initiation provides the organising metaphor and evokes the deepening of understanding that accrues to long-term field research (Clifford 1988: 81). Many monographs relate how the researcher gradually learns about the secrets of the Other. The ethnographer undergoes a 'parallel' initiation: 'As an initiate, the researcher receives and interprets revelations' (Clifford 1988: 84). The metaphor of initiation in Griaule's work has been fully documented, but is not restricted to his ethnography. In fact, Marxist anthropologists have just as artfully employed the trope. Let me quote from Maurice Godelier's *The Making of Great Men* (1986), an ethnography on male domination among the New Guinea Baruya:

> One may easily imagine, on reading these pages, just how much time and confidence it must have taken on the part of the Baruya to introduce me to their way of thinking and allow me to see (as they have expressed it) not only the leaves, branches, and the trunk, but also some of the most secretly buried roots of their thought. (Godelier 1986: xiii)

Godelier confidently asserts that he was trusted by the Baruya – a precondition for successful fieldwork. He suggests that, due to the appropriate conduct of fieldwork, the Baruya themselves took the initiative to part with their secret knowledge and allowed him to see 'the most secretly buried roots of their thought'. Ethnographies often portray fieldwork as 'a gradual penetration in which surface appearances – facades – give way to deeper truths' (Gable 1997: 227). These deeper truths are often understood to constitute the core of culture. Indeed, when ethnographers talk about male initiation, secrecy and secret societies, they often assume they are dealing with the hard core of culture. In a parallel initiation, the ethnographer accesses the deep, hidden truths of the Other. The deep truths of the Other are subsequently revealed to us by the ethnographer. Let us return to Gode-lier's preface:

> I must ask the reader who may sometimes be tempted, according to the lights of his or her own philosophy or mood, to regard the secrets confided to me by the Baruya as derisory, grotesque, or even obscene, to remember that for them they are an essential part of their identity, a vital, sacred force inherited from the past, on which they depend in order to withstand all those voluntary or involuntary pressures that our world brings to bear upon them, often enough in perfectly good faith, but more often still deliberately. (Godelier 1986: xiii)

This is a complex sentence, in which negative evaluations of Baruya secrets are suggested to the reader who is not initiated and as yet unaware of the real meanings of the secrets. The author, in contrast, recognises the impor-tance of secrets to the Baruya: they constitute an essential part of their identity, even a sacred force inherited from the past. Godelier defines the secrets as the core of Baruya culture – an essential core that remains in times of turmoil – on which the Baruya depend in order to withstand change. Change, however, comes to the Baruya from outside, from 'our world'. Godelier is sympathetic towards the Baruya, and the allegory of redemption voluntarily offered to the Baruya is clearly noticeable (Clifford 1986). But it seems the Baruya stand little chance of surviving in a world in which pres-sures are deliberately brought to bear upon them.

Godelier's preface is not idiosyncratic. Secrets are often portrayed as the hard core of culture, which anthropologists have set themselves the task of revealing. While my argument only relates to the metaphors of secrecy and revelation, I hypothesise that a good deal of narrative anthropology, even if it does not use the trope of initiation in a literal sense, still displays a similar rhetorical structure. We expect monographs to make a cumulative argument, and we always hope for a final, deep ethnographic 'plot' that makes the parts of the monograph fit. The 'plot' provides ethnographic cohesion. In other words, ethnography often takes the form of a narrative of gradual revelation, whereby facades give way to deeper truths. In fact, Geertzian 'thick description' casts the anthropological narrative into a mould that privileges gradual revelation (Geertz 1973). As a form of layered description, it suggests that a cultural core is only accessible through a series of revelations.

MY 'INITIATION'

The literary turn in anthropology relegated scientific approaches and emphasised that ethnography is first of all an exercise in writing. The literary turn also established that cultural knowledge is created in conversa-tions between fieldworkers and informants. Anthropological texts, it was asserted, need to be self-reflexive about the process of writing culture, from the first fieldnote to the final epilogue. Since the literary turn, we have realised that authors construct authority for their ethnographies by writing about their own initiations.

Many monographs that explicitly analyse initiation ceremonies give an account of how the author (usually a man) was initiated into the secrets of the tribe. The authors claim to have been allowed to attend 'secret' rituals. It is part of the same rhetoric to suggest that such permission can only be obtained as a result of an established rapport. Reading such claims always gives me a certain feeling of envy. For one reason or another, I never established such apparently good relations, or, if I did, my introduction to the 'secret' proved disappointing. What had been concealed to me proved of very limited relevance once it was revealed. Or the revelation of the secret happened in such a way that my access to the esoteric lore was immediately framed as illegitimate. Invariably, my presence at secret places was taken as a violation of established modes of revelation (cf. Taussig 1999).

At no point during my fieldwork in Casamance did I undergo one of the local initiation ceremonies. I was not given the occasion to become initiated. Others have entered the sacred forest, although to my knowledge none of the anthropologists working in Casamance have been initiated. Elsewhere, however, anthropologists have been initiated and have acquired full command of esoteric lore. Several authors give particularly dramatic and moving accounts of their initiations, often driven by the experience of exclusion (Van Binsbergen 1991). Indeed, power relations remain central to the performance of secrecy and initiation. Although I never submitted myself to formal procedures of initiation in order to establish a rapport and productive relationships, exclusion certainly made me eager to learn more about the secret. This is apparent, for instance, from my experiences in a particular initiation ceremony, which I was able to attend because the sons of my host were participating in it. I travelled with my host and his family to his village of birth where several of his sons were to be initiated by means of a week of seclusion in the bush. The elder sons of my host who had already been initiated and therefore were allowed to enter and leave the initiation camp informed me about it. They complained about the bad organisation of the entire ceremony and, remarkably, shared their misgivings with me. Again, the secrecy pertaining to everything that happens in the sacred forest was not so carefully observed. Although I was informed about the proceedings in the sacred forest I also felt terribly excluded when, after a week of seclusion, the initiates were taken to the river for a ritual bath and I was the only man in the village not allowed to accompany them, being left in the company of women who profited from the men's absence by mocking them and their religious piety. Unclassifiable as a man, I found myself in the company of women who ignored my presence. I had become invisible.

Surprisingly, after the ritual bath of the initiates my host invited me to visit the sacred forest. He suggested that I should make a gift to the initiates, who would then pray for me. I was eager enough to accept such a *mise en scène*. So we set out for the sacred forest, going past the bend in the path that had for days marked the edge of the forbidden. While heading for the forest, we met a number of men returning from it and some politely asked where I was going. All seemed satisfied with the explanation provided by my host, but when we finally got to the place where the initiates were gathered, I felt uneasy. The initiates were gathered in the shade of some mango trees, while their guardians and elders oversaw them. There was not much else to see. My host informed the elders about the reasons for my presence. There was confusion. My host then showed the 1,000 francs, explaining I wanted to offer the money to the initiates. One man stood up and told my host: 'Youssouf, what you have done no one has ever done before!' The men started a heated discussion and I wanted to leave, but my assistant said the harm had already been done. Then people calmed down and actually started praying. All of them sank to their knees and raised their hands. Dozing boys were woken up to join the prayer. I was in utter confusion. Luckily, the prayer lasted for only half a minute and everyone got up. My host then suggested I should take some pictures, and although I had been told on numerous occasions that there is no worse sacrilege than a photograph of the secret, I could not resist the request. Some men explicitly asked to be photographed. Having taken a few pictures, I left, complaining to my host about the awkward position he had put me in. I was very embarrassed.

This set of transactions was utterly complex. While my curiosity drove me towards accepting the offer of my host, I was from the outset most hesitant. I had in fact become sensitive to the game of secrecy, and had acquired a measure of understanding of its practice. When we approached the sacred forest, I felt excitement and anxiety about the intrusion I was about to make. My intrusion into the realm of the secret did not fail to produce the expected results. However, once the men had calmed down there seemed to be no real issue. My awkwardness and embarrassment may be taken as indicative of the empathy conventionally required of the anthropologist: I had internalised the attitudes to secrecy of my hosts. A formal initiation was not required to acquire a measure of cultural competence in the performance of secrecy. Indeed, secrecy is an intersubjective experience that draws the excluded in.

FORBIDDEN REPRESENTATIONS

It goes without saying that the representation of secret practices is hazardous, certainly for those formally required to keep the secret. Only under certain conditions can the secret be represented and these conditions are to a large extent determined by politics. Let me give a vignette of an experience I had photographing a mask. When I conducted my research on the Kankurang masquerade, I was very eager to take a picture of the masked figure. So when I finally had the opportunity, I focused my camera on the Kankurang dancing on the backs of his guardians lying stretched out on the street. But one of the guardians suddenly appeared before me, demanded my camera and grabbed it out of my hands. This left me puzzled but after some negotiating, I was allowed to 'buy' my camera back. Of course, this can be interpreted as a seizure triggered by the atmosphere of licence that prevails at Kankurang performances, but the guardians legitimised their action by claiming that I could reproduce the photograph and turn it into a postcard. This, they said, is what they wanted to prevent. I assured them this was not my intention and I was allowed to keep the film.

Time and again I was told that the mask should not be photographed. Indeed, there is a widespread belief in Casamance that close observation of the mask deprives the mask of its mystical power. Undoubtedly, this belief is partly informed by the conditions for a successful performance. The mask's terrifying character must not be taken lightly by non-initiates. Spectators, even if they do not believe in the mask's occult power, should at least feign fear so as not to undermine its mystical reputation. This is why bystanders are forbidden to photograph the mask and thus nullify its awesome nature. The performers want to prevent the 'objectification' of the masquerade. Their imposition of a prohibition on representation is a protest against ethnographic objectification. The secret is thus reproduced in interaction with the anthropologist. Secrecy thus engages with the anthropological project and includes the anthropologist in the performance by denying him any possibility to exercise the gaze.

The prohibition on representation does not only apply to masquerades, but to anything shrouded in secrecy. At the male initiation celebration in Thionck Essyl, a French team had permission to record the ceremony on film. The permission was given in a contract with dignitaries of one of the two factions in the village (Chapter 4). In exchange for the permission, the ward was given electronic equipment for their youth club. The documentary that resulted from the collaboration was broadcast on Senegalese television. Apart from showing the preparations and public processions in the village, the documentary also showed the ritual bath of the novices. The indignation over what was thus revealed was immense among the inhabitants of the other wards of the village. According to the members of this faction, some of the things in the documentary were taboo (*nyau-nyau*) and should never have been shown on television: they should not have been recorded in the first place. In contrast, the members of the ward that had allowed the film to be made argued that the ritual bath was a public affair and that no secrets were revealed. More precisely, they argued that this ritual bath took place after the public demonstration of the novices at the edge of the sacred forest, and that the novices were no longer subject to prohibitions by the time they had their ritual bath.

The case shows that the recording of a particular performance, in denying its secret character, was seen, by some, as a desecration. But what can be recorded and what cannot is clearly subject to negotiation and not determined by a set of formal rules. Hegemony is never realised and the secret always requires a measure of voluntary complicity on the part of the excluded. Such complicity can be withheld and in a number of preceding chapters demonstrations of such non-compliance have been given. The secret is always threatened by exposure by those whose interests are not at stake. And even when the excluded do not contest their exclusion, their complicity does not necessarily amount to awesome reproduction of the secret. In fact, various chapters demonstrated how the secret is time and again exposed, transgressed, reinvented and restored. Secrets always need to be negotiated between those 'in the know' and the excluded. Secrecy therefore always amounts to a performance of power.

ETHNOGRAPHIC REVELATIONS

In the field I noticed a wide variety of reactions towards my professed aim of studying 'traditions'. Some people – but only some – showed outright hostility to my research and were not prepared to transmit secret knowledge. One sacred forest officiant refused to talk with me, saying, 'Whites only want to discover our secrets and disclose them in their books.' Fieldwork is not always a matter of dialogue. I frequently found myself excluded as men and women denied me access to certain places and performances. However, while secrecy may create boundaries, it nevertheless engages those excluded from the secret, even without formalised initiation. For anthropologists who depend on revelations – even if their significance remains to be established – secrecy produces a moral binding. As a result of this, the presentation of secret lore in ethnography is often presented as a moral issue (Godelier 1986; Baum 1999; Reed 2003). Anthropologists have always been cautious to reveal what they see as secret information. While the ethnographer's rapport enables him to penetrate secrets, his moral obligations arguably prohibit him/her from bringing secret knowledge into the public domain. The disclosure of secrets is indeed a morally ambiguous area, but the representation of secrets need not necessarily be seen as a disclosure. After all, ethnography cannot be reduced to revelation of the secrets of the Other. This would be tantamount to conceptualising ethnography as revelation only. Ethnography is something else: it contextualises secrets in text. Whereas the moral binding of secrecy belongs to the field, the writing of ethnography separates secrets from the field. Ethnography transforms experience in the field into writing on the field, objectifying what was once a subjective experience. This objectification is comparable to the project that the performers of secrecy try to accomplish: writing secrets is complicit in the production of locality.

This study of secrecy has demonstrated that the performance of secrecy in Casamance mediates and mitigates the impact of the global market economy and the postcolonial state. Secrecy enables the inhabitants of Casamance to translate and transform these powers and bring them within their grasp. While secrecy as a mode of cultural performance may thus provide a popular mode of political action, it is clear that its efficacy resides primarily in performance. In performance secrecy can contribute to the production of locality, a sense of place. Ethnography is not a performance of secrecy, but may do justice to it. The revelations here are thus not meant to expose secrets, but to demonstrate how secrecy contributes to the production of an alternative modernity in which the performers of secrecy are at home. In April 2006 I received the following e-mail from a young friend in Senegal:

> I write this letter to greet you, to ask about your health and that of your family. As far as I am concerned, thank God. I remind you that our initiation ceremony will probably be held towards the 16th of July. For me this is the moment to quench myself with Jola civilisation. It is the most important occasion for a young Jola to learn about his own culture. I also like to know how life is in England. Is it a hospitable country?

NOTES

CHAPTER 1

1. See Tefft 1980 for a cross-cultural comparison of secret societies in a variety of settings. See also Blok's historical study on the evolution of the Sicilian Mafia in a context of Italian state formation (Blok 1988). There too, secrecy operates in a modern context.
2. For a critical discussion of Horton's theory, see Van Binsbergen 1981 and Baum 1999.
3. See Van der Klei 1989 for a Marxist analysis of the Jola initiation. His contribution will be discussed in subsequent chapters.
4. Gable criticises the rhetorical form making fieldwork appear as a gradual penetration in which surface appearances – facades – give way to deeper truths (1997: 227). My fieldwork vignettes primarily serve to establish how I myself gradually learnt the language of secrecy, not secrets.
5. Goffman writes about the 'empty' and the 'inside' secret: 'These are ones whose possession marks an individual as being a member of a group and helps the group feel separate and different from those individuals who are not "in the know". Inside secrets give objective intellectual content to subjectively felt social distance' (Goffman 1959: 142). Of course, the latter observation can be reversed to account for the performative nature of secrecy: inside secrets may be performed to *create* social distance.
6. Secrecy is not necessarily the prerogative of the powerless. Cohen demonstrates that the Creoles of Sierra Leone, in organising themselves informally in freemason lodges, ascertained their access to the centre of the state (Cohen 1971, 1981). Their cohesion was effectuated through frequent socialising in secret lodges.
7. In his book on the African state, Bayart (1993) abandoned the notion of *mode populaire d'action politique* that he himself had coined a decade earlier. 'Politics of the belly' focuses entirely on how African elites appropriate the state and – in my view – overlooks the historical modes of resistance to the state. *L'État rhizome*, however, rampant, has its limits in the penetration of society and therefore continues to meet resistance.
8. The very concept of context has recently been criticised in an interesting collection of essays that examine the various ways in which anthropologists, and scholars in other disciplines, use and understand it (Dilley 1999). I do not claim to tackle the many and multifarious problems of this concept, but see my attempts below.
9. In her essay on the emerging paradigm of practice, Ortner had already predicted a turn towards this new research interest: '[...] until very recently, little effort has been put toward understanding how society and culture themselves are

produced and reproduced through human intention and action' (Ortner 1984: 158).

10. I borrow the term 'extraversion' from Bayart's work (1993), and use his spelling of the term. After all, its meaning in anthropological analysis differs substantially from its connotations in psychology.

CHAPTER 2

1. See Geschiere and Van der Klei 1987 and 1988; Barbier-Wiesser 1994; Darbon 1988; Diop 2002; Diouf 1994 and 2004; Evans 2003; Faye 1994; Foucher 2002; Gasser 2002; Marut 1999; and the special issue of the *Canadian Journal of African Studies* 39 (2), (2005): 'Contested Casamance/Discordante Casamance'.

2. Jola male initiation has been studied by quite a few scholars: Thomas 1965; Girard 1969; Schloss 1988; Van der Klei 1989; Linares 1992; Mark 1985 and 1992; and Baum 1999. Their contributions to our understanding of the ritual are discussed in Chapter 6. Jola female initiation has been examined by Thomas 1959; Linares 1992; Baum 1999; and Langeveld 2003.

3. In the local dialect (Gusilay, one of the numerous Jola dialects), the term used to denote male initiation is *garur*. Depending on the dialect, the Jola use different terms to denote male initiation. In Fogny, initiation is called *futamp* (cf. Linares 1992). The Jola of Niomoun (Thomas 1965), Diatock (Van der Klei 1989) and Esulalu (Linares 1992; Baum 1999) call their initiation *bukut*. The Ehing use the word *kombutsu* (Schloss 1988). The term *garur* only applies to male initiation in Thionck Essyl.

4. See Sapir 1970: 1346, note 2; Snyder 1981: 24; Van der Klei 1989: 94; Linares 1992: 63, 229, note 8.

5. See Loquay 1979: 261; Snyder 1981: 70–2; Van der Klei 1989: 122; Linares 1992: 56; Baum 1999: 29.

6. In most Jola villages, only the men have rice fields, but in Thionck Essyl women also inherit land. In Thionck Essyl each conjugal household has full control over its land.

7. Elsewhere in Lower Casamance, these shrines are called *ukin* (singular *bukin*). For an elaborate discussion of the meaning, form, ownership and location of the shrines, see Thomas 1959: 590 ff.; Mark 1985: 79–81 discusses their transformed meaning as a result of Islamisation. Linares 1992 has studied the impact of mandinkisation and Islamisation on the pivotal role shrines play in the regulation of social life. Baum 1999 demonstrates that the traditional Jola religion was capable of dealing with the social transformations that resulted from the Jola's insertion in the world economy.

8. This probably happened to the guardianship of the sacred forest of Thionk's subward Kafanta. The officiant Diuwaluti Diatta (*gatunum* Babudiubor) left his native subward Kafanta (Niaganan ward) to settle in another ward (Batine) and subsequently handed over the guardianship of Kafanta's sacred forest to his sister's son Udienkalil Niassy (see Chapter 4 for a discussion of the disputed legitimacy of this transfer).

9. The term used to denote the 'coming out' (*gapurem*) of the drums is also used for the 'coming out' of initiates from the sacred forest (or for masks coming out of the sacred forest). The term connotes the crossing of the boundary from the sacred to the profane.

10. See Douglas, who comments that 'ritual recognises the potency of disorder' (Douglas 1966: 95). Durkheim thought of effervescence as a requirement for making the sacred present (1915: 245–51).

11. In Diatock, a nearby Jola village, the same device is called *angheringheri*. The term is very similar to Mandinko *ngheringharo*, which suggests that *angheringheri* is a loanword (the prefix a- designates the singular). Schloss gives an accurate description of a similar practice among the Ehing in Lower Casamance (Schloss 1988: 71 ff.). He translates the Ehing term *apia kalu* as 'master of the forest'.

12. The meaning of the name of Assaye is in itself significant. In other contexts, the term *assaye* (plural *ussaye*) designates sorcerers. Thus the name Assaye itself denotes mystical power.

13. In Batine ward, several of the initiates were carrying *ejumbi* masks for the occasion. For a discussion of the meaning of the *ejumbi* mask (plural *sijumbi*) in Thionck Essyl's 1994 initiation, see Mark, De Jong and Chupin 1998: 42 ff. The history and meaning of this mask are more extensively discussed by Mark 1992.

14. In the past, sons were not initiated in the initiation following that of their fathers and had to wait for the next one. There had always been an intermediate generation between fathers and their sons. In 1962, however, sons were allowed to enter the sacred forest in the initiation following that of their fathers for the first time. Some Jola villages have recently allowed sons to be initiated *together* with their fathers. This is revolutionary because only a decade ago it was considered a grave transgression for a non-initiate to have children. The result is that today's initiation creates age sets in which fathers and sons are 'equal'.

15. According to Baum, the ostentatious killing of cattle as is characteristic of *bukut* (the name for the male initiation in Esulalu) is why *kahat* was abandoned and *bukut* became the preferred way of initiating men. The increased wealth of families resulting from their participation in the late eighteenth-century slave trade could thus be manifested (1999: 125).

16. See Chapter 3 for an analysis of the meaning of dress in initiations.

17. Enda Tiers-monde published a report containing quantitative data on female excision in Senegal (Mottin Sylla 1990). According to this report, 94 per cent of the Jola women (N = 147) were excised collectively and 6 per cent individually. Of all the Jola women 58 per cent had also undergone initiation (ibid.: 62). I cannot judge how representative these data are but it is clear that the number of respondents is small.

18. See Pélissier 1966: 797; Leary 1971: 242 ; Quinn 1972: 125 ; Mark 1985: 70 ; Linares 1992: 94.

19. Not all Muslim Jola are Qadiriyya, and some of them belong instead to the Tijaniyya brotherhood (Pélissier 1966: 808–11). In Thionck Essyl, where most of the research for this study was conducted, the Tijaniyya *tariqa* is disproportionately well-represented owing to the work by the Tukulor marabout Tierno Sy, who lived in the village (Mark 1985: 102–3; Pélissier 1966: 810; Loquay 1979: 9). Thomas and Cruise O'Brien note that Mouride proselytisers were particularly unsuccessful at converting the Jola (Thomas 1959: 778–9; Cruise O'Brien 1971: 194).

20. For a specification of these regional differentiations, see Pélissier 1966: 802–4 and Linares 1992. See Loquay 1979: 280–1 for a discussion of mandinkisation and labour division in Thionck Essyl, where part of the research for this study was conducted.

21. There are still many important differences between *gassus* and the girls' excision as performed among the Mandinko of Pakao. In Pakao, girls' excision and initiation are one and the same ritual (Schaffer and Cooper 1980: 99–101), in contrast to the Jola practice in Thionck Essyl where circumcision and initiation are separate rituals. The women of Thionck Essyl do not merely imitate Mandinko traditions; they reconfigure them in the process of imitation. Their

circumcision and initiation rituals are probably also patterned after the *male* model prevalent in Thionck Essyl.

CHAPTER 3

1. See Thomas 1959 and 1965; Girard 1969; Mark 1985 and 1992; Van der Klei 1989; Linares 1992; Baum 1999; and Langeveld 2003.
2. Thomas 1959, II: 702–3; Girard 1969: 87–115; Baum 1999: 101–3.
3. Cf. Thomas 1965: 97; Mark 1985: 122; Schloss 1988: 66; Van der Klei 1989: 155–7.
4. Opposition to the initiation also used to be strong among the Catholic missionaries (Baum 1990).
5. Mark asserts that in Thionck Essyl, the 1962 initiation was probably the last for these libations (1985: 123). I was unable to obtain unambiguous data about the sacrifices at the sacred forest. In this particular aspect, secrecy has served to conceal the possibly anti-Islamic nature of sacrifices at the sacred forest. Some anthropologists managed to enter the sacred forest and witnessed palm wine libations (Thomas 1965; Schloss 1988), but their communities of research were not Muslim. The only ethnography (Van der Klei 1989) that gives elaborate information about male initiation in a Muslim community does not address the issue of prayers and sacrifices at the sacred forest.
6. For a fine iconological analysis of the masks used during the initiation ritual, see Mark 1992.
7. There is no consensus among historians and anthropologists on when the Jola started to practise circumcision. The question is whether the Jola have always practised circumcision, or introduced this practice after conversion to Islam. The data provided by the various authors do not support an unambiguous answer. In non-Muslim communities on the southern shore of the Casamance River, circumcision is practised on the first day of the initiation retreat (Schloss 1988: 74–6). In 1965, in the non-Muslim village of Niomoun, the novices were also circumcised (Thomas 1965: 109). But in an earlier publication, Thomas suggests that circumcision among the Jola had always consisted of a symbolic incision. Removal of the foreskin was, he argues, a consequence of Islamisation (Thomas 1959, II: 700–1). Mark argues that novices normally undergo circumcision except in Muslim communities where most youths have already been circumcised. In that case, they receive a ritual scarification (Mark 1992: 38). This position suggests that circumcision was indeed practised by the Jola even before they converted to Islam. This observation is corroborated by Van der Klei, who suggests that, before the Jola's conversion to Islam, circumcision was practised in the initiation ritual (Van der Klei 1989: 185). Thus the Jola have probably always practised circumcision. I think this conclusion is supported by two arguments. First, non-Muslim communities on the southern shore practise circumcision. Second, the symbolic incision is probably made on novices *because* they have previously been circumcised, but initiation requires some kind of physical marker, which is why a symbolic incision is made.
8. This discrepancy may be due to the fact that the other authors did their research in the early 1980s (Van der Drift up to 1990) whereas I did mine in 1994. Rapid transformations may account for the differences in research findings.
9. Cf. Geschiere and Gugler 1998, especially pp. 310–11, emphasise the mutual support the urban–rural connection provides to villagers and migrants.
10. Some young men even think the Kaaba was formerly a sacred forest. Apparently, the global religion is increasingly appropriated in a local idiom. However, it is true that the Kaaba is located at a pre-Islamic sacred site.

11. This demonstrates that, although initiation is considered compatible with Islam, the ritual is sometimes also thought of as a religious expression.

12. One piece of cloth is provided by the father, the other by the mother. Thus, while the cloth signifies their changing social status, the rules governing its provenance reaffirm kinship ties in their new status as adult men.

CHAPTER 4

1. For recent contributions to this ongoing debate, see the thematic issue of *Africa Today* 45 (3–4), 1998, the thematic issue of *Africa* on 'primary patriotism' 68 (3), 1998, the volume on 'civil society' edited by John and Jean Comaroff 1999 and the *CODESRIA Bulletin* 1, 2000.

2. Interestingly, Robert Sagna legitimised his initiation in Thionck on the same grounds as the MFDC rebels who were initiated in July. As a matter of course I do not suggest an affinity in political orientation, but an affinity in cultural performance.

3. This regionalisation of the administration is at least partly a reaction of the central government to the demands of the MFDC. However, the separatist movement was not engaged in discussions about the regionalisation, does not approve of it and, instead of accepting regional autonomy, maintains its claims to political independence.

4. Interestingly the population of Brin, the village of Sagna's birth, is generally identified as Bainunk. His Bainunk background posed no obstacle to his initiation in Thionck Essyl. During our interview, Sagna stated that he considered himself both Jola and Bainunk. Indeed, the Casamance ethnic discourse classifies Bainunk as a sort of Jola. However, the fact that Sagna opted for initiation in a Jola village was politically wise. Consider the numbers of Jola and Bainunk in the administrative *région* of Ziguinchor: the Jola made up 60.7 per cent of the population in the 1988 population census. Since they are a negligible minority the Bainunk are not registered under a separate entry (République du Sénégal, 1992: 21).

5. In early 1999 the Senegalese government indeed gave Robert Sagna full responsibility for the negotiations with the MFDC (Marut 1999: 76).

6. Many administrators in the Ziguinchor region, such as the governor and the prefect of Boulouf, are of Serer extraction. There is a joking relationship between the two ethnic groups. The appointment of Serer to crucial positions in the local administration is, I presume, a Senegalese policy to enhance administrative relations with the Jola population. See de Jong 2005.

7. A photograph of the governor as a full participant in the ritual, carrying a stick, and decorated with beads, appeared in the national paper *Le Soleil* (2 August 1994).

8. When I did my fieldwork in 1994, I lived in the only Niaganan sub-ward (Kafanta) that organised its initiation in collaboration with the other wards of Thionck Essyl. When I tried to find out why the three sub-wards had acted on their own, my research results were coloured by my affiliation with my host and his place of residence.

9. Circumcision used to be practised on the first day of the seclusion at the sacred forest. In a week, the novices had probably sufficiently recovered from the operation to withstand an attack.

10. In fact, this Niassy-white segment had already independently assumed important ritual responsibilities since guardianship of Kafanta's sacred forest had been transferred to them through a maternal uncle–sister's son relationship (*assebul* relationship). The former officiant of the sacred forest, who belonged to the

Diatta-Balèn lineage, had left Kafanta and subsequently settled in Batine. He transferred the guardianship of Kafanta's sacred forest to his sister's son, who belonged to the Niassy-black family. However, this version of the transfer of this ritual responsibility to the Niassy family was also contested in various ways. Indeed, no claim remained undisputed.

11. See Barker 1973; Cruise O'Brien 1975: 147–85; Coulon 1978; Hesseling 1985: 372–3; Fatton, Jr 1986. With regard to political factionalism in Senegal, Barker says that '[t]he tendency is for the two or three clans at each level to align themselves with clans at the next higher level. The existence of these vertical alignments is apparent only in moments of conflict among national leaders and during elections' (Barker, 1973: 289).

12. Members of the Tijaniyya brotherhood resist initiation (see Chapter 3). Sadio's father was a Tijani.

13. A similar intertwinement of initiation and modern politics is observed in other societies of the Upper Guinea Coast (cf. Ellis 1999; Ferme 1999).

14. These figures were not obtained from official sources. Figures from the official sources were contested; in Senegal election results are *always* contested as presumably manipulated.

15. I should like to thank Linda Beck for pointing this out to me: personal communication, 30 June 1997, Dakar.

CHAPTER 5

1. At the time of the 1988 population census, the urban population of the *Région de Ziguinchor* consisted of eight major ethnic groups. The Jola were the largest ethnic group, comprising 35.5 per cent of the urban population, the Fulani were second with 15.1 per cent (the Fulani from Upper Casamance and the transnational migrant Fulani from the Futa Jalon are included in one category), and the Mandinko were third with 13.7 per cent (République du Sénégal 1992: 22). Note that these figures pertain to the urban population of the entire *Région de Ziguinchor*, comprising Ziguinchor and a few minor cities (Bignona and Oussouye). Population figures for Ziguinchor alone are not avalaible.

2. All the villages in the vicinity of Ziguinchor are Bainunk villages. In his interpretation of the meaning of place names in the Senegambian region, Bühnen argues that all the place names with a suffix -or were founded by the Bainunk (Bühnen 1992).

3. See Weil 1976, Fassin 1987 and Langeveld 2003 for discussions of this association.

4. In the 1980s the Senegalese government brought these organisations under state control, and registration is now compulsory. This encapsulation has not led to the abandonment of these organisations, which can be seen as a form of civil society as they tend to operate independently of political parties. Associations explicitly aim to counteract ethnic sentiments.

5. These figures are based on the 1988 population census. The figures pertain to the department of Ziguinchor which includes several villages in addition to the *Commune de Ziguinchor*. More precise data for Ziguinchor are not available.

6. For example, Creole is the lingua franca in Santhiaba, Mandinko in Peyrissac and Jola in Soucoupapaye.

7. Attempts at desecration of the mask usually result in serious punishments, certainly when they involve undressing the mask (see Chapter 6).

8. For an excellent discussion of the status of blacksmiths in Mande society and the powers attributed to them, see McNaughton 1988. Together with woodworkers (*lawbe*), leatherworkers (*garankew*), bards (*jèliw*) and Islamic praise singers

(*finew*), the blacksmiths (*numuw*) make up the status category of *nyamakalaw*. The *nyamakalaw* consist of endogamous groups that each has a monopoly on the exercise of their profession. In addition, there are two other status groups in Mande society, the 'free men' or nobles (*horonw*) and, nowadays often unrecognised, the slaves (*jonw*). The status of the *nyamakalaw* – whom scholars and colonial administrators often termed 'castes' – is the subject of a study that tries to break away from the rigid notion of caste and proposes a more dynamic analysis of status groups in Mande society (Conrad and Frank 1995).

9. *Kungfano* refers to 'the power to see in the past, present, and future – the ability to perceive evil, to identify sorcerers or witches, to detect the presence of spirits' (Weil 1971: 282). Among the Badyaranké of Upper Casamance, blacksmiths are also considered 'seers': 'All blacksmiths are thought to be seers, and by virtue of this power, they work fearlessly with fire and have the task of circumcising the young boys' (Simmons 1971: 80).

10. In Casamance, the patronym Kanté is identified with a blacksmith clan. The name Kanté also figures in the Sunjata epic, in which the legendary founder of the Mali Empire fights Sumanguru Kanté, who is identified as a blacksmith. See the version of the Sunjata epic edited by Niane 1960: 73 ff.

11. One of the protective devices mentioned is a bull-roarer. Bull-roarers are used in initiation rituals throughout West Africa, and indeed also among the Jola (see Chapter 2).

12. McNaughton 1988: 140 mentions a song of the *kòmò* association that refers to a sorcerer woman. Oral traditions have it that she tried to observe the *kòmò* mask dance which, as a non-initiate, she was not allowed to do. The *kòmò* mask subsequently killed her.

13. Although secrecy was observed after circumcision, the act of circumcision itself was public and observed by women. At night, 'their Devvil' called *Ho-re* frightened people with its loud roarings (Jobson, 1968: 105 ff.). This could well have been a bull-roarer (see note 11, this chapter).

14. The description of male initiation in Mandinko communities of Pakao by Schaffer and Cooper 1980: 95–9 resembles the descriptions men gave me of *past* male initiations in Ziguinchor.

15. The Prophet Muhammed is not reported to have had any sons. The informant may not have been aware of this. It shows that his understanding of the initiation, although informed by Muslim convictions, was a local understanding of Islam.

16. The term *iblissa* is derived from the Arabic *iblis*.

17. A calabash is put on the floor and all the novices are ordered to sit around it and put their fingers on the calabash's edge. The instructor sings the various lines of the song while tapping the calabash with a stick. The novices respond by repeating the lines, all the while rhythmically tapping the calabash. A description of this practice (*passindiro*) is also given by Father Doutremépuich 1939: 486. Apparently, there has been continuity in this practice from the 1930s onwards.

18. On the technicalities of the *kin* rhythm, see Knight 1974: 30–1, who refers to the rhythm as *Chingo*. His article examines various Mandinko rhythms from an ethnomusicological perspective.

19. The blacksmith was probably remunerated in kind. He could impose tasks on the novices while they were in seclusion, such as the collection of firewood and straw (Doutremépuich 1939: 490).

20. Cf. Argenti 1998, who argues that masquerades in the Cameroon Grassfields have always embodied the powers of alterity. In precolonial times, alterity was represented by the bush and the wild animals that inhabited it. Recently, the

category of alterity has been expanded to include the powers of modernity. Masquerading in the Grassfields now consists of a mimesis of the Other.

21. The colonial state rejected the celebration of initiation because of the intrinsic destruction of wealth. The early postcolonial state opposed the ritual for similar reasons. The Senegalese paper that usually reflects the government point of view commented in June 1972, '[I]l est devenu urgent pour le gouvernement de fixer un calendrier pour ce genre de manifestations et restreindre les dépenses somptueuses occasionnées dans de pareilles circonstances' (*Le Soleil*, 30 June 1972, cited in Trincaz 1981: 94–5).

CHAPTER 6

1. There is an extensive literature, comprising among others: Butt-Thompson 1929; Little 1949, 1965, 1966; Fulton 1972; Murphy 1980; Bellman 1979, 1984; Ferme 1999, 2001.
2. His later work focuses on questions with regard to the Kankurang's costume (Mark 1992).
3. Weil develops an elaborate categorisation of Kankurang types and defines the categories by means of a combination of eight criteria. The Kankurang discussed here belongs to his all-bark type (Weil 1995: 9–15).
4. See Girard 1969: 96; Mark 1985: 44; Roche 1985: 41; Schaffer and Cooper 1980: 102; Weil 1971: 281.
5. See among others: Little 1965; Henderson 1972: 352–78; Kasfir 1985: 11–12.
6. The article appeared in *Le Soleil* (30 April to 5 May 1987) and was entitled 'Meurtres collectifs à Marsassoum' (Collective killings in Marsassoum) and written by J. Lopy.
7. The court document reports verbatim: 'Avant d'en arriver à la sanction, le problème de l'imputabilité se passe. Qui a tué, qui a mis le feu? Qu'on nous le dise donc!' (République du Sénégal 1996: 7).
8. The court document reports verbatim: 'En mettant à nu le Kankuran, Solo Thiouda a foulé au sol la culture Mandingue donc il mérite une sanction' (République du Sénégal 1996: 7). In 1991, some of my interlocutors told me that the suspects had not been sentenced since the judge agreed that Solo's violation of Mandinko tradition was indeed a serious offence. The idea that the protagonists should not be sentenced was apparently judged reasonable (but my interlocutors may have been implicated in the execution).
9. The court document reports verbatim: 'On ne sait pas qui a frappé qui. Le kankuran c'est qui, c'est quoi, vous pouvez le dire Messieurs de la Cour?' (République du Sénégal 1996: 7).
10. In this respect, it is surprising that Diato Djiba, the masker, had not been summoned. It is altogether unclear why only five of the twenty-six men who were arrested were actually tried.
11. *Sopi*, 30 September 1988, and an unpublished article by J. Lopy for *Le Soleil*, 1 October 1988.
12. These accusations were subsequently cited in the newspaper *Sopi (le Journal du Changement)* of the opposition Senegalese Democratic Party (PDS).
13. 'There is unto these youthes allowed a certaine licentious liberty, whereat they may steale and take away peoples hennes, or poultry; nay from the Fulbies [Fulani], a biefe or cattle to eat and banquet themselves without any offence to the lawes, or government of the countrey' (Jobson 1968: 146).
14. The decision reads verbatim: 'La Commission sur l'Affaire des KANKOU-RANGS, s'est réunie le Dimanche 16 Octobre 1994 à l'Ecole Moussa BARRY en présence de toutes les Communautés et les délégués sus-visées. [...] DECIDE:

l'interdiction totale des KANKOURANGS pendant 5 ans pour compter du 30 Octobre 1994 à l'intérieur du territoire communal jusqu'à l'organisation des grandes cérémonies d'initiation par les différentes Communautés conformément à la réglementation en vigueur et au respect des coutumes des différentes communautés.'

15. See: 'Circoncision de Thionck-Essyl: L'Annonce faite aux futurs initiés', *Le Soleil*, 1 March 1990; 'Circoncision: Tendimane à l'heure du bukut', *Le Soleil*, 26 August 1992; 'Bukut de Thionck-Essyl: A la conquête du statut d'homme social', *Le Soleil*, 2 August 1994.

16. See among others: 'Le viol des masques', *Le Soleil*, 30 April 1987; 'Tradition contre modernité', *Le Soleil* 17 September 1988; 'L'Evolution controversée du Kankourang', *Le Soleil*, 1 March 1990; 'Force et faiblesse d'un mythe', *Sud Quotidien*, 6 September 1993.

CHAPTER 7

1. Girard 1965: 68–9 gives a detailed description of the technical aspects of Kumpo's costume.

2. There are a few masquerades in Africa that are entirely performed by women. For a discussion of female masquerading, see Phillips 1978 and Langeveld 2003.

3. The perception of the mask is differential, depending on the social position of the observer (cf. Weil 1988), resulting in differential behaviour vis-à-vis the mask.

4. Girard 1965: 43–4 and Van der Klei 1989: 218 share this point of view. Mark, however, suggests that Kumpo might have been introduced to Jola villages well before the nineteenth century (1985: 50).

5. Jones 1988 observes that fashion is very likely to have played an important role in the appearance and disappearance of Nigerian masked performances.

6. Thomas 1959, I: 221–2, Girard 1965: 80–1, Mark 1985: 45–6 and Madge 2000 also attribute an important role in social control to Kumpo.

7. For descriptions of other masks introduced in the 1940s and 1950s, see Thomas 1959, I: 221 and Girard 1965: 68–77.

8. Cf. Snyder's (1978) account of legal innovation by a youth association in a Banjal village on the southern shore of the Casamance River. The village-wide association of unmarried men of marriageable age took many initiatives comparable to the activities of the Diatock association. Snyder focuses on their initiative to form a ranger patrol in order to prevent cattle damaging crops. The innovation failed due to a lack of support by the village elders.

9. Personal communication, Kirsten Langeveld, July 1994.

10. Personal communication, Mark Davidheiser, 28 October 2005.

11. See http://www.casamance.net/traditions/photos/kankuran.html. The same page displays various pictures of the Kankurang mask. The accompanying text reads: 'Tradition ancestrale, Kankuran et Kumpo sont deux personnages clés de la culture casamançaise.'

CHAPTER 8

1. Interestingly, the tradition–modernity discourse thus recaptures the old cosmological opposition of 'bush' versus 'town', as is performed in Mandinko male initiation.

2. The other institution is the state-sponsored cultural centre that houses a library and a permanent exhibition of Casamance art.

3. The exhibition catalogue reads verbatim: 'Le respect de la diversité sociale et

l'amorce de sentiments de respects passent nécessairement par les échanges culturels.'

4. Verbatim from the opening address: '... les cultures Mandingues et Diolas sont deux piliers de la culture Casamançaise et donc Sénégalaise.'

5. From *Wal Fadjri*: 'Si la paix en Casamance repose sur le dialogue, ce doit d'abord être un dialogue des cultures.' The article was written by a journalist from Ziguinchor, publishing under a pseudonym.

6. It was not entirely impossible to openly support the peace process. A few weeks after the exhibition, secondary school students took to the street and held a peace march.

BIBLIOGRAPHY

Abbink, Jan. 1997. 'Ethnicity and constitutionalism in contemporary Ethiopia', *Journal of African Law* 41, 159–74.

Achebe, Chinua. 1971. *Arrow of God*. London: Heinemann.

Africa. 1998. Thematic issue on 'Primary Patriotism', 68 (3).

Africa Today. 1998. Thematic issue on 'Citizenship in Africa', 45 (3–4).

Amselle, Jean-Loup and Elikia M'Bokolo (eds). 1985. *Au coeur de l'ethnie: ethnies, tribalisme et état en Afrique*. Paris: La Découverte.

Anderson, Benedict. 1992. *Long-distance Nationalism: World Capitalism and the Rise of Identity Politics*. Wertheim Lecture 1992. Amsterdam: Centre for Asian Studies Amsterdam.

Appadurai, Arjun. 1986a. 'Introduction: commodities and the politics of value', in A. Appadurai (ed.), *The Social Life of Things: Commodities in Cultural Perspective*, pp. 3–63. Cambridge: Cambridge University Press.

—— (ed.). 1986b. *The Social Life of Things: Commodities in Cultural Perspective*. Cambridge: Cambridge University Press.

——. 1995. 'The production of locality', in R. Fardon (ed.), *Counterworks: Managing the diversity of knowledge*, pp. 204–25. London and New York: Routledge

——. 1996. *Modernity at Large: Cultural Dimensions of Globalization*. Minneapolis, MN and London: University of Minnesota Press.

Argenti, Nicolas. 1998. 'AirYouth: performance, violence and the state in Cameroon', *Journal of the Royal Anthropological Institute* 4, 753–81.

Barbier-Wiesser, François-George (ed.). 1994. *Comprendre la Casamance: chronique d'une intégration contrastée*. Paris: Karthala.

Barker, Jonathan. 1973. 'Political factionalism in Senegal', *Canadian Journal of African Studies* 9 (1), 23–42.

Barth, Fredrik (ed.). 1969. *Ethnic Groups and Boundaries: The Social Organization of Culture Difference*. Oslo: Universitets Forlaget.

——. 1975. *Ritual and Knowledge among the Baktaman of New Guinea*. New Haven, CT: Yale University Press.

Baum, Robert. 1990. 'The emergence of a Diola christianity', *Africa* 60: 370–98.

——. 1999. *Shrines of the Slave Trade: Diola Religion and Society in Precolonial Senegambia*. New York and Oxford: Oxford University Press.

Baumann, Gerd. 1996. *Contesting Culture: Discourses of Identity in Multi-ethnic London*. Cambridge: Cambridge University Press.

Bausinger, Hermann. 1990. *Folk Culture in a World of Technology*. Bloomington and Indianapolis, IN: Indiana University Press (first German edition 1961).

Bayart, Jean-François. 1983a. 'La revanche des sociétés africaines', *Politique africaine* 11: 95–127.

——. 1983b. 'Les sociétés africaines face à l'Etat', *Pouvoirs* 25, 23–39.

——. 1986. 'Civil Society in Africa', in P. Chabal (ed.), *Political Domination in Africa:*

Reflections on the Limits of Power, pp. 109–25. Cambridge: Cambridge University Press.

——. 1993. *The State in Africa: The Politics of the Belly*. London and New York: Longman.

——, Achille Mbembe and Comi Toulabor. 1992. *Le politique par le bas en Afrique noire: contributions à une problématique de la démocratie*. Paris: Karthala.

Beidelman, T. O. 1997. *The Cool Knife: Imagery of Gender, Sexuality, and Moral Education in Kaguru Initiation Ritual*. Washington, DC and London: Smithsonian Institution Press.

Bellman, Beryl L. 1979. 'The social organization of knowledge in Kpelle ritual', in B. Jules-Rosette (ed.), *The New Religions of Africa*, pp. 39–56. Norwood, NJ: Ablex.

——. 1984. *The Language of Secrecy: Symbols and Metaphors in Poro Ritual*. New Brunswick, NJ: Rutgers University Press.

Bloch, Maurice. 1986. *From Blessing to Violence: History and Ideology in the Circumcision Ritual of the Merina of Madagascar*. Cambridge: Cambridge University Press.

Blok, Anton. 1988. *The Mafia of a Sicilian Village, 1860–1960*. Prospect Heights, IL: Waveland Press (first printed 1974).

Bok, Sissela. 1982. *Secrecy: On the Ethics of Concealment and Revelation*. New York: Pantheon Books.

Bravmann, René A. 1974. *Islam and Tribal Art in West Africa*. Cambridge: Cambridge University Press.

Bruneau, Jean-Claude. 1979. *La croissance urbaine dans les pays tropicaux: Ziguinchor en Casamance, une ville moyenne du Sénégal*. Bordeaux: Centre d'Etudes de Géographie Tropicale.

Bühnen, Stephan. 1992. 'Place names as an historical source: an introduction with examples from southern Senegambia and Germany', *History in Africa* 19, 45–101.

Burnham, Philip. 1996. *The Politics of Cultural Difference in Northern Cameroon*. Edinburgh: Edinburgh University Press for the International African Institute.

Butt-Thompson, F. W. 1929. *West African Secret Societies: Their Organisations, Officials and Teaching*. London: Witherby.

Canadian Journal of African Studies. 2005. Thematic issue on 'Contested Casamance/Casamance discordante', 39 (2).

Clifford, James. 1986. 'Introduction: partial truths', in J. Clifford and G. E. Marcus (eds), *Writing Culture: The Poetics and Politics of Ethnography*, pp. 1–26. Berkeley and Los Angeles, CA: University of California Press.

——. 1988. *The Predicament of Culture: Twentieth-century Ethnography, Literature, and Art*. Cambridge, MA and London: Harvard University Press.

——. 1989. 'The Others: beyond the "salvage" paradigm', *Third Text* 6, 73–7.

——. 1997. *Routes: Travel and Translation in the Late Twentieth Century*. Cambridge, MA and London: Harvard University Press.

—— and G.E. Marcus. 1986. *Writing Culture: The Poetics and Politics of Ethnography*. Berkeley and Los Angeles, CA: University of California Press.

CODESRIA Bulletin. 2000. Thematic issue on 'Civil Society and the Public Space', (1).

Cohen, Abner. 1969. *Custom and Politics in Urban Africa: A Study of Hausa Migrants in Yoruba Towns*. London: Routledge & Kegan Paul.

——. 1971. 'The politics of ritual secrecy', *Man* n.s. 6 (3), 427–48.

——. 1981. *The Politics of Elite Culture: Explorations in the Dramaturgy of Power in a Modern African Society*. Berkeley, CA: University of California Press.

Cohen, Anthony P. 1989 [1985]. *The Symbolic Construction of Community*. London: Routledge.

Comaroff, Jean. 1985. *Body of Power, Spirit of Resistance: The Culture and History of a South African People*. Chicago: University of Chicago Press.

—— and John Comaroff (eds). 1993. *Modernity and Its Malcontents: Ritual and Power in Postcolonial Africa*. Chicago and London: University of Chicago Press.

Comaroff, John and Jean Comaroff (eds). 1999. *Civil Society and the Political Imagination in Africa: Critical Perspectives*. Chicago and London: University of Chicago Press.

Connerton, Paul. 1989. *How Societies Remember*. Cambridge: Cambridge University Press.

Conrad, David C. and Barbara E. Frank (eds). 1995. *Status and Identity in West Africa: Nyamkalaw of Mande*. Bloomington and Indianapolis, IN: Indiana University Press.

Copans, Jean. 1978. 'Idéologies et idéologues du tourisme au Sénégal: fabrications et contenus d'une image de marque', in J.-L. Boutillier et al. (eds), *Le tourisme en Afrique de l'ouest: panacée ou nouvelle traite*, pp. 108–28. Paris: François Maspero.

——. 1988. *Les marabouts de l'arachide: la confrérie mouride et les paysans du Sénégal*. Paris: L'Harmattan (orginally published in 1980 by Le Sycomore).

Coulon, Christian. 1978. 'Élections, factions et idéologies au Sénégal', in Centre d'Étude d'Afrique noire (ed.), *Aux urnes l'Afrique! Elections et pouvoirs en Afrique noire*, pp. 149–86. Paris: Éditions A. Pedone.

——. 1981. *Le marabout et le prince: islam et pouvoir au Sénégal*. Paris: Pedone.

——. 1999. 'The *grand magal* in Touba: a religious festival of the Mouride brotherhood of Senegal', *African Affairs* 98, 195–210.

Crain, Mary M. 1998. 'Reimagining identity, cultural production and locality under transnationalism: performances of San Juan in the Ecuadorean Andes', in F. Hughes-Freeland and M. M. Crain (eds), *Recasting Ritual: Performance, Media, Identity*, pp. 135–60. London and New York: Routledge.

Cruise O'Brien, Donal B. 1971. *The Mourides of Senegal: The Political and Economic Organization of an Islamic Brotherhood*. Oxford: Clarendon Press.

——. 1975. *Saints and Politicians: Essays in the Organisation of a Senegalese Peasant Society*. Cambridge: Cambridge University Press.

——. 1998. 'The shadow-politics of wolofisation', *Journal of Modern African Studies* 36 (1), 25–46.

Darbon, Dominique. 1988. *L'administration et le paysan en Casamance: essai d'anthropologie administrative*. Paris: Pédone.

De Jong, Ferdinand. 1999a. 'Trajectories of a mask performance: the case of the Senegalese *Kumpo*', *Cahiers d'études africaines* 153, 49–71.

——. 1999b. 'The production of translocality: initiation in the sacred grove in southern Senegal', in R. Fardon, W. van Binsbergen and R. van Dijk (eds), *Modernity on a Shoestring: Dimensions of Globalization, Consumption and Development in Africa and Beyond*, pp. 315–40. Leiden and London: EIDOS.

——. 2000. 'Secrecy and the state: the Kankurang masquerade in Senegal', *Mande Studies* 2: 153–73.

——. 2002. 'Politicians of the sacred grove: citizenship and ethnicity in southern Senegal', *Africa* 72 (2), 203–20.

——. 2004. 'The social life of secrets', in W. van Binsbergen and R. van Dijk (eds), *Situating Globality: African Agency in the Appropriation of Global Culture*, pp. 257–76. Leiden and Boston: Brill.

——. 2005. 'A joking nation: conflict resolution in Senegal', *Canadian Journal of African Studies* 39 (2), 389–413.

——— and Geneviève Gasser. 2005. 'Contested Casamance: introduction', *Canadian Journal of African Studies* 39 (2): 213–29.

Diaw, Aminata and Mamadou Diouf. 1992. 'Ethnies et nation au miroir des discours identitaires: le cas sénégalais.' Unpublished paper, Université Cheikh Anta Diop, Dakar.

Dilley, Roy (ed.). 1999. *The Problem of Context.* New York and Oxford: Berghahn Books.

Diop, Momar-Coumba (ed.). 2002. *Le Sénégal contemporain.* Paris: Karthala.

Diouf, Makhtar. 1994. *Sénégal: les ethnies et la nation.* Paris: L'Harmattan.

Diouf, Mamadou. 1994. 'L'échec du modèle démocratique du Sénégal, 1981–1993', *Afrika Spektrum* 1, 47–64.

———. 1999. 'The French colonial policy of assimilation and the civility of the *originaires* of the four communes (Senegal): a nineteenth century globalization project,' in B. Meyer and P. Geschiere (eds), *Globalization and Identity: Dialectics of Flow and Closure*, pp. 71–96. Oxford: Blackwell.

———. 2004. 'Between ethnic memories and colonial history in Senegal: the MFDC and the struggle for independence in Casamance', in B. Berman et al. (eds), *Ethnicity and Democracy in Africa*, pp. 218–39. Oxford and Athens, OH: James Currey and Ohio University Press.

Dirks, Nicholas B. 1990. 'History as a sign of the modern', *Public Culture* 2 (2), 25–32.

Douglas, Mary. 1966. *Purity and Danger: An Analysis of the Concepts of Pollution and Taboo.* London and New York: Routledge.

Doutremépuich, E. 1939. 'Visite à un "camp" de circoncis en Casamance', *Les Missions Catholiques* 72, 474–7, 486–92.

Durkheim, Emile. 1915. *The Elementary Forms of the Religious Life*, trans. Joseph W. Swain. New York: Free Press.

Ebong, Ima. 1991. 'Negritude between mask and flag: Senegalese cultural ideology and the "Ecole de Dakar"', in S. Vogel and I. Ebong (eds), *Africa Explores: 20th Century African Art*, pp. 198–209. New York and Munich: Center for African Art and Prestel.

Ebron, Paulla. 2002. *Performing Africa.* Princeton, NJ and Oxford: Princeton University Press.

Ellis, Stephen. 1999. *The Mask of Anarchy: The Destruction of Liberia and the Religious Dimension of an African Civil War.* London: Hurst.

Englund, Harri and James Leach. 2000. 'Ethnography and the meta-narratives of modernity', *Current Anthropology* 41 (2), 225–48.

Errington, Frederick and Deborah Gewertz. 1996. 'The individuation of tradition in a Papua New Guinean modernity', *American Anthropologist* 98 (1), 114–26.

Evans, Martin. 2003. 'The Casamance, Senegal: 'War Economy' or Business as Usual?' PhD dissertation, University of London.

Evans-Pritchard, E. E. 1940. *The Nuer: A Description of the Modes of Livelihood and Political Institutions of a Nilotic People.* New York and Oxford: Oxford University Press.

Fabian, Johannes. 1990. *Power and Performance: Ethnographic Explorations through Proverbial Wisdom and Theater in Shaba, Zaire.* Madison, WI: University of Wisconsin Press.

———. 1996. *Remembering the Present: Painting and Popular History in Zaire.* Berkeley, CA: University of California Press.

———. 1998. *Moments of Freedom: Anthropology and Popular Culture.* Charlottesville, VA and London: University of Virginia Press.

Fall, Yoro. 1989. 'Les Wolof au miroir de leur langue: quelques observations', in

J.-P. Chrétien and G. Prunier (eds), *Les ethnies ont une histoire*, pp. 117–23. Paris: Karthala.

Fassin, Didier. 1987. 'Rituels villageois, rituels urbains: la reproduction sociale chez les femmes joola du Sénégal', *L'Homme* 104, XXVII (4), 54–75.

Fatton, Robert, Jr. 1986. 'Clientelism and patronage in Senegal', *African Studies Review* 29 (4), 61–78.

Faye, Ousseynou. 1994. 'L'instrumentalisation de l'histoire et de l'ethnicité dans le discours séparatiste en Basse Casamance (Sénégal)', *Afrika Spektrum* 29 (1), 65–77.

Ferguson, James. 1999. *Expectations of Modernity: Myths and Meaning of Urban Life on the Zambian Copperbelt*. Berkeley, CA: University of California Press.

Ferme, Mariane. 1999. 'Staging *politisi*: the dialogics of publicity and secrecy in Sierra Leone', in John Comaroff and Jean Comaroff (eds), *Civil Society and the Political Imagination in Africa: Critical Perspectives*, pp. 160–91. Chicago and London: University of Chicago Press.

——. 2001. *The Underneath of Things: Violence, History, and the Everyday in Sierra Leone*. Berkeley, CA: University of California Press.

Fisiy, Cyprian and Peter Geschiere. 1990. 'Judges and witches, or how is the state to deal with witchcraft? Examples from southeastern Cameroon', *Cahiers d'études africaines* 118, 135–56.

——. 1996. 'Witchcraft, violence and identity: different trajectories in postcolonial Cameroon', in R. Werbner and T. Ranger (eds), *Postcolonial Identities in Africa*, pp. 193–221. London and New York: Zed Books.

Foucher, Vincent. 2002. 'Les "évolués," la migration, l'école: pour une nouvelle interprétation de la naissance du nationalisme casamançais', in Momar-Coumba Diop (ed.), *Le Sénégal contemporain*, pp. 375–424. Paris: Karthala.

——. 2003a. 'Le "retour au religieux" et la recherche de la paix en Casamance', *Studia Africana* 14, 40–4.

——. 2003b. 'Church and nation: the Catholic contribution to war and peace in Casamance', *Le Fait missionaire* 13, 7–40.

——. 2005. 'La guerre des dieux? Religions et séparatisme en Basse Casamance', *Canadian Journal of African Studies* 39 (2), 361–88.

Friedman, Jonathan. 1990. 'Being in the world: globalization and localization', in M. Featherstone (ed.), *Global Culture: Nationalism, Globalization and Modernity*, pp. 311–28. London, Newbury Park, CA and New Delhi: Sage.

——. 1994. *Cultural Identity and Global Process*. London: Sage.

Fulton, Richard M. 1972. 'The political structures and functions of Poro in Kpelle society', *American Anthropologist* 74, 1218–33.

Gable, Eric. 1997. 'A secret shared: fieldwork and the sinister in a West African village', *Cultural Anthropology* 12 (2), 213–33.

Gandalou, Justin-Daniel. 1989. *Au coeur de la Sape: moeurs et aventures des Congolais à Paris*. Paris: L'Harmattan.

Gasser, Geneviève. 2002. '"Manger ou s'en aller": que veulent les opposants armés casamançais?', in Momar-Coumba Diop (ed.), *Le Sénégal contemporain*, pp. 459–98. Paris: Karthala.

Geertz, Clifford. 1973. *The Interpretation of Cultures*. London: Fontana Press.

——. 1988. *Works and Lives: The Anthropologist as Author*. Cambridge: Polity Press.

Gellar, Sheldon. 1995. *Senegal: An African Nation between Islam and the West*, 2nd edn. Boulder, CO: Westview Press.

Geschiere, Peter. 1997. *The Modernity of Witchcraft: Politics and the Occult in Post-colonial Africa*. Charlottesville, VA and London: University of Virginia Press.

Geschiere, Peter and Josef Gugler. 1998. 'The urban–rural connection: changing issues of belonging and identification', *Africa* 68 (3), 309–19.

Geschiere, Peter and Jos van der Klei. 1987. 'La relation État–paysans et ses ambi-valences: modes populaires d'action politique chez les Maka (Cameroun) et les Diola (Casamance)', in E. Terray (ed.), *L'État contemporain en Afrique*, pp. 297–340. Paris: L'Harmattan.

——. 1988. 'Popular protest: the Diola of south Senegal', in P. Quarles van Ufford and M. Schoffeleers (eds), *Religion and Development: Towards an Integrated Approach*, pp. 209–29. Amsterdam: Free University Press.

Girard, Jean. 1965. 'Diffusion en milieu diola de l'association du Koumpo baïnouk', *Bulletin de l'IFAN*, XXVII sér. B (1–2), 42–98.

——. 1969. *Genèse du pouvoir charismatique en Basse Casamance (Sénégal)*. Dakar: IFAN.

Godelier, Maurice. 1973. 'Le concept de tribu: crise d'un concept ou crise des fondements empiriques de l'anthropologie?', in M. Godelier, *Horizon, trajets marxistes en anthropologie*, pp. 93–131. Paris: Maspero.

——. 1986. *The Making of Great Men: Male Domination and Power Among the New Guinea Baruya*. Cambridge: Cambridge University Press.

Goffman, Erving. 1959. *The Presentation of Self in Everyday Life*. Harmondsworth: Penguin.

Graburn, Nelson H. H. (ed.) 1976. *Ethnic and Tourist Arts: Cultural Expressions from the Fourth World*. Berkeley, CA: University of California Press.

Griaule, Marcel. 1948. *Dieu d'eau: entretiens avec Ogotemmêli*. Paris: Editions de Chêne.

Greenwood, Davydd J. 1977. 'Culture by the pound: an anthropological perspective on tourism as cultural commoditization', in V. L. Smith (ed.), *Hosts and Guests: The Anthropology of Tourism*, pp. 129–38. Philadelphia: University of Pennsylvania Press.

Gupta, Akhil, and James Ferguson. 1992. 'Beyond "culture": space, identity and the politics of difference', *Cultural Anthropology* 7 (1), 6–23.

Habermas, Jürgen. 1989. *The Structural Transformation of the Public Sphere: An Inquiry into a Category of the Bourgeois Society*, trans. T. Burger with F. Lawrence. Cambridge, MA: MIT Press.

Handler, Richard. 1988. *Nationalism and the Politics of Culture in Quebec*. Madison, WI: University of Wisconsin Press.

Hannerz, Ulf. 1987. 'The world in creolisation', *Africa* 57 (4), 546–59.

——. 1990. 'Cosmopolitans and locals in world culture', in M. Featherstone (ed.), *Global Culture: Nationalism, Globalization and Modernity*, pp. 237–51. London, Newbury Park, CA and New Delhi: Sage.

Harney, Elizabeth. 2004. *In Senghor's Shadow: Art, Politics, and the Avant-garde in Senegal, 1960–1995*. Durham, NC and London: Duke University Press.

Henderson, Richard N. 1972. *The King in Every Man: Evolutionary Trends in Onitsha Ibo Society and Culture*. New Haven, CT: Yale University Press.

Hesseling, Gerti. 1985. *Histoire politique du Sénégal: institutions, droit, société*. Paris: Karthala.

Hobsbawm, Eric and Terence Ranger (eds). 1983. *The Invention of Tradition*. Cambridge: Cambridge University Press.

Hodgson, Dorothy L. 1999. '"Once intrepid warriors": modernity and the production of Maasai masculinities', *Ethnology* 38 (2), 121–50.

Horton, Robin. 1971. 'African conversion', *Africa* 41 (2), 85–108.

Huizinga, Johan. 1985. *Homo Ludens: proeve ener bepaling van het spelelement der cultuur*. Groningen: Wolters Noordhoff (reprint of orig. 1938 edition).

James, Allison, Jenny Hockey and Andrew Dawson (eds). 1997. *After Writing Culture:*

Epistemology and Praxis in Contemporary Anthropology. London and New York: Routledge.

Jewsiewicki, Bogumil. 1991. 'Painting in Zaire: from the invention of the West to the representation of social self', in S. Vogel and I. Ebong (eds), *Africa Explores: 20th Century African Art*, pp. 130–51. New York and Munich: Center for African Art and Prestel.

Jobson, Richard. 1968. *The Golden Trade.* Amsterdam and New York: Theatrum Orbis Terrarum and Da Capo Press (reprint of orig. 1623 edition).

Johnson, G. Wesley, Jr. 1971. *The Emergence of Black Politics in Senegal: The Struggle for Power in the Four Communes, 1900–1920.* Stanford, CA: Stanford University Press.

Jones, G. I. 1988. 'The Niger-Cross River hinterlands and their masks', in S. L. Kasfir (ed.), *West African Masks and Cultural Systems*, pp. 109–22. Tervuren: Musée Royal de l'Afrique Centrale.

Juillard, Caroline. 1991. 'Le plurilinguisme au quotidien: Ziguinchor au Sénégal', *Afrique contemporaine* 158, 31–52.

——. 1994. 'Demain, Ziguinchor, ville plurielle? Indices de la wolofisation en cours', in F.-G. Barbier-Wiesser (ed.), *Comprendre la Casamance: chronique d'une intégration contrastée*, pp. 401–13. Paris: Karthala.

Jules-Rosette, Bennetta. 1984. *The Messages of Tourist Art: An African Semiotic System in Comparative Perspective.* New York: Plenum Press.

Kasfir, Sidney L. 1985. *Art in History, History in Art: The Idoma Ancestral Masquerade as Historical Evidence.* Paper of the African Studies Center, Boston University.

——. 1988a. 'Masquerading as a cultural system', in S. L. Kasfir (ed.), *West African Masks and Cultural Systems*, pp. 1–16. Tervuren: Musée Royal de l'Afrique Centrale.

—— (ed.). 1988b. *West African Masks and Cultural Systems.* Tervuren: Musée Royal de l'Afrique Centrale.

Kesteloot, Lilyan. 1994. 'Les Mandingues de Casamance: kankourang, castes et kora', in F.-G. Barbier-Wiesser (ed.), *Comprendre la Casamance: Chronique d'une intégration contrastée*, pp. 97–111. Paris: Karthala.

Knight, Roderic. 1974. 'Mandinka drumming', *African Arts* VII (4), 24–35.

Kopytoff, Igor. 1986. 'The cultural biography of things: commoditization as process', in A. Appadurai (ed.), *The Social Life of Things: Commodities in Cultural Perspective*, pp. 64–91. Cambridge: Cambridge University Press.

Kratz, Corrine A. 1994. *Affecting Performance: Meaning, Movement and Experience in Okiek Women's Initiation.* Washington, DC and London: Smithsonian Institution.

La Fontaine, Jean. 1985. *Initiation: Ritual Drama and Secret Knowledge Across the World.* Harmondsworth: Penguin.

Lambert, Michael C. 1998. 'Violence and the war of words: ethnicity *v.* nationalism in the Casamance', *Africa* 68 (4), 585–602.

——. 2002. *Longing for Exile: Migration and the Making of a Translocal Community in Senegal, West Africa.* Portsmouth, NH: Heinemann.

Langeveld, Kirsten. 2003. *Het Geheim van het Masker: maskerrituelen en genderrelaties in de Casamance, Senegal.* PhD dissertation, University of Utrecht.

Leary, Frances A. 1971. 'The role of the Mandinka in the Islamization of the Casamance, 1850–1901', in C. T. Hodge (ed.), *Papers on the Manding*, pp. 227–48. Bloomington, IN: Indiana University Press.

Linares, Olga F. 1992. *Power, Prayer and Production: The Jola of Casamance.* Cambridge: Cambridge University Press.

——. 1996. 'Cultivating biological and cultural diversity: urban farming in Casamance, Senegal', *Africa* 66 (1), 104–21.

Little, Kenneth. 1949. 'The role of the secret society in cultural specialization', *American Anthropologist* 51 (2), 199–212.

——. 1965. 'The political functions of the Poro, I', *Africa* 35: 349–65.

——. 1966. 'The political functions of the Poro, II', *Africa* 36, 62–72.

Loquay, Annie. 1979. 'Thionck-Essyl en Basse Casamance: évolution récente de la gestion des ressources renouvelables. Thèse de 3e cycle, Université de Bordeaux.

MacCormack, Carol P. 1979. 'The public face of a secret society', in B. Jules-Rosette (ed.), *The New Religions of Africa*, pp. 27–37. Norwood, NJ: Ablex.

McLaughlin, Fiona. 1995. 'Haalpulaar identity as a response to wolofization', *African Languages and Cultures* 8 (2), 153–68.

McNaughton, Patrick. 1988. *The Mande Blacksmiths: Knowledge, Power, and Art in West Africa*. Bloomington, IN and Indianapolis: Indiana University Press.

Madge, Clare. 2000. 'Forest spirits and the negotiation of ethnicity and gender among the Jola', in R. Cline-Cole and C. Madge (eds), *Contesting Forestry in West Africa*, pp. 124–47. Aldershot and Burlington: Ashgate.

Mafeje, Archie. 1971. 'The ideology of "tribalism"', *Journal of Modern African Studies* 9 (2), 253–61.

Malkki, Liisa H. 1995. *Purity and Exile: Violence, Memory and National Cosmology Among Hutu Refugees in Tanzania*. Chicago: Chicago University Press.

Mamdani, Mahmood. 1996. *Citizen and Subject: Contemporary Africa and the Legacy of Late Colonialism*. Princeton, NJ: Princeton University Press.

Mark, Peter. 1976. 'Economic and Religious Change Among the Diola of Boulouf (Casamance), 1890–1940: Trade, Cash Cropping and Islam in Southwestern Senegal.' PhD dissertation, Yale University.

——. 1977. 'The rubber and palm produce trades and the Islamization of the Diola of Boulouf (Casamance), 1890–1920', *Bulletin de l'IFAN*. 39 (sér. B, no 2), 341–61.

——. 1978. 'Urban migration, cash cropping, and calamity: the spread of Islam among the Diola of Boulouf (Senegal), 1900–1940', *African Studies Review* 21 (2), 1–14.

——. 1985. *A Cultural, Economic, and Religious History of the Basse Casamance since 1500*. Stuttgart: Franz Steiner Verlag.

——. 1992. *The Wild Bull and the Sacred Forest: Form, Meaning, and Change in Senegambian Initiation Masks*. Cambridge: Cambridge University Press.

——. 1994. 'Art, ritual, and folklore: dance and cultural identity among the peoples of the Casamance', *Cahiers d'études africaines* 136, XXXIV (4), 563–84.

——, Ferdinand de Jong and Clémence Chupin. 1998. 'Ritual and masking traditions in Jola men's initiation', *African Arts* 31 (1), 36–47, 94–5.

Marut, Jean-Claude. 1995. 'Solution militaire en Casamance', *Politique africaine* 58, 163–9.

——. 1999. 'La question de Casamance (Sénégal): une analyse géopolitique.' Doctoral dissertation, Université Paris 8.

——. 2002. 'Le problème casamançais est-il soluble dans l'État-nation', in Momar-Coumba Diop (ed.), *Le Sénégal contemporain*, pp. 425–58. Paris: Karthala.

Mauss, Marcel. 1954. *The Gift: Forms and Functions of Exchange in Archaic Societies*, trans. Ian Cunnison. London: Cohen & West.

Mbembe, Achille. 1992. 'Provisional notes on the postcolony', *Africa* 62 (1), 3–37.

M'Bengue, Mamadou S. 1973. *Cultural Policy in Senegal*. Paris: Unesco.

Meyer, Birgit. 1999. *Translating the Devil: Religion and Modernity Among the Ewe in Ghana*, International African Library 21. Edinburgh: Edinburgh University Press.

—— and Peter Geschiere (eds). 1999. *Globalization and Identity: Dialectics of Flow and Closure*. Oxford: Blackwell.

Mitchell, J. Clyde. 1956. *The Kalela Dance: Aspects of Social Relationships Among Urban Africans in Northern Rhodesia*. Manchester: Manchester University Press.

Mitchell, Timothy. 2000. 'The stage of modernity', in T. Mitchell, *Questions of Modernity*, pp. 1–34. Minneapolis, MN and London: University of Minnesota Press.

Moore, Francis. 1738. *Travels into the Inland Parts of Africa*. London: Edward Cave.

Moreau, Marie-Louise. 1994. 'Demain, la Casamance trilingue? Valeurs associées au diola, au français et au wolof', in F.-G. Barbier-Wiesser (ed.), *Comprendre la Casamance: chronique d'une intégration contrastée*, pp. 413–28. Paris: Karthala.

Mottin Sylla, Marie Hélène. 1990. *Excision au Sénégal*. Dakar: Enda tiers-monde.

Murphy, William P. 1980. 'Secret knowledge as property and power in Kpelle Society: elders versus youth', *Africa* 50 (2), 193–207.

Myers, Fred M. 1994. 'Culture-making: performing aboriginality at the Asia Society Gallery', *American Ethnologist* 21 (4), 679–99.

Napier, David. 1988. 'Masks and metaphysics: an empirical dilemma', in S. L. Kasfir (ed.), *West African Masks and Cultural Systems*, pp. 231–40. Tervuren: Musée Royal de l'Afrique Centrale.

Niane, Djibril T. 1960. *Soundjata ou l'épopée mandingue*. Paris and Dakar: Présence Africaine.

Nooter, Mary H. (ed.). 1993. *Secrecy: African Art that Conceals and Reveals*. New York and Munich: Museum for African Art and Prestel.

Nunley, John W. 1987. *Moving with the Face of the Devil: Art and Politics in Urban West Africa*. Urbana and Chicago: University of Illinois Press.

Ortner, Sherry B. 1984. 'Theory in anthropology since the sixties', *Comparative Studies in Society and History* 26, 126–66.

Osaghae, Eghosa E. 1991. 'A re-examination of the conception of ethnicity in Africa as an ideology of inter-elite competition', *African Study Monographs* 12 (1), 43–61.

Ottenberg, Simon. 1975. *Masked Rituals of Afikpo: The Context of an African Art*. Seattle, WA: University of Washington Press.

Pélissier, Paul. 1966. *Les paysans du Sénégal: les civilisations agraires du Cayor à la Casamance*. Saint-Yrieix: Fabruègue.

Pels, Peter. 1996. '*Kizungu* rhythms: Luguru christianity as *ngoma*', *Journal of Religion in Africa* XXVI (2), 173–205.

——. 1999. *A Politics of Presence: Contacts Between Missionaries and Waluguru in Late Colonial Tanganyika*. Chur: Harwood Academic.

Phillips, Ruth B. 1978. 'Masking in Mende Sande society initiation rituals', *Africa* 48 (3), 265–77.

Piot, Charles. 1993. 'Secrecy, ambiguity, and the everyday in Kabre Culture', *American Anthropologist* 95 (2), 353–70.

——. 1999. *Remotely Global: Village Modernity in West Africa*. Chicago and London: University of Chicago Press.

Poppi, Cesare. 1993. 'Sigma! The pilgrim's progress and the logic of secrecy', in M. H. Nooter (ed.), *Secrecy: African Art that Conceals and Reveals*, pp. 197–203. New York and Munich: Museum for African Art and Prestel.

Quinn, Charlotte A. 1972. *Mandingo Kingdoms of the Senegambia: Traditionalism, Islam, and European Expansion*. London: Longman.

Rabinow, Paul. 1977. *Reflections on Fieldwork in Morocco*. Berkeley, Los Angeles and London: University of California Press.

Ranger, T. O. 1975. *Dance and Society in Eastern Africa 1890–1970: The Beni Ngoma.* Berkeley, CA: University of California Press.

Rea, William R. 1998. 'Rationalising culture: youth, elites and masquerade politics', *Africa* 68 (1), 98–117.

Reboussin, Daniel A. 1995. 'From Affiniam-Boutem to Dakar: Migration from the Casamance, Life in the Urban Environment of Dakar, and the Resulting Evolutionary Changes in Local Diola Organizations.' PhD dissertation, University of Florida.

Reed, Daniel. 2003. *Dan Ge Performance: Masks and Music in Contemporary Côte d'Ivoire.* Bloomington and Indianapolis, IN: Indiana University Press.

République du Sénégal. 1988a. *Répertoire des villages: région de Kolda.* Dakar: Direction de la prévision et de la statistique.

——. 1988b. *Répertoire des villages: région de Ziguinchor.* Dakar: Direction de la prévision et de la statistique.

——. 1992. *Recensement général de la population et de l'habitat de 1988: rapport régional (résultats définitifs): Ziguinchor.* Dakar: Direction de la prévision et de la statistique.

——. 1993. *Recensement général de la population et de l'habitat de 1988: rapport national (résultats définitifs).* Dakar: Direction de la prévision et de la statistique.

——. 1996. *Cour d'Assises; audience du 06 mars 1996; affaire du Kankuran de Marsassoum.* Ministère de la Justice, Tribunal régional de Ziguinchor.

Richards, Paul. 1996. *Fighting for the Rain Forest: War, Youth and Resources in Sierra Leone.* Oxford: James Currey.

Roberts, Allen F. and Mary Nooter Roberts. 2003. *A Saint in the City: Sufi Arts of Urban Senegal.* Los Angeles: UCLA Fowler Museum of Cultural History.

Roche, Christian. 1985. *Histoire de la Casamance: conquête et résistance: 1850–1920.* Paris: Karthala (reprint of orig. 1976 edition).

Said, Edward. 1989. 'Representing the colonized: anthropology's interlocutors', *Critical Inquiry* 15, 205–27.

Sanjek, Roger (ed.). 1990. *Fieldnotes: The Makings of Anthropology.* Ithaca, NY and London: Cornell University Press.

Sapir, David. 1970. 'Kujaama: symbolic separation among the Diola-Fogny', *American Anthropologist* 72, 1330–48.

Schaffer, Matt and Christine Cooper. 1980. *Mandinko: The Ethnography of a West African Holy Land.* New York: Holt, Rinehart & Winston.

Schloss, Marc. 1988. *The Hatchet's Blood: Separation, Power, and Gender in Ehing Social Life.* Tucson, AZ and London: University of Arizona Press.

Scott, James C. 1985. *Weapons of the Weak: Everyday Forms of Peasant Resistance.* New Haven, CT and London: Yale University Press.

Simmel, Georg. 1967. 'The secret and the secret society', in *The Sociology of Georg Simmel,* trans., ed. and intro. Kurt H. Wolff, pp. 307–76. New York: Free Press (first print 1950).

——. 1968. *Soziologie: Untersuchungen über die Formen der Vergesellschaftung (Gesammelte Werke).* Berlin: Duncker & Humblot (first published in 1908).

Simmons, William S. 1971. *Eyes of the Night: Witchcraft Among a Senegalese People.* Boston: Little, Brown.

Skurnik, Walter A. E. 1965. 'Léopold Sédar Senghor and African socialism', *Journal of Modern African Studies* 3 (3), 349–69.

Smith, Valene L. (ed.). 1977. *Hosts and Guests: The Anthropology of Tourism.* Philadelphia: University of Pennsylvania Press.

Snipe, Tracy. 1998. *Arts and politics in Senegal, 1960–1996.* Trenton, NJ and Asmara: Africa World Press.

Snyder, Francis G. 1978. 'Legal innovation and social change in a peasant community: a Senegalese village police', *Africa* 48 (3), 231–47.

———. 1981. *Capitalism and Legal Change*. New York: Academic Press.

Steiner, Christopher B. 1994. *African Art in Transit*. Cambridge: Cambridge University Press.

Svašek, Maruška. 1997. 'Identity and style in Ghanaian artistic discourse', in J. MacClancy (ed.), *Contesting Art: Art, Politics, and Identity in the Modern World*, pp. 27–61. Oxford: Berg.

Szombati-Fabian, Ilona and Johannes Fabian. 1976. 'Art, history and society: popular painting in Shaba, Zaire', *Studies in the Anthropology of Visual Communication* 3, 1–21.

Taussig, Michael. 1999. *Defacement: Public Secrecy and the Labor of the Negative*. Stanford, CA: Stanford University Press.

Tefft, Stanton K. (ed.). 1980. *Secrecy: A Cross-cultural Perspective*. New York: Human Sciences Press.

Thoden van Velzen, H. U. E. and W. van Wetering. 1988. *The Great Father and the Danger: Religious Cults, Material Forces, and Collective Fantasies in the World of the Surinamese Maroons*. Dordrecht: Foris.

Thomas, Louis-Vincent. 1959. *Les Diola: essai d'analyse fonctionnelle sûr une population de Basse-Casamance*, 2 vols. Dakar: IFAN.

———. 1965. 'Bukut chez les diola-Niomoun', *Notes africaines* 108, 97–118.

Tilley, Christopher. 1997. 'Performing culture in the global village', *Critique of Anthropology* 17 (1), 67–89.

Tomàs, Jordi. 2005. '"La parole de paix n'a jamais tort." La paix et la tradition dans le royaume d'Oussouye (Casamance, Sénégal)', *Canadian Journal of African Studies* 39 (2), 389–441.

Tonkin, Elizabeth. 1979. 'Masks and powers', *Man* n.s. 14 (2), 237–48.

———. 1988. 'Cunning mysteries', in S. L. Kasfir (ed.), *West African Masks and Cultural Systems*, pp. 241–52. Tervuren: Musée Royal de l'Afrique Centrale.

Trincaz, Jacqueline. 1981. *Colonisations et religions en Afrique noire: l'exemple de Ziguinchor*. Paris: L'Harmattan.

Trincaz, Pierre Xavier. 1984. *Colonisation et régionalisme: Ziguinchor en Casamance*. Paris: ORSTOM.

Turner, Victor. 1967. *The Forest of Symbols: Aspects of Ndembu Ritual*. Ithaca, NY and London: Cornell University Press.

———. 1987. *The Anthropology of Performance*. New York: PAJ Publications.

Urry, John. 1990. *The Tourist Gaze: Leisure and Travel in Contemporary Societies*. London: Sage.

Vail, Leroy (ed.). 1989. *The Creation of Tribalism in Southern Africa*. London and Berkeley, CA: James Currey and the University of California.

Van Binsbergen, Wim M. J. 1981. *Religious Change in Zambia: Exploratory Studies*. London: Kegan Paul International.

———. 1984. 'Socio-ritual structures and modern migration among the Manjak of Guinea-Bissau: ideological reproduction in a context of peripheral capitalism', *Antropologische Verkenningen* 3 (2), 11–43.

———. 1985. 'From tribe to ethnicity in western Zambia: the unit of study as an ideological problem', in W. M. J. van Binsbergen and P. L. Geschiere (eds), *Old Modes of Production and Capitalist Encroachment*, pp. 181–234. London and Boston: Kegan Paul International.

———. 1991. 'Becoming a sangoma: religious anthropological fieldwork in Francistown, Botswana', *Journal of Religion in Africa* XXI (4), 309–44.

———. 1992. *Tears of Rain: Ethnicity and History in Central Western Zambia*. London and New York: Kegan Paul International.

——. 1994. 'Ethnicity as cultural mediation and transformation in Central Western Zambia', *African Studies* 53 (29), 92–125.

——. 1995. 'Popular culture: the dynamics of African cultural and ethnic identity in a context of globalization', in J. van der Klei (ed.), *Popular Culture: Beyond Historical Legacy and Political Innocence*, pp. 7–40. Utrecht: CERES/CNWS.

——. 1999. 'Globalization and virtuality: analytical problems posed by the contemporary transformation of African societies', in B. Meyer and P. Geschiere (eds), *Globalization and Identity: Dialectics of Flow and Closure*, pp. 273–303. Oxford: Blackwell.

Van de Laar, Irene. 1995. '"True love exists no more": confusion about choosing a partner, love and marriage among the young in Senegal', in J. van der Klei (ed.), *Popular Culture: Beyond Historical Legacy and Political Innocence*, pp. 151–84. Utrecht: CERES/CNWS.

Van der Drift, Roy. 1992. 'Arbeid en Alcohol: de dynamiek van de rijstverbouw en het gezag van de oudste bij de Balanta Brassa in Guinee Bissau.' PhD dissertation, University of Leiden.

Van der Klei, Jos. 1985. 'Articulation of modes of production and the beginning of labour migration among the Diola of Senegal', in W. van Binsbergen and P. Geschiere (eds), *Old Modes of Production and Capitalist Encroachment*, pp. 71–93. London: Kegan Paul International.

——. 1989. *Trekarbeid en de Roep van het Heilige Bos: het gezag van de oudste en moderne veranderingen bij de Diola van Zuid-Senegal*. Nijmegen: Iken.

Van Dijk, Rijk. 1997. 'From camp to encompassment: discourses of transsubjectivity in the Ghanaian Pentecostal diaspora', *Journal of Religion in Africa* 27 (2), 135–60.

Van Gennep, Arnold. 1960. *The Rites of Passage*. Chicago: University of Chicago Press.

Villalón, Leonardo A. 1995. *Islamic Society and State Power in Senegal: Disciples and Citizens in Fatick*. Cambridge: Cambridge University Press.

Vogel, Susan and Ima Ebong (eds). 1991. *Africa Explores: 20th Century African Art*. New York and Munich: Center for African Art and Prestel.

Weil, Peter M. 1971. 'The masked figure and social control: the Mandinka case', *Africa* 4 (4), 179–93.

——. 1976. 'The staff of life: food and female fertility in a West African Society', *Africa* 46 (2), 182–95.

——. 1988. 'Fighting fire with fire: the Mandinka Sengko mask', in S. L. Kasfir (ed.), *West African Masks and Cultural Systems*, pp. 153–94. Tervuren: Musée Royal de l'Afrique Centrale.

——. 1995. *The Kankurang Mask Category: A Problem of Mande Cultural History*. Paper presented at the international conference on Mande studies, Leiden University.

—— and Bala Saho. 2005. 'Masking for money: the commodification of Kankurang and Simba mask performances in urban Gambia', in S. Wooten (ed.), *Wari Matters: Ethnographic Explorations of Money in the Mande World*, pp. 162–77. Münster: Lit Verlag.

Werbner, Richard. 1996. 'Introduction: multiple identities, plural arenas', in R. Werbner and T. Ranger (eds), *Postcolonial Identities in Africa*, pp. 1–25. London and New York: Zed Books.

Werbner, Richard (ed.). 2002. *Postcolonial Subjectivities in Africa*. London and New York: Zed Books.

Wolf, Eric. 1982. *Europe and the People without History*. Berkeley, CA: University of California Press.

INDEX